THE NEW MERMAIDS

Bartholmew Fair

THE NEW MERMAIDS

General Editor
BRIAN GIBBONS
Professor of English Literature, University of Zürich

Previous general editors of the series have been:
PHILIP BROCKBANK
BRIAN MORRIS
ROMA GILL

Bartholmew Fair

BEN JONSON

Edited by G. R. HIBBARD

Emeritus Professor of English,
University of Waterloo, Ontario

LONDON/A & C BLACK

NEW YORK/W W NORTON

Reprinted 1991
by A & C Black (Publishers) Limited
35 Bedford Row, London WR1R 4JH
ISBN 0-7136-3531-2

First published in this form 1977
by Ernest Benn Limited

Published in the United States of America
by W. W. Norton and Company Inc.
500 Fifth Avenue, New York, N.Y. 10110

Printed in Great Britain by
Whitstable Litho Printers Ltd.,
Whitstable, Kent

CONTENTS

ACKNOWLEDGEMENTS

My main debt is to the Herford and Simpson edition of the play. I have also benefited from the editions by E. A. Horsman, Edward Partridge, and E. M. Waith.

Waterloo, Ontario G. R. H.

ABBREVIATIONS

1. *Texts of* Bartholmew Fair

F	the edition of 1631.
Alden	C. S. Alden, ed., *Bartholomew Fair*, *Yale Studies in English*, 25 (1904).
Spencer	Hazelton Spencer, ed., *Elizabethan Plays*, Boston, 1933.
H & S	C. H. Herford and Percy and Evelyn Simpson, eds., *The Works of Ben Jonson*, 11 vols., 1925–52.
Horsman	E. A. Horsman, ed., *Bartholomew Fair*, The Revels Plays, 1960.
Waith	Eugene M. Waith, ed., *Bartholomew Fair*, The Yale Ben Jonson, 1963.

2. *Other works*

Chambers	E. K. Chambers, *The Elizabethan Stage*, 4 vols., 1923.
Nashe	R. B. McKerrow, ed., *The Works of Thomas Nashe*, 5 vols., 1904–10.
OED	*The Oxford English Dictionary*.
Pepys	R. Garnett, ed., *Diary of Samuel Pepys*, Everyman's Library, 2 vols., 1906.
Shakespeare	Peter Alexander, ed., *The Complete Works of William Shakespeare*, 1951.
Stow	Henry B. Wheatley, ed., John Stow's *The Survey of London* (1598), Everyman's Library, 1912.
Tilley	Morris P. Tilley, *A Dictionary of the Proverbs in England in the Sixteenth and Seventeenth Centuries*, Ann Arbor, 1950.

3. *Journals*

PMLA	*Publications of the Modern Language Association of America*
SEL	*Studies in English Literature 1500–1900*
UTQ	*University of Toronto Quarterly*

ed.	this editor
Ed.	an earlier editor
s.d.	stage direction
s.p.	speech prefix.

INTRODUCTION

THE AUTHOR

WE KNOW MORE about Jonson's life—some of it from his own lips—than we do about the life of any other major dramatist of the time. Colourful, adventurous, and varied, it conforms, unlike Shakespeare's, to the popular connotation of the word 'Elizabethan', and it brought him into intimate contact with all conditions of men from the lowest to the highest, King James I himself. Born in 1572, either in or near London, he was the posthumous son of a poor gentleman who had eventually become 'a grave minister of the gospel'. Not long after his father's death, his mother took a second husband, a master-bricklayer of Westminster. As a consequence, presumably, of this remarriage, Jonson was 'brought up poorly' in his earliest years, but then had the good fortune to attract the interest of 'a friend', who put him to school at Westminster, where he was taught by the great scholar and historian William Camden. The friendship that grew up between them was one of the main formative influences on Jonson's life. Camden imbued the boy with his own passion for learning; and, later on, the poet acknowledged his debt and repaid it by making his old master the subject of one of his finest epigrams, xiv, in which he addresses him as:

> CAMDEN, most reuerend head, to whom I owe
> All that I am in arts, all that I know.

How long Jonson remained at Westminster School we do not know, but it would seem that he did not finish his course there, for he told the Scots poet William Drummond of Hawthornden that he was 'taken from it, and put to ane other Craft'—bricklaying in all probability—'which he could not endure'. His removal from school must have happened about 1588–89. At some time between that date and 1597, he served as a volunteer in the war in Flanders. When he arrived there the war was languishing. Disappointed at the lack of action, he took on some misguided individual on the other side in single combat 'in the face of both the Campes', killed him, stripped him of his arms in the best classical manner, and carried them back with him to his own lines. Having demonstrated in this very practical manner his belief in the Renaissance ideal of the unity of learning and action, Jonson 'betook himself to his wonted studies', whatever that may mean. He also married, at some date between 1592 and 1595, a wife whom he would later describe to Drummond as 'a shrew yet honest'. She bore him two children: a daughter, who died at the age of six months, and a son who survived to the age of seven, 'BEN. IONSON his best piece of *poetrie*', as his father called him in the moving epigram, xlv, which he wrote on the child's death in 1603.

How did Jonson live during this time? The information we have is not altogether reliable, since it comes from Thomas Dekker's play *Satiro-mastix* (1601) in which Jonson is attacked, but in essence it rings true. From it we learn that he belonged to a troupe of strolling players and that he took the leading role in Thomas Kyd's *The Spanish Tragedy*. From the highway he graduated to the London stage and to trouble. In the summer of 1597 Thomas Nashe had handed over to the players part of an unfinished satirical comedy called *The Isle of Dogs*. It was completed by one of them, the young Ben Jonson, without, according to Nashe, his consent. Its performance, at some time prior to 28 July, resulted in information being laid before the Privy Council to the effect that it was 'a lewd play . . . contanynge very seditious and sclandrous matter'. Taking prompt action, the Privy Council had 'some of the Players' apprehended and imprisoned, 'whereof one . . . was not only an Actor, but a maker of parte of the said Plaie'. Jonson spent over two months in gaol, and was not released until 8 October. It is a significant beginning to his career as a playwright, for he was to run foul of the authorities again.

On his release, Jonson continued to write plays, and, by September 1598, he was already sufficiently well known to have his name mentioned by Francis Meres, in his *Palladis Tamia*, among those who 'are our best for Tragedie'. In the middle of the same month came his first great success. *Every Man in His Humour* was played by Shakespeare's company, the Lord Chamberlain's Men, to delighted audiences, with Shakespeare himself acting one of the parts. Near-disaster followed. On 22 September, Jonson, pugnacious as ever, quarrelled with an actor called Gabriel Spencer, fought a duel with him, killed him, and was arrested for felony. Tried at the Old Bailey, in October, he pleaded guilty, but managed to escape from the gallows by claiming 'benefit of clergy'. His goods were confiscated and his thumb branded.

At this point in his career, Jonson's urge to experiment, coupled with his readiness to castigate those of his contemporaries whose work he disapproved of, led him into what looks in retrospect something of a blind alley. His romantic comedy *The Case is Altered* did well when it was performed by the Children of the Chapel towards the end of 1598, but *Every Man Out of His Humour*, put on by the Lord Chamberlain's Men at their new theatre, the Globe, late in 1599 or early in 1600, met with a more mixed reception. Boldly announcing itself as a 'Comicall Satyre' when it was first published in 1600, this comedy is highly original. Dispensing with story almost completely, it depicts fools and gulls in profusion. The audience is taken on an extended tour, as it were, of a great gallery full of living caricatures, exhibited to arouse their derision, and, Jonson would have said, to ensure their edification. The bright young men of the court and the Inns of Court enjoyed it enormously and read it avidly; three quarto editions appeared in 1600. But the ordinary playgoer seems to have been less enthusiastic. He wanted more in the way of story than the dramatist offered him, and may well have sensed that this play was moving away from the central concerns of humanity to matters of a more peripheral and ephemeral kind. It also had the effect of antagonizing some of the other dramatists, especially John Marston, whose bizarre diction it had ridiculed. Not surprisingly, Marston retorted in kind by satirizing Jonson in his *Jack Drum's Entertainment* (1600), and thus precipitated a 'war of the theatres'. Jonson's further contributions to it, *Cynthia's Revels* and *Poetaster*, both performed in 1601 by the Children of the Chapel, are not without their brilliance, but they are 'caviary to the general', because 'the general' have the sense to recognize that one cannot live on caviare and that bread and cheese is a far better diet. Moreover, the pungency of the satire in *Poetaster* had made fresh enemies for Jonson, including men of power and influence. Threatened with prosecution, he retired for a time from the stage.

He returned to it in 1603, when his tragedy *Sejanus* was played by the King's Men, with Shakespeare once again taking one of the parts. Still underrated by many critics, this is, in fact, one of the greatest political plays of the time; but its massive achievement did not save it from the wrath of the groundlings who could not tolerate its long speeches. It was damned, and, to make matters worse, Jonson found himself in trouble over what some took to be satirical allusions to contemporary matters in it. He was called before the Privy Council; but there the matter seems to have ended. Characteristically, he was soon in hot water again. In 1604 he collaborated with Chapman and Marston in the writing of *Eastward Ho!*, a superb send-up of citizen comedy. Unfortunately, the comedy also contained some incidental satire on the Scots and a gibe at King James. Along with his two collaborators, Jonson went to gaol again, but was eventually released.

It was his last brush with authority; he did not go to gaol any more. Instead, he settled down to a decade of high dramatic endeavour, producing a series of superb comedies that no audience could resist. *Volpone* (1605), *Epicoene* (1609–10), *The Alchemist* (1610), and

Bartholmew Fair (1614) make up a massive achievement, the great central bastion in the Jonsonian *oeuvre*, establishing him as the master of the comic mode. In this same period he composed another Roman tragedy, *Catiline*. Played by the King's Men in 1611, it was, much to the annoyance of its author, unequivocally damned on its first performance. In 1616 came a further comedy, *The Devil is an Ass*, which leaves one in no doubt about Jonson's continued grasp on and attitude to the social and economic realities of the time.

He wrote no play for the next nine years. He did not need to. Since the Christmas of 1604, he had been composing masques for the court, and bringing the art of the masque to perfection in the process. He had also been busy writing the lyrical and ethical poetry which won him the admiration and the discipleship of numerous younger poets who liked to think of themselves as belonging to 'the tribe of Ben'. He was a dominant force in the many literary activities which had their focus in the London taverns he loved to frequent, and he found himself a welcome visitor at the country houses of the great. Oxford University acknowledged his scholarship by making him a Master of Arts in 1619; and in the previous year he had demonstrated his physical fitness by walking to Scotland and back. It was in Scotland that he stayed with Drummond of Hawthornden, who had the good sense to make a record of what Jonson told him during the course of their *Conversations*.

By the time *The Staple of News* was first played in 1626, however, things were going wrong for him. The death of James I, in 1625, was a serious blow, since Charles I did not share his father's admiration for Jonson and his work, nor was he as generous as his father had been. Short of money, the poet, now in his fifties, was forced to resort to the stage once more. The plays he wrote, though far from being 'dotages', were out of touch with the taste and the temper of the time. They did not succeed. Worse still, he was stricken with paralysis in 1628, and seems not to have left his chamber thereafter, though he lived on for another nine years. He died on 6 August 1637, and was buried in Westminster Abbey, under a tombstone bearing the inscription: 'O rare Ben Jonson'. According to William Oldys (1696–1761), there was a tradition that these words represent 'the popular applause of this Play [*Bartholmew Fair*] after his solemn Catiline had been coldly received by the Audience' (H & S, i, 183).

DATE, STAGE HISTORY, AND SOURCES

The title-page of the first printed version (1631) informs us that the play was acted in 1614 by the Lady Elizabeth's Servants. The

Induction (62–9) is even more specific, giving the date of the opening performance as 31 October 1614, and the place as the Hope Theatre. The Prologue and the Epilogue, both addressed to the King, show that there was a performance at court for James I; and the Chamber Accounts, recording a payment of £10 to 'Nathan ffeilde in the behalfe of himselfe and the rest of his fellowes . . . for . . . Bartholomewe Fayre' (Chambers, iv, 183), provide the date 1 November 1614 for that performance. The Revels Accounts reveal that on the same occasion a payment was made to cover the cost of 'Canvas for the Boothes and other necessaries for a play called Bartholomewe Faire' (ibid.).

No further record of performance prior to 1661 has been found, though one of Samuel Pepys's remarks, quoted below, would, if it can be taken literally, indicate that the comedy continued to be played, without excision of the puppet-shew, until 1621 or thereabouts. It was revived after the Restoration, and proved popular. Pepys saw it on 8 June 1661, 'the first time it was acted now-a-days', and described it then as 'a most admirable play and well acted, but too much prophane and abusive'. The puppet-shew was omitted from this performance, and from the second on 27 June, but not from a further performance on 7 September, which led the diarist to make the following comment:

> And here was 'Bartholomew Fayre', with the puppet-showe, acted today, which had not been these forty years, it being so satyricall against Puritanism, they [the players] durst not till now, which is strange they should already dare to do it, and the King [who was present] to countenance it, but I do never a whit like it the better for the puppets, but rather the worse (Pepys, i, 170 and 191).

Beginning its second life thus, *Bartholmew Fair* continued to be acted for the next seventy years, up to 1731, after which it was seen no more on the stage for the best part of two centuries. Its disappearance coincides with a general decline in its author's reputation. Dubbed 'classical' and seen as the antithesis of Shakespeare, Jonson did not appeal to an age dominated by romanticism. A renewal of interest in his work, as in that of the Metaphysical Poets, his contemporaries, came in the second decade of the twentieth century. T. S. Eliot's important essay on him appeared in 1919. Two years later, on 26 June 1921, *Bartholmew Fair* was played by the Phoenix Society at the New Oxford Theatre. Since that time, it has received several amateur productions, usually in universities, and at least three professional ones. George Devine directed the Old Vic Company in it at the Edinburgh Festival in 1949, and then, in 1950, at the Old Vic itself. It was given by the Bristol Old Vic in 1966, and, finally, by the Royal Shakespeare Company at the Aldwych in the autumn of 1969.

For *Bartholmew Fair*, as for most of Jonson's comedies, no source, in the usual sense of that word, is known, and none is likely to be found, for his way of working was radically different from Shakespeare's. Shakespeare's interest seems to have been caught by story, and, when he was writing comedy, often by story of a romantic, improbable, even fantastic kind. He therefore enriches and deepens the characterization he finds in his sources as a means of conferring an illusion of reality on fanciful material. Jonson, on the other hand, was primarily interested in the variety, absurdity, and eccentricity of human nature. For him, consequently, the characters come first, and he then devises an appropriate intrigue or fable carefully designed to shew those characters in action.

This is emphatically the case in *Bartholmew Fair*. It is, among other things, a skit on plays, such as John Marston's *The Malcontent* and Shakespeare's *Measure for Measure*, which shew the ruler moving about in disguise among his people. But there is no specific debt to these plays or to others like them. There is a fairly close parallel between the purse-cutting scene, III.v, and one of the stories in Robert Greene's *The Third and Last Part of Cony-Catching* (1592); but collusion between ballad-singer and cutpurse was a well-worn topic when Greene took it up. The same scene may have been influenced by the story about Sir Thomas More which Nightingale alludes to at lines 98–100 (see note), but that story itself smacks of the jest-book. Jonson uses popular legend much as he uses his knowledge of the classics, making it serve his purpose. The intrigue, however, is, so far as we know, his own; and the source of it is his intimate acquaintance with and observation of the life of the times.

THE PLAY

Towards the end of IV.ii, Cokes the simpleton and Trouble-all the madman meet for the first time. Since entering the Fair, Cokes has been robbed of both his purses, of his sword, cloak, and hat, and of a handkerchief given to him by Grace Wellborn, to whom he is contracted in marriage. Furthermore, he has lost Grace in the crowd and, finally, he has lost himself. He therefore asks Trouble-all to take him home to Justice Overdo's house. Trouble-all, however, will do nothing without Overdo's warrant, and, when Cokes says, 'Pray thee guide me to the house', the madman answers:

> Sir, I'll tell you. Go you thither yourself first alone; tell your worshipful brother [Overdo] your mind; and but bring me three

> lines of his hand, or his clerk's, with 'Adam Overdo' underneath. Here I'll stay you, I'll obey you, and I'll guide you presently.
> (IV.ii, 96–100)

There is an exquisitely crazy logic about this speech, as it moves forward, step by step, from its absurdly impossible initial suggestion to its totally superfluous end. It is the kind of thing that, allowing for differences of language, might well have come out of the Goon Show. Nor does it stand alone. In IV.iv, for instance, Wasp, who is impelled in everything he says or does by the spirit of contradiction, takes part in the foolish game of vapours, which consists in opposing 'the last man that spoke'. Assured by Whit that he is in the right, Wasp retorts:

> I am not i' the right, nor never was i' the right, nor never will be i' the right, while I am in my right mind. (IV.iv, 61–3)

Ridiculous though this outburst is in its assertion that to be in the wrong is a proof of sanity, it has its own kind of truth in so far as Wasp is concerned, and goes far towards explaining his behaviour.

Often described as a realistic play, because it is so firmly rooted in the streets, the sights, the sounds, and the smells of Jacobean London, *Bartholmew Fair* has, in fact, many of the characteristics that one associates with surrealism. An exuberant fancy, coupled with a readiness to push things to their ultimate logical conclusion, no matter how absurd that conclusion may be, plays over the ordinary and the commonplace, transforming it into something wild and strange, that yet has its own inner coherence. The extreme zealots among the Puritans of the early seventeenth century were capable of much in their eagerness to identify and destroy relics of paganism and popery, but even they did not go to the lengths of taking dolls and gingerbread figures for idols or of engaging in disputations with puppets, as Zeal-of-the-land Busy does. Larger than life and twice as vocal, Busy is not so much a satirical portrait of the worst kind of Puritan preacher as an enormous inflated caricature of him. The possibilities inherent in a combination of reliance on the motion of the spirit and deliberate wilful ignorance are given their full scope. The result is a gigantic figure of fun, with an appetite to match. It is positively Gargantuan; Knockem remarks of Busy, in III.vi, that he has eaten two and a half sucking pigs at a sitting and 'drunk a pailful' of ale. Observation has contributed to his making, but essentially he is a product of the same imagination that gave birth to Volpone and Sir Epicure Mammon.

So is the play in which he lives. Like Ursla the pig-woman, whose booth is the focus for so much of its action, *Bartholmew Fair* is large, vital, and vulgar. One of the longest of Jonson's comedies—and he never gave his audience short measure—it is filled, almost to overflowing, with sharply differentiated characters, each endowed with his own distinctive idiom, even though this may amount to no more in some cases than a street-cry. Within the play proper there are no fewer than thirty-four speaking parts; and to these the Induction adds another three. Moreover, all these characters belong to the *vulgus*, the common people, coming either from the middle class or from the lower orders of society. Bartholmew Cokes, 'an esquire of Harrow', is one of the minor landed gentry, and Grace Wellborn is of the same rank. Winwife and Quarlous are 'gentlemen', meaning that they have some social standing, some education, acquired, by Quarlous at any rate, at the Inns of Court, and, most importantly, that they do not work for their living; nor, as their conduct amply demonstrates, have they any intention of doing so in a world where marriage to a woman of means can free a man from the curse of Adam. The rest of the characters are either citizens and their wives or traders, sharpers, hangers-on, and crooks who live in the Fair. Consequently, there is no one among them who has the unquestioned and unquestionable authority that birth and position give to so many of Shakespeare's dukes, for example.

This motley crowd is involved in a multiplicity of actions, none of which can be unequivocally labelled as the most important. Similarly, there is no single figure whose activities and fortunes ultimately become the dominant centre of interest. *Bartholmew Fair* is a play without a hero. This does not mean, however, that it is shapeless. On the contrary, it is a marvel of organization. The action falls into three distinct parts, each of which has its own locale. It begins outside the Fair at the home of Littlewit, where the whole of the expository first act takes place. From thence it moves to a loosely defined area of the Fair in and around Ursla's booth, where roast pig, the special attraction of the Fair, is sold. Here there are a number of playing places: the booth itself, the place where Leatherhead and Trash have their stalls, the street where Nightingale sings his ballads, and the stocks. Acts II, III, and IV, the 'busy part' of the play, as Jonson would have called them, are all set in this area. Then, for Act V, the denouement, the scene changes to another part of the Fair altogether, the place where Leatherhead has his puppet theatre.

One place, many places in and around one place, one place; concentration, expansion, concentration; the pattern is already clear and significant. *Bartholmew Fair* may well appear a mighty maze at first sight, but it is not without a plan. Further evidence of careful planning is to be seen in the structure of the individual acts. Each contains six scenes and takes the same course. It begins quietly with either one or a few characters on stage. Then, more and more people appear, and, as they do so, the pace quickens, the action becomes more and more tumultuous, insults fly, tempers become frayed, quarrels break out, fights and beatings follow. Finally, at the very end of the sixth scene, and especially in the last scene of the last act, there is an anticlimax. Win Littlewit shamefacedly tells her husband that she must find somewhere to make water; the Watch gaze in dumbfounded amazement at the empty stocks; Overdo has to abandon the great scene of revelation and condemnation for the sake of which he has endured so much. The play dramatizes disorder on a large scale, but it does so in a most orderly fashion.

The swirling crowd of characters who take part in this action fall, as Richard Levin has convincingly shown in his admirable analysis of the play's structure,[1] into two sharply contrasted halves. On the one side, there are the denizens of the Fair. For them this fair-day is much like any other fair-day, except that it ends with their being invited to Overdo's house for supper. They go about their usual business, whether it be the provision of food and drink, the sale of trumpery, the procuring of prostitutes, or the picking of purses. Competing with one another for custom and engaging in the slanging matches expected of them, they are also capable of banding together for mutual profit or protection. While much happens to them in one way—Ursla, for example, scalds her leg, and Edgworth the cutpurse is in danger of being hanged—nothing whatever happens to them in another way; they are exactly the same at the end of the day as they were at its beginning. And the fact that they do not change, but remain the same loosely knit community throughout, is a guide to their place and function in the comedy. Sharp-witted, loud-mouthed, keen of eye to see an opportunity for gain, and quick of hand to seize it, the people of the Fair, fascinating though they are in themselves, exist to create and provide the conditions in which the main drama can take place. They are not the subject of that drama. It is their job to keep the try-pot a-boiling, as it were; and they carry out this task to perfection.

Over against the inhabitants of the Fair are set the visitors to it, drawn thither, for the most part, by the strong enticing odours that emanate from its seething cauldron of activity. Jonson's own stage direction, at III.ii, 73, is particularly instructive on this score. It reads: 'BUSY *scents after it like a hound*'. The 'it' is roast pig; the Fair's appeal is to the appetite. But the word 'appetite' covers much, even within the context of a fair, ranging from the simple elementary gluttony of Busy to the inordinate desire of Overdo to 'wind [smell]

[1] 'The Structure of *Bartholomew Fair*', *PMLA*, 80 (1965), 172–9.

out wonders of enormity' (II.ii, 110). Like 'scent after', 'wind out' is part of the technical terminology of hunting; and the play is shot through and through with references to hunting and falconry, because the world it depicts is very decidedly a predatory one. The dominant appetite is the appetite for prey of one kind or another. Most of the characters in it, visitors to the Fair and natives of the Fair alike, are out to 'apprehend' something or someone: a purse, a rich widow, or, in the case of Overdo, a big haul of wrongdoers.

Unlike the fair-people, on whom the vicissitudes of the day leave no mark, the fair-goers not only experience much that is new and unexpected but also feel the effects of it. Some of the more important among them are even changed by it. The one significant exception here is Cokes, whom nothing can change. Apart from Overdo, who is in a special category of his own and does not appear until the first scene of Act II, they are all introduced in the first act, which is devoted entirely to them. At this stage they fall into three discrete groups, each of which has its own motives for going to the Fair. The first group is the citizen family, made up of John Littlewit, his wife Win-the-fight, her mother Dame Purecraft, and Purecraft's spiritual father Zeal-of-the-land Busy. Their ostensible reason for going is the need to satisfy the pregnant Win's simulated longing for roast pig; their real reason sheer gluttony, and more importantly, where Littlewit is concerned, his desperate desire to see the performance in the Fair of the puppet-play he has written. The second group, also four in number, is another family party: Cokes, his married sister Mistress Overdo, his tutor Wasp, and his betrothed Grace Wellborn, who is Justice Overdo's ward. The moving spirit here is Cokes, avid for toys and novelties, and determined to see the Fair because it bears his name, Bartholmew, and is therefore his fair. Finally come Winwife, a suitor for the hand of Dame Purecraft, and his friend Quarlous. It is only after they have made the acquaintance of Cokes and his party that these two decide on a visit to the Fair in order to watch the antics of Cokes and Wasp in particular, who, says Winwife, are bound to 'engender us excellent creeping sport' (I.v, 127–8).

Even within Act I, however, it is already plain that two of these groups lack cohesion. Littlewit and Win practise deception on Purecraft and Busy, and have no illusions about the true nature of these two characters. Littlewit describes Purecraft as 'a most elect hypocrite' (I.v, 149), and both he and Win voice their contempt for Busy—in his absence, of course. The divisions in Cokes's party are even deeper. Wasp is horrified, as well he might be, at the prospect of his rattle-brained charge let loose in the Fair, and only agrees to accompany him out of a sense of duty. Grace has no wish to see the Fair at all, and, as she reveals in an aside (I.v, 77), loathes the idea of being married to Cokes. Nor has Cokes the slightest affection for her; the toy-like Win is far more to his taste. There are even some signs of cracks in the relationship of Quarlous and Winwife. The freedoms Quarlous takes with Win jar on Winwife, and, when he expresses his dislike of them, Quarlous retorts with a violent diatribe against Winwife's 'widow-hunting'.

In the unrestrained atmosphere of the Fair, where the satisfaction of one appetite merely serves to stimulate another and it is easy to detach oneself from unwanted 'friends', the groups break up completely, and new alliances are formed. When the last scene opens, Winwife is married to Grace, Quarlous to Dame Purecraft, Win, masked and dressed as a prostitute, is with Edgworth the cutpurse, and Mistress Overdo, similarly disguised, is sunk in a drunken stupor by the side of Whit the pimp and procurer. Cokes and Wasp, after a long period of separation from each other, have eventually been reunited in V.iv, and are together again, but on a new basis, since Wasp, recognizing what is now an accomplished fact, has abandoned all pretence of exercising any authority over Cokes. Learning from Cokes that his charge knows he has been set in the stocks, Wasp remarks ruefully:

> Does he know that? Nay, then the date of my authority is out; I must think no longer to reign, my government is at an end. He that will correct another must want fault in himself. (V.iv, 89–91)

Wasp's realization that he has lost his authority, such as it was, and with it all right to be censorious prefigures a similar realization by the Puritan elder and the Justice of the Peace, whose experiences so far have run parallel to his. All three have been in the stocks together, put there by the rogues: Busy at the instance of Leatherhead, suborned by Littlewit; Overdo on the instigation of the cutpurse; and Wasp through the agency of Whit, who brings in the Watch. Not the least of the joys that *Bartholmew Fair* has to offer is its total subversion of order. It is a comedy in which, in the words of the Duke in *Measure for Measure*:

> liberty plucks justice by the nose;
> The baby beats the nurse, and quite athwart
> Goes all decorum. (I.iii, 29–31)

When Wasp confesses his inadequacy in V.iv, Busy and Overdo still have to recognize theirs. Busy is forced into doing so in V.v, where he turns up at the puppet-shew, mouthing the stock complaints against the theatre which its enemies had been uttering and printing for the best part of forty years. Confident in the rightness of his cause and in his own ability to uphold it, he engages in a disputation with the puppet Dionysius, and suffers absolute defeat when, in answer to his charge that 'the male among you putteth on the apparel of the female, and the female of the male', the puppet lifts up its garments to reveal that it has no sex at all. Crying 'the cause hath failed me', Busy accepts Leatherhead's invitation to be converted and let the play go on, saying explicitly: 'Let it go on. For I am changed, and will become a beholder with you!' (V.v, 105–6). His collapse is at once farcical and logical, a superb demonstration of his abysmal ignorance of the real issues about which he has been so positive and ranted so long. Even his language has changed. For the first time in the play, he has actually managed to say three different things in two brief sentences, instead of saying the same thing over and over again at greater and greater length, until it ceases to mean anything at all.

Delighted with this outcome of the disputation, Cokes cries 'On with the play!', but at this point Overdo throws off the disguise he is wearing—the second he has adopted during the course of the action—and begins to savour his moment of triumph, 'wherein', as he puts it in gleeful anticipation, 'I will break out in rain and hail, lightning and thunder, upon the head of enormity' (V.ii, 5–6). He has endured much in order to reach this Jove-like, as he imagines it, position. Entering the play in II.i, under the disguise of 'Mad Arthur of Bradley', he explains, in soliloquy, his motives for donning it. They are not entirely foolish. A city magistrate, he distrusts his subordinates, and not without reason, for Haggis, Bristle, and Pocher, when they do appear, prove themselves master bunglers. He is therefore determined to find out the truth for himself. But his characteristic tendency to 'overdo' things is immediately evident in his description of what he expects to discover, for while a fair is likely to produce petty crime in plenty, it does not run to 'enormity', nor do its activities have any effect on the commonwealth, of which Overdo sees himself as the pillar and defender.

Attempting to combine the roles of Cicero and Sherlock Holmes, Overdo makes one mistake after another and suffers a series of indignities. He takes the cutpurse for a civil young man who must be saved from the debauched company he keeps, he is beaten by Wasp on the suspicion of being an accomplice of the cutpurse, then put into the stocks for the same reason. While there, he discovers that Trouble-all the madman, once one of his officers, has been driven mad by Overdo's severity in dismissing him from his post, and, in an effort to make the madman some recompense, he hands over what is virtually a blank cheque to Quarlous, who has disguised himself as Trouble-all. Quarlous promptly turns it into a deed of gift that makes him, not Overdo, the guardian of Grace Wellborn.

Blithely unaware, in spite of, and even because of, his arduous detective activities, of what has in fact happened during the day, Overdo is all set for his great scene. It is to be a truth-showing, such as that which comes at the end of *Measure for Measure*, followed by a grand judgement on the offenders. Firmly in command of the situation, as he thinks, he begins to put the characters in their places. To his surprise, he discovers that Winwife and Grace are married. It ought to give him pause, but it does not. Extolling himself as a great discoverer, comparable to such men as Columbus and Drake, he begins to sort the sheep, including Edgworth, from the goats, and unmasks Mistress Littlewit. Trouble-all comes rushing in, and Overdo has to recognize that Quarlous cannot be Trouble-all, but even this does not shake his confidence in himself and in his superior knowledge. But at this moment the masked Mistress Overdo awakens from her drunken stupor, calls for a basin, and is promptly sick. It is a magnificent anticlimax. Overdo is put to silence; and Quarlous, a much better detective, proceeds to acquaint him with the truth in all its humiliating detail and to draw a practical moral from it:

> . . . remember you are but Adam, flesh and blood! You have your frailty. Forget your other name of Overdo, and invite us all to supper.
> (V.vi, 93–5)

With no other choice open to him, Overdo accepts this advice; and the entire company, rogues and all, go off to the feast which so often concludes an Elizabethan or Jacobean comedy.

Interpreted along these lines, *Bartholmew Fair* emerges as the festive comedy its title leads one to expect, and also as the didactic comedy that its author's reputation as a moralist and his emphasis on the capacity of drama to teach should naturally lead to: Wasp, Busy, and Overdo have all learnt to know themselves better and, as a consequence, will be less censorious of their fellow-men in future. But is this neat package what the play really offers, or all that it offers? There are at least three major obstacles in the way of accepting this interpretation *in toto*. The first is the conversions. Of these, Overdo's is the most convincing. He, after all, has regretted his treatment of Trouble-all and tried to make some amends for it before the last scene begins. He has begun to change as early as IV.i. But will Wasp give up scolding or Busy abandon ranting for good? It seems inconceivable; these activities are their life-blood. The second difficulty, which will be shelved for the time being, is that it is Quarlous who comes out on top and who provides the solution; yet how can his conduct be regarded as in any way exemplary? Finally, the reading proposed takes no account whatever of Cokes, who is, in many ways, the most interesting figure in the play.

From an early stage in his career Jonson had shown a deep

interest in fools. In *Every Man in His Humour* (1598) he had depicted three of them. Wellbred lures his friend Edward Knowell from the country to the City by promising to have two fine specimens, Master Mathew and Bobadill, on exhibition for his delectation; and Knowell makes his own contribution to the feast by taking his cousin, Master Stephen, along with him. Master Stephen, 'the country gull', as he is called, is the first sketch, so to speak, out of which will ultimately come Cokes, the finished masterpiece. Brainless, conceited, and affected, Master Stephen is quite simply an object of derision. Cokes is not. There is nothing affected about him; he is the thing itself, natural uninhibited folly in all the exuberance and witlessness of youth. Incapable of keeping his mind on any subject for more than a few moments and responding immediately and instinctively to every distraction that springs up before him, he is actuated in all he does by a simple love of pleasure, and he can find pleasure in the most trivial things. Tall and gangling—Quarlous on his first view of him talks of his 'Sir Cranion legs' (I.v, 90)—he is often referred to as a bird or an insect, and with good reason. As soon as he reaches the Fair, he flits, like some demented butterfly, from object to object, from stall to stall, picking up one toy or trifle after another. Ill-advisedly, Wasp, in an attempt to curb him, resorts to irony, telling him: 'No, the shop; buy the whole shop, it will be best; the shop, the shop!' (III.iv, 74–5). Predictably, the irascible command has the opposite effect to that intended, for Cokes, impervious to irony, goes on to buy not one shop but two. So untouched by care is he that there are moments when one almost envies him; and there is even an infectious quality about his folly. When he takes part in the refrain of Nightingale's ballad, one feels very much like joining him.

His progress through the Fair is, of course, a process of being plucked and picked clean. Reduced to his doublet and hose, he eventually reaches the puppet-shew penniless, borrows some money from Littlewit, and finds himself in his element. As Winwife remarks on seeing him there, he has 'gotten in among his playfellows' (V.iv, 1). He has indeed; among the puppets, whom he regards as miniature live actors, he is thoroughly at his ease; and, after Overdo has issued his invitation to the company to join him at supper, Cokes has the last word as he says: 'Yes, and bring the actors along, we'll ha' the rest o' the play at home'. (V.vi, 110–11).

There are very good reasons why these final words should be given to Cokes and why they should be the final words. The puppets are the perfect playfellows for him, because he himself is an extreme example of man as puppet. He reacts immediately and predictably, as the fair-people are quick to realize, to any stimulus from without. The brilliantly hilarious central scene, III.v, puts this matter at its clearest and funniest. No sooner has Nightingale, urged on by Edgworth who already has Cokes's measure, begun to sing than Cokes responds by crying out 'Ballads!'—the single word denoting delighted recognition of something desirable is one of the most marked features of his whole manner of speech. He then becomes wholly absorbed in the pleasures of the song and in his own scheme to entrap the cutpurses by exhibiting the purse that contains his gold and challenging them to snatch it. It is while he is in this state that Edgworth, to quote Jonson's own stage direction, '*gets up to him, and tickles him in the ear with a straw twice, to draw his hand out of his pocket*'. Needless to say, the trick works. Cokes scratches his ear, and Edgworth robs him of his purse and handkerchief. Nightingale and Edgworth, the puppet-masters, have manipulated him exactly as they intended.

The scene demonstrates in the plainest possible manner something that is basic for the whole comedy. Cokes is the most obvious puppet in it, but he by no means stands alone. The people of the Fair behave like automata as they cry their wares in exactly the same terms time after time. Moreover, they have one-track minds, as their speech so clearly indicates. Knockem, for example, thinks and talks entirely in terms of horse, while Ursla is a pig-woman not only because she cooks and sells pig but also because she looks like a pig and has a vocabulary that is as greasy as her person. A mistress in the not so gentle art of vulgar abuse, she pours scorn on her opponents and enemies by her unfailing ability to draw them into and make them part of that world of animals and cooking which is the only world she knows. Edgworth, who plays so skilfully on the puppet-like nature of Cokes, becomes the puppet of Quarlous. Win and Mistress Overdo have to obey the dictates of their distended bladders—as we all must at times—and then succumb to the blandishments of Knockem and Whit, who turn them into a couple of prostitutes.

But the most sophisticated puppets are those who are jerked into motion by their ruling passions or their *idées fixes*. Wasp, Busy, and Overdo all fall into this class. Wasp, the simplest case of the three, is driven in all he does by his irascibility, his urge to contradict, and his love of scolding. It is the last of these impulses, incidentally, that attaches him so closely to Cokes, for Cokes, who is constantly doing things that deserve scolding and remains completely unaffected by any scolding he receives, is the ideal host for Wasp's parasitic temper to batten on. A creature of his own passions, Wasp reacts in such a predictable way that Edgworth can tell Quarlous, near the end of IV.iii, that stealing the licence from him will be so easy as not to be 'worth speaking on'. Nor is it.

Busy is far more complicated. As befits a hypocrite, there are two of him not one: he is both puppet-master and puppet. The first, the subterranean Busy, so to speak, is a character we never see in action, we merely hear about him. But what we hear is very important. As early as I.ii, we find from Littlewit and Win that he is sponging on Dame Purecraft (I.ii, 58–67). Then, in the following scene, come more revelations: he was once a baker, and ruined a grocer who was so foolish as to trust him with currants, but 'has given over his trade'. Certainly he has ceased to be a baker, but has he abandoned business altogether? We are left to assume that he has until we reach V.ii, the scene in which Dame Purecraft offers herself in marriage to the disguised Quarlous, under the mistaken impression that he is the madman Trouble-all, whose clothes he has stolen. There, after confessing the devious and fraudulent methods she has employed to make herself worth six thousand pounds, Purecraft goes on to say:

> Our elder, Zeal-of-the-land, would have had me; but I know him to be the capital knave of the land, making himself rich by being made feoffee in trust to deceased brethren, and cozening their heirs by swearing the absolute gift of their inheritance. (V.ii, 63–7)

Busy has switched from baking to the more profitable and less laborious business of cooking wills and swindling heirs. His Puritanism is a mask and a lever. He uses it to win men's confidence in order to defraud them. He is a puppet-master, a manipulator of others for his own ends, which have nothing to do with religion.

How does he do it? By talking, of course; the Busy we do see and hear makes that plain enough. Not that he ever says anything; he does not need to, for he has discovered the art of making something out of nothing, or almost. In his mouth the most elementary statement swells into a monstrous preachment, as repetition is piled on repetition and variation on variation. Moreover, it all acquires a kind of sham authority from the scriptural references with which it is so liberally studded and, as Jonas A. Barish has so well shown,[2] from the Biblical cadences into which it falls. Busy is the complete Aeolist, some eighty years before Jonathan Swift defined and identified that tribe in his *A Tale of a Tub*, and, like Swift's madman, the first proselyte he has made is himself.[3] He has become the creature of his own yeasty rhetoric. The tongue cries 'Satan', 'the Beast', or 'Dagon', and the rest of the man responds with a reflex action. *Vox et praeterea nihil*, Busy is a hollow man, the puppet of his own rantings, which bear no relation to observable facts.

[2] *Ben Jonson and the Language of Prose Comedy*, Cambridge, Mass., 1960, pp. 197–204.

[3] *A Tale of a Tub &c.*, ed. A. C. Guthkelch and D. Nichol Smith, Oxford, 1920, pp. 150–61 and 171.

As for Overdo, he is, like Volpone, like Volpone's dupes, and like the dupes in *The Alchemist*, a product of Jonson's perception that the last thing a man will abandon is his illusions, and especially his illusions about himself. Although his hopes are for glory, not criminal gain, he is, nonetheless, in exactly the same state of mind as the birds of prey in *Volpone*, of whom Mosca says:

> Each of 'hem
> Is so possest, and stuft with his own hopes,
> That any thing, vnto the contrary,
> Neuer so true, or neuer so apparent,
> Neuer so palpable, they will resist it—. (V.ii, 23–7)

The beating Overdo receives from Wasp is palpable enough, so are the stocks in which he is set; but, buoyed up by his image of himself as a Lucius Junius Brutus and a Cicero, and lured forward by his dream of the great scene, something like Prospero's at the end of *The Tempest*, that he will ultimately stage, he continues on his self-appointed course until the sight of his wife, dressed as a whore, accompanied by the infamous Whit, and vomiting into a basin, demonstrates the vanity of his wishes in a fashion which even he cannot ignore. He ceases to be a puppet when he recognizes things as they are, instead of, in Bacon's phrase, 'submitting the shows of things to the desires of the mind'.[4]

The significance of puppetry in the play is endorsed by the fact that it is to the puppet-show that the action moves and there finds its resolution. Furthermore, the puppet-play itself is, as several critics have observed, a re-enactment of the preceding human drama, characterized by the same name-calling, the same crude insults, raucous din, pointless quarrelling, and senseless brawling. At times it is a carbon copy of the main drama. In IV.v, Knockem and Whit get rid of the whore Ramping Alice, who has become troublesome, by literally kicking her out of Ursla's booth. In the puppet-play, Damon and Pythias, invited to 'Kiss the whore [Hero!] o' the arse', reply 'So we will, so we will' (V.iv, 281–2), and, deliberately mistaking the word 'kiss', proceed to kick her backside. The puppets behave like the human characters because they are imitating a way of life in which human beings behave like puppets.

The exceptions to this generalization are Grace and, to a lesser degree, Quarlous and Winwife. Grace has no wish to visit the Fair, and does her best to deter Cokes and the rest of his party from going by describing it as a form of entertainment that is not frequented by those 'of any quality or fashion' (I.v, 119). But her plea falls on deaf

[4] *The Advancement of Learning*, Bk. II, iv. 2; p. 102 in the edition by William Aldis Wright, Oxford, 1900.

ears; and she has to go along, because, being a ward, she has no more option in this matter than she has in that of being contracted in marriage to Cokes. The law has made a puppet of her, and she has no illusions about the matter. When Quarlous asks her how she came to be Overdo's ward, she answers, without bitterness but with a sober appreciation of her own position:

> Faith, through a common calamity: he bought me, sir. And now he will marry me to his wife's brother, this wise gentleman that you see, or else I must pay value o' my land. (III.v, 263–5)

Her freedom from illusions about herself and her recognition of things as they are give Grace the strength to take action, when the chance comes, in order to escape from her puppet-like state. They also serve to set her off from the rest of the group among which she first appears. Before she has so much as spoken a word, Quarlous and Winwife have noticed how incongruous a figure she is, because, unlike her companions, 'She seems to be discreet, and as sober as she is handsome' (I.v, 51). And, though it is never made quite explicit, the interest they find in her would seem to be one of the reasons why they decide to go to the Fair, for they make that decision immediately after expressing their realization of the disparity between her and Cokes (I.v, 123–8).

The motive Quarlous and Winwife do give for their visit to the Fair is 'sport'. They will go to watch the fair-goers in much the same spirit as Democritus, according to the quotation from Horace which Jonson placed on his title-page, would go to watch the audience at a play rather than the play itself. In fact, however, they do no such thing. While Winwife is reluctant to become involved in the activities of the place, Quarlous, whose name appears to be a combination of 'quarrellous', meaning 'quarrelsome', and 'parlous', meaning 'dangerously clever', is not. He is soon at odds with Knockem; then both he and Winwife engage in a tremendous flyting with Ursla; and, finally, he comes to blows with Knockem. All this happens in II.v. The Fair destroys Quarlous's pose of detached observer in no time. Then, having met Cokes and his party in III.iv, they begin to talk to Grace and, when Cokes and the rest of his party go off, leaving her behind them, they ask her to trust herself to their company, which she does readily enough. At the same time, however, each becomes suspicious of the other. At the opening of IV.iii, they '*enter with their swords drawn*' quarrelling over her. They have become a typical part of the Fair, doing what the other people in it are only too ready to do. But their quarrel does not end in a fight, because Grace takes over. Asked to choose between them, she refuses to do so, saying:

> How can I judge of you, so far as to a choice, without knowing you more? You are both equal and alike to me, yet; and so indifferently affected by me, as each of you might be the man, if the other were away; for you are reasonable creatures; you have understanding and discourse. (IV.iii, 29–34)

Her balanced lucid prose—and she speaks thus throughout the play—is in marked contrast to the speech of every other character, except Winwife, and tells much about her. Clear-eyed and free from all illusions about her own desperate position, she is ready to take either of them as a husband rather than Cokes, because they 'are reasonable creatures', at least to the extent that they have listened to her instead of fighting, and are therefore capable of being educated. They are also, as she recognizes, the only alternatives to Cokes that there are; and, since she must make a decision at once between them, she very sensibly leaves the matter to chance, bearing in mind the old proverb 'Hanging and wiving go by destiny'. She is, of course, making herself a puppet of fortune, but who is not? By exercising her intelligence she has freed herself from the puppet-like condition in which the law had placed her. Moreover, the husband that destiny, in the shape of the madman Trouble-all, gives her is the more suitable of the two, for Winwife, though rather thin and colourless by the side of Quarlous, is also more refined and more amenable to education than his companion.

Even so, however, Grace is dependent for her escape on the ingenuity of Quarlous; and what is one to make of him? This much can be said with certainty: he is, by far and away, the cleverest person in the play. Drawn into the activities of the Fair by the irresistible opportunities it provides for a release of the abusive and aggressive instincts in him that are so evident on his first appearance in I.iii, he contrives to remain sufficiently detached from them to observe them with care and to use them for his own purposes. He blackmails Edgworth into stealing the licence from Wasp; adopts a disguise, like Overdo but far more effectively, in order to find out whether he or Winwife is to be the husband of Grace; and then, quick-wittedly, puts it to further use in extracting a blank charter from Overdo. By the end of the play, he is in the omniscient position that the Justice had hoped to be in and so clearly is not, and is therefore able to impose his own tolerant solution on the action.

But much that Quarlous says and does leaves a sour taste in the mouth. His marriage to Dame Purecraft, although it involves a complete reversal of the attitude expressed in his coarse and violent attack on widow-hunting in I.iii, can be partly condoned on the grounds that it is not he who makes advances to her but she who offers herself to him, albeit under the mistaken notion that he really is the Trouble-all he pretends to be, and that he has just learnt that Grace has fallen to the lot of Winwife. But does this excuse his taking 'this six thousand pound' which he knows has been made through fraud? Furthermore, there is something especially repellent in the self-righteous tone in which he rejects Edgworth's offer to share his whore with him (IV.vi, 19–25). Having immersed himself in pitch, he seeks to wash himself clean with the plea that 'it was for sport' (IV.vi, 27), but by the end of the play this will not do. It was for power and for gain. Quarlous equivocates with himself, and there is much that is equivocal in Jonson's presentation of him. The closest parallel to it is his presentation of that other clever rogue Face in *The Alchemist*. Both roles seem to carry the implication that in a world of knaves and fools the cleverest knave will come out on top.

Men can learn from experience and change themselves for the better; men are the puppets of their own natures and illusions; men can free themselves from a puppet-like condition imposed on them from without by using their intelligence; the world is a wicked place, so the best thing one can do is to accept the fact and adopt a wholly pragmatic attitude to life. *Bartholmew Fair* raises all these possibilities and, in the end, leaves them all open, because it is an authentic drama. Jonson presents his characters in action, leaving the business of interpretation to that judicious element in the audience that he mentions at line 72 of the Induction, where he also makes it clear, in typically Jonsonian fashion, that good judgement is synonymous with approval of the play. The Induction is a less genial and more two-edged piece of theatre criticism than many commentators on it would suggest.

Open-ended in the general attitude to life that it expresses, *Bartholmew Fair* is specific and definite in what it has to say about the two social issues that it raises. After reading it, one is in no doubt as to what Jonson thought about wardship. Grace's laconic comment on her own situation 'he bought me, sir' (III.v, 263) tells us all we need to know in this connection. Jonson disapproved, and expected his audience to disapprove, of the sale of human beings conducted by the Court of Wards; and it says much for his courage that he was prepared to make his position clear in a play that was to have its second performance before James I, one of whose sources of income was that same Court, which had been under heavy attack in Parliament. Moreover, it is Overdo, a Justice of the Peace, who has bought Grace, in order to marry her and her fortune to his foolish brother-in-law Cokes. Finding 'enormity' in the petty frauds and swindles of the Fair, he is blind to the true though legal enormity of his treatment of Grace.

Wardship and its abuses, though they have their place in the comedy, are not, however, the main target of its satiric thrust. That place is occupied by the enemies of poetry in general and of the theatre in particular. When *Bartholmew Fair* was written the theatre had been under attack for the best part of forty years, and from two main directions. The City fathers disapproved of it on grounds that were largely social and economic. They complained that the congregation of people at plays helped to spread the plague, provided whores and pickpockets with a golden opportunity to ply their trades, lured apprentices and journeymen into absenteeism from work, and so forth. The more austere Protestants denounced it because the playing of plays on Sundays kept people away from their sermons; because plays, like May-games and similar traditional festivals, were, in their view, a survival from the Roman Catholic past and, ultimately, from paganism; because tragedies dealt with such sins as anger and murder, and comedies with 'loue, bawdrie, cosenage, flattery, whordome, adulterie' (Chambers, iv, 223); and because the Fathers of the Church had set their faces against the degenerate theatre of Ancient Rome. The list of 'enormities' practised in or encouraged by the theatre could be extended to almost any length; and the tone adopted by the preachers is well represented in a sermon given at Paul's Cross in 1608 by William Crashaw, the father of the poet Richard Crashaw, part of which runs thus:

> The vngodly Playes and Enterludes so rife in this nation: what are they but a bastard of Babylon, a daughter of error and confusion, a hellish deuice (the diuels owne recreation to mock at holy things) by him deliuered to the Heathen, from them to the Papists, and from them to vs. (Chambers, iv, 249)

The attack was, as Sir Philip Sidney saw and made clear in his *Defence of Poesie*, written about 1583 but not published until 1595, an attack on imaginative writing in general. How did the dramatists and their allies react to it? For the most part they made the fatal mistake of trying to meet the enemy on his own grounds and with his own weapons, seeking to show through prose treatises, such as Thomas Heywood's *An Apology for Actors* (1608?), that the theatre was a sound moral agent, reproving and exposing vice and extolling and encouraging virtue. Alternatively, they contented themselves with some skirmishing by holding Puritan hypocrisies up to ridicule in some of their plays. The single big exception to this rule is Jonson. In *Bartholmew Fair* a great playwright deploys his skills as a dramatist, not to apologize for the theatre, but to mount a comprehensive and hard-hitting counter-attack against its opponents and detractors. In the Prologue to the play he describes himself as 'The Maker', deliberately adopting Sidney's name for the poet, and, dropping all pretence to educate or improve, he offers his comedy for the King's 'true delight'. He then sets about the enemy: the City authorities, embodied in Overdo, who, on several occasions, voices his dislike of and contempt for poetry, which he regards as the ruin of a potentially good citizen—Edgworth!—and the preachers, whose excesses and absurdities are epitomized and pilloried in the rantings of Busy. Fanaticism, bigotry, and ignorance are defined, exposed, and placed for what they are by Jonson's good sense, his concern for humanistic values, and his profound respect for tradition, including the tradition of fun.

Needless to say, *Bartholmew Fair* could not change the course of history. Twenty-eight years after it was written the theatres were closed. But they were reopened in 1660; and, within a year of their reopening, it was being staged once more. There is something symbolically appropriate about that.

A NOTE ON THE TEXT

THE SOLE AUTHORITY for the text of *Bartholmew Fair* is the folio printed by John Beale, in 1631, for Robert Allot. This folio also included *The Devil is an Ass*, first played in 1616, and *The Staple of News*, first played in 1626. However, no publication, so far as is known, followed on the printing. In July 1637 Mary Allot, whose husband had died, transferred her rights in *Bartholmew Fair* and *The Staple of News—The Devil is an Ass* appears to have been overlooked—to John Legatt and Andrew Crooke. They, in turn, though no record of the transaction survives, would seem to have sold the sheets of the 1631 printing to Richard Meighen, who issued them, in 1640, with a new title-page, describing the three plays as 'The Second Volume' of Jonson's 'Workes'.

The collation of *Bartholmew Fair* in the folio text of 1631 is A1 blank; A2 recto, the title-page; A2 verso, blank; A3 recto, the Prologue; A3 verso, the Persons of the Play; A4 recto to A6 verso, the Induction; B to M in fours, paged 1 to 88, with pages 12, 13, and 31 wrongly numbered as 6, 3, and 13 respectively, the text of the play and the Epilogue.

The copy for the text was, as the massed entries at the beginning of each scene and the rhetorical punctuation indicate, almost certainly a carefully prepared manuscript in Jonson's own hand. He was, therefore, justifiably very annoyed when Beale did a thoroughly bad job on it. In a letter he wrote to the Earl of Newcastle, when sending him a copy of *The Devil is an Ass*, he mentions that he has already sent a copy of *Bartholmew Fair*, but that he cannot extract a copy of *The Staple of News* from Beale, whom he calls 'the Lewd Printer'. He also complains that as a consequence of Beale's 'delayes and vexation, I am almost become blind' (H & S, i, 211). It was probably Beale's incompetence, and his own inability to force the printer into putting things right, that led Jonson, whose standards of accuracy were high, to drop the project of publishing a second volume of his Works, with the result that the three plays were not issued until three years after his death in 1637.

In setting up the play Beale and his men committed one common error after another, and, to make matters even worse, some kind of accident happened to the forme containing L2 recto (V.iii, 79–121) and L3 verso (V.iv, 83–122), so that it had to be reset. Most of their mistakes fall into definite groups. First, there is a fine crop of misprints. They begin, appropriately enough, on the title-page, where, in the penultimate line of the quotation from Horace, '*asello*' appears as '*assello*'. They continue in 'The Persons of the Play' with 'WHTCHMEN' (l. 24) for 'WATCHMEN', thence into the Induction, where 'Soueraigne' (l. 67) is turned into 'Soueragine', and so on into the main body of the play right down to the final scene, which gives 'fot' (l. 12) instead of 'for'. This last error, due to foul case, is one of a number of such: 'wirh' for 'with' (III.v, 11), 'Heatt' for 'Heart' (III.v, 288), and 'rhe' for 'the' (IV.vi, 40). Similarly, there are several instances of *c* for *e*: 'Licencc' for 'Licence' (I.ii, 22), 'shce' for 'shee' (I.ii, 43), 'fatnessc' for 'fatnesse' (II.ii, 112), and so on. Secondly, letters are omitted, giving 'Her's' for 'Here's' (I.i, 3), 'littl' for 'little' (I.iv, 111), 'scury' for 'scuruy' (I.iv, 113), and the like. Thirdly, words are printed in the wrong order, for instance, 'do good' for 'good do' (I.ii, 39). Fourthly, words are omitted. A clear example is 'is, taken' for 'is, is taken' (IV.iii, 55), but as some of my emendations indicate, there are, I think, others. Fifthly, there is much pointless repetition of words: 'of of' for 'of' (II.i, 40), 'then then' for 'then' (III.v, 27), 'and and' for 'and' (III.vi, 35). Sixthly, words are misspaced, beginning with 'hiseighteene' for 'his eighteene' (Ind. 86); and, finally, there are, in my opinion, a number of minim errors: 'drunke' for 'drinke' (I.iii, 24) seems an obvious case.

Jonson, we know, was very careful indeed about his punctuation, which is designed to assist the actor's delivery of the lines. It is rhetorical, that is to say, the stops are intended primarily to denote the duration of pauses rather than the grammatical units into which a sentence falls. The heavier the stop, the longer the pause is to be. Beale, however, seems to have worked on the principle that one stop is as good as another. As early as I.i, 23, he prints 'And. her' for 'And, her' or possibly 'And her'; and from this point onwards goes his own way, often producing sentences which have neither a rhetorical nor a grammatical basis.

In the present edition printer's errors of the obvious kind have been silently corrected, but all departures of substance from the copy text have been noted at the foot of the page on which they occur. All additions to the copy text, with the one exception of the speech prefix before the opening speech in each scene (see the note to the stage direction at the beginning of I.i), are enclosed in square brackets. The spelling has been modernized; but colloquial forms, such as 'o' the', meaning 'of the' or 'on the', and the like, have been retained. So have the abbreviated forms of personal names ('Barthol-mew' for 'Bartholomew', 'Ursla' for 'Ursula', etc.). The punctuation presented a special problem. Jonson's rhetorical pointing is, in any case, disconcerting to the modern reader. When blurred and confused by the bunglings of Beale, it becomes very difficult indeed. It has therefore been replaced by modern punctuation. This policy has meant that on some occasions one possible sense has been suppressed in favour of another. In such cases the original pointing is given at the foot of the page.

The edition is based on a photocopy of the British Museum copy of the three plays of 1631 with the press-mark 642.1.29.

FURTHER READING

Barish, Jonas A., *Ben Jonson and the Language of Prose Comedy*, Cambridge, Mass., 1960, pp. 187–239.

Barton, Anne, *Ben Jonson, Dramatist*, Cambridge, 1984, pp. 194–218.

Blissett, William, 'Your Majesty is Welcome to a Fair', in *The Elizabethan Theatre IV*, ed. G. R. Hibbard, Toronto, 1974, pp. 80–105.

Donaldson, Ian, *The World Upside-Down*, Oxford, 1970, pp. 1–23 and 46–77.

Duncan, Douglas, *Ben Jonson and the Lucianic Tradition*, Cambridge, 1979, pp. 203–13.

Dutton, Richard, *Ben Jonson: To the First Folio*, Cambridge, 1983, pp. 156–74.

Heffner, Ray L., Jr, 'Unifying Symbols in the Comedy of Ben Jonson', in *English Stage Comedy*, ed. W. K. Wimsatt, New York, 1954, pp. 74–97; rptd. in *Elizabethan Drama: Modern Essays in Criticism*, ed. R. J. Kaufmann, New York, 1961, pp. 170–86.

Levin, Richard, 'The Structure of *Bartholomew Fair*', *PMLA* 80 (1965), 172–9.

Parker, R. B., 'The Themes and Staging of *Bartholomew Fair*', *UTQ*, 39 (1970), 293–309.

Riggs, David, *Ben Jonson: A Life*, Cambridge, Mass., 1989, pp. 206–14.

Townsend, Freda L., *Apologie for Bartholomew Fayre: The Art of Jonson's Comedies*, New York, 1947.

Waith, Eugene M., 'The Staging of *Bartholomew Fair*', *SEL*, 2. 2 (1962), 181–95.

Womack, Peter, *Ben Johnson*, Oxford, 1986, pp. 144–52.

BARTHOLMEW FAYRE:

A COMEDIE,

ACTED IN THE YEARE, 1614.

By the Lady *ELIZABETHS* SERVANTS.

And then dedicated to King IAMES, of *moſt Bleſſed Memorie;*

By the Author, BENIAMIN IOHNSON.

Si foret in terris, rideret Democritus: *nam*
Spectaret populum ludis attentiùs ipſis,
Vt ſibi præbentem, mimo ſpectacula plura.
Scriptores autem narrare putaret aſello
Fabellam ſurdo. Hor. lib. 2. Epiſt. 1.

LONDON,
Printed by *I. B.* for ROBERT ALLOT, and are to be ſold at the ſigne of the *Beare,* in *Pauls* Church-yard. 1631.

BARTHOLMEW FAYRE. The full form of the name *Bartholomew* occurs only once in the play, at I. i, 3, where, significantly, Littlewit is reading the licence for Cokes's marriage. Everywhere else the preferred form, preserved in this edition, is *Bartholmew* (probably pronounced *Bartlemy*), a spelling which persisted into the nineteenth century.

From 1120 till 1855 a great fair was held annually in Smithfield on 24 August, the feast of St Bartholomew.

the Lady ELIZABETHS SERVANTS. This company of players seems to have come into being in 1611, when a patent was issued to them on 27 April. After various vicissitudes, they established themselves at the newly built theatre called the Hope in the autumn of 1614. See Chambers, ii. 246–58.

Si foret . . . surdo. Quoted from Horace, *Epistles*, II.i. 194–200, with lines 195–6 omitted, *nam* for *seu*, and *asello* misprinted as *assello*. 'If Democritus were still in the land of the living, he would laugh himself silly, for he would pay far more attention to the audience than to the play, since the audience offers the more interesting spectacle. But as for the authors of the plays—he would conclude that they were telling their tales to a deaf donkey'. Characteristically, Jonson is telling his audience what he thinks of them and of the state of the drama.

I.B. The initials of the printer John Beale.

Pauls Church-yard. The churchyard of old St Paul's Cathedral was the centre of the book-trade in London in the sixteenth and early seventeenth centuries.

THE PROLOGUE *TO* THE KING'S MAJESTY

Your Majesty is welcome to a Fair;
Such place, such men, such language, and such ware,
You must expect; with these, the zealous noise
Of your land's Faction, scandalized at toys,
As babies, hobby-horses, puppet-plays,
And such like rage, whereof the petulant ways
Yourself have known, and have been vexed with long.
These for your sport, without particular wrong,
Or just complaint of any private man
Who of himself or shall think well or can,
The Maker doth present; and hopes tonight
To give you, for a fairing, true delight.

4 *toys* trifles
5 *babies* dolls
6 *rage* mad folly
8 *particular wrong* injurious reference to any individual
11 *Maker* author
12 *fairing* present given at or bought at a fair

PROLOGUE. This prologue took the place of the Induction when the play was presented before James I at court on 1 November 1614.

4 *your land's Faction.* Ever since the breakdown of the Hampton Court Conference in 1604 James I had been embroiled with the Puritans.

THE PERSONS OF THE PLAY

JOHN LITTLEWIT, *a proctor*
[SOLOMON, *his man*]
WIN LITTLEWIT, *his wife*
DAME PURECRAFT, *her mother and a widow*
ZEAL-OF-THE-LAND BUSY, *her suitor, a Banbury man*
WINWIFE, *his rival, a gentleman*
QUARLOUS, *his companion, a gamester*
BARTHOLMEW COKES, *an esquire of Harrow*
HUMPHREY WASP, *his man*
ADAM OVERDO, *a Justice of Peace*
DAME OVERDO, *his wife*
GRACE WELLBORN, *his ward*
LANTERN LEATHERHEAD, *a hobby-horse-seller*
JOAN TRASH, *a gingerbread-woman*
EZEKIEL EDGWORTH, *a cutpurse*
NIGHTINGALE, *a ballad-singer*
URSLA, *a pig-woman*
MOONCALF, *her tapster*
JORDAN KNOCKEM, *a horse-courser, and ranger o' Turnbull*
VAL CUTTING, *a roarer*
CAPTAIN WHIT, *a bawd*

1 *proctor* legal agent, attorney
2 SOLOMON, *his man* Ed. (omitted F)
7 QUARLOUS combination of 'quarrellous' (= contentious) and 'parlous' (= dangerously clever)
gamester (i) gambler (ii) rake (iii) inveterate jeerer
8 COKES dupe, simpleton
17 URSLA shortened form of Ursula, Latin for 'little she-bear'
18 MOONCALF born fool
19 *horse-courser* horse-dealer, expert in sharp practice
ranger o' Turnbull gamekeeper of Turnbull Street in London, the 'game' being the prostitutes for whom the street was notorious
20 *roarer* noisy bully
21 WHIT term of abuse of uncertain meaning, also used by Jonson in *The Alchemist* (IV, vii, 45)

---

5 *a Banbury man*. Banbury, in Oxfordshire, was proverbially famous for its cheese, cakes, and ale, and, by the early seventeenth century, it had come to be regarded as a centre of Puritanism. Busy, a glutton as well as a Puritan, has been a baker (cf. I.iii, 110–20).

PUNK ALICE, *mistress o' the game*
TROUBLE-ALL, *a madman*
[HAGGIS, BRISTLE,] } *watchmen*
[POCHER, *a beadle*]
[A] COSTARD-MONGER
[A CORNCUTTER]
[A TINDERBOX-MAN]
[NORTHERN, *a*] *clothier*
[PUPPY, *a*] *wrestler*
[FILCHER, SHARKWELL,] } *doorkeepers [at the puppet-shew]*
PUPPETS
[PASSENGERS]

The Scene: Smithfield

22 *the game* prostitution
24–6 HAGGIS . . . *beadle* Ed. (WHTCHMEN, three. F)
27 A COSTARD-MONGER Ed. (COSTARD-monger. F) costermonger (originally a vendor of costards, i.e., apples)
28 A CORNCUTTER Ed. (omitted F)
29 A TINDERBOX-MAN Ed. (MOVSETRAP-man. F)
30 NORTHERN, *a* Ed. (CLOTHIER. F)
31 PUPPY, *a* Ed. (WRESTLER. F)
32–3 FILCHER, SHARKWELL, *doorkeepers at the puppet-shew* Ed. (DOORE-KEEPERS. F)
35 PASSENGERS Ed. (PORTERS F)

THE INDUCTION ON THE STAGE

[*Enter*] STAGE-KEEPER

STAGE-KEEPER

Gentlemen, have a little patience, they are e'en upon coming, instantly. He that should begin the play, Master Littlewit, the Proctor, has a stitch new fallen in his black silk stocking; 'twill be drawn up ere you can tell twenty. He plays one o' the Arches, that dwells about the Hospital, and he has a very pretty part. But for the whole play, will you ha' the truth on't?—I am looking, lest the poet hear me, or his man, Master Brome, behind the arras—it is like to be a very conceited scurvy one, in plain English. When't comes to the Fair once, you were e'en as good go to Virginia for anything there is of Smithfield. He has not hit the humours, he does not know 'em; he has not conversed with the Bartholmew-birds, as they say; he has ne'er a sword-and-buckler man in his Fair, nor a little Davy to take toll o' the bawds there, as in my time, nor a Kindheart, if anybody's teeth should chance to

s.d. STAGE-KEEPER man employed to set and sweep the stage
4 *tell* count
8 *arras* tapestry hanging
9 *conceited* fanciful, unrealistic
11 *hit the humours* hit off the typical oddities of behaviour
12 *Bartholmew-birds* roguish denizens of the Fair (cf. 'jail-birds')
13 *sword-and-buckler man* Ed. (Sword, and Buckler man F) swash-buckler, bragging bully

---

5 *one o' the Arches.* The Court of Arches, where Littlewit practises, was held in Bow Church and was the court of appeal from the diocesan courts.
the Hospital. 'St. Bartlemew, in Smithfield, an hospital of great receipt and relief for the poor . . . is endowed by the citizens' benevolence' (Stow, 438).

7–8 *his man, Master Brome.* Richard Brome was for a time Jonson's 'faithful servant', learned from him how to write plays, and eventually became a dramatist in his own right. Jonson's tribute to him is printed in H & S, viii. 409.

14 *little Davy.* Referred to in several works of the early seventeenth century, this individual seems to have been a professional bully.

15 *Kindheart.* An itinerant tooth-drawer who gave his name to Henry Chettle's pamphlet *Kind-Harts Dreame* (1593).

ache in his play; nor a juggler with a well-educated ape to come over the chain for the King of England, and back again for the Prince, and sit still on his arse for the Pope and the King of Spain! None o' these fine sights! Nor has he the canvas cut i' the night for a hobby-horse-man to creep in to his she-neighbour and take his leap there! Nothing! No, an some writer that I know had had but the penning o' this matter, he would ha' made you such a jig-a-jog i' the booths, you should ha' thought an earthquake had been i' the Fair! But these master-poets, they will ha' their own absurd courses; they will be informed of nothing. He has, sir-reverence, kicked me three or four times about the tiring-house, I thank him, for but offering to put in with my experience. I'll be judged by you, gentlemen, now, but for one conceit of mine! Would not a fine pump upon the stage ha' done well for a property now? And a punk set under upon her head, with her stern upward, and ha' been soused by my witty young masters o' the Inns o' Court? What think you o' this for a shew, now? He will not hear o' this! I am an ass! I! And yet I kept the stage in Master Tarlton's time, I thank my stars. Ho! an that man had lived to have played in *Bartholmew Fair*, you should ha' seen him ha' come in, and

20 *hobby-horse-man* (i) seller of hobby-horses (ii) frequenter of hobby-horses (prostitutes)

21 *take his leap* technical term for the copulation of a stallion with a mare
an if

23 *jig-a-jog* jogging motion (with sexual innuendo)

26–7 *sir-reverence* (originally 'save reverence') I apologize for mentioning it

27–8 *tiring-house* backstage area where the dressing-rooms were

28 *put in* intervene, help him out

30 *conceit* bright idea

31 *punk* whore

32 *soused* soaked to the skin

33 *witty* clever, facetious

---

33 *young masters o' the Inns o' Court.* The Inns of Court—Lincoln's Inn, the Inner Temple, the Middle Temple, and Gray's Inn—where students studied the law, were virtually a third university.

35 *in Master Tarlton's time.* Richard Tarlton, who died in 1588, was the most celebrated clown of his time. A member of the Queen's Men from the time of that company's foundation in 1583, he became something of a legend, and there were numerous stories and anecdotes about him.

ha' been cozened i' the cloth-quarter, so finely! And Adams, the rogue, ha' leaped and capered upon him, and ha' dealt his vermin about as though they had cost him nothing. And then a substantial watch to ha' stolen in upon 'em, and taken 'em away with mistaking words, as the fashion is in the stage practice.

[Enter] BOOK-HOLDER, SCRIVENER, *to him*

BOOK-HOLDER

How now? What rare discourse are you fallen upon, ha? Ha' you found any familiars here, that you are so free? What's the business?

STAGE-KEEPER

Nothing, but the understanding gentlemen o' the ground here asked my judgement.

BOOK-HOLDER

Your judgement, rascal? For what? Sweeping the stage? Or gathering up the broken apples for the bears within? Away, rogue, it's come to a fine degree in these spectacles when such a youth as you pretend to a judgement.

[Exit STAGE-KEEPER]

And yet he may, i' the most o' this matter i'faith; for the author hath writ it just to his meridian, and the scale of the grounded judgements here, his play-fellows in wit.

40 *vermin* fleas?

42 *mistaking words* malapropisms (cf. Dogberry and Verges in *Much Ado About Nothing*)

43 s.d. BOOK-HOLDER prompter

45 *free* free of speech, forward

52 *pretend* lay claim

54 *just to his meridian* exactly calculated to the limit of his understanding

55 *grounded* (i) well-grounded, proficient (ii) standing on the ground, in the pit

---

38 *cozened i' the cloth-quarter.* The cloth-quarter, originally the most important part of the Fair, was by the north wall of St Bartholomew's Church. An anecdote in the anonymous *Tarltons Jests* (1611) tells how the comedian was cheated of his clothes there.

Adams. John Adams was another member of the Queen's Men at the same time as Tarlton (Chambers, ii. 296).

47 *understanding gentlemen o' the ground.* A punning reference to the groundlings who stood under, i.e. below, the stage, in the pit.

50 *the bears within.* The Hope Theatre, which opened in 1614, was both a playhouse and a bear-garden. The stage was removed on the days when bear-baiting was the entertainment offered.

Gentlemen, not for want of a prologue, but by way of a new one, I am sent out to you here, with a scrivener and certain articles drawn out in haste between our author and you; which if you please to hear, and as they appear reasonable, to approve of, the play will follow presently. Read, scribe; gi' me the counterpane.

SCRIVENER

Articles of Agreement, indented, between the spectators or hearers at the Hope on the Bankside, in the County of Surrey, on the one party, and the author of *Bartholmew Fair*, in the said place and county, on the other party, the one and thirtieth day of October, 1614, and in the twelfth year of the reign of our Sovereign Lord, James, by the grace of God King of England, France, and Ireland; Defender of the Faith; and of Scotland the seven and fortieth.

INPRIMIS, It is covenanted and agreed by and between the parties above-said . . . and the said spectators and hearers, as well the curious and envious as the favouring and judicious, as also the grounded judgements and understandings, do for themselves severally covenant and agree to remain in the places their money or friends have put them in, with patience, for the space of two hours and an half, and somewhat more. In which time the author promiseth to present them, by us, with a new sufficient play called *Bartholmew Fair*, merry, and as full of noise as sport, made to delight all, and to offend none—provided they have either the wit or the honesty to think well of themselves.

It is further agreed that every person here have his or their

61 *counterpane* other half of the indenture
72 *curious* hypercritical
envious hostile
78 *sufficient* up to standard, of good quality

63 *the Bankside*. An area on the south side of the river Thames, and therefore not within the jurisdiction of the City of London, which, during the decade 1590–1600, became the theatrical centre.

71 *above-said . . . and* ed. (abouesaid, and F). It is very difficult to make sense of the long sentence 'It is . . . more.' (ll. 70–7) as it stands in the Folio. One expects the initial statement 'It is . . . abovesaid', to be followed by 'that', as it is in each of the subsequent articles. The present editor assumes that the compositor has omitted a line of Jonson's manuscript. The difficulty can be got over in the theatre by having the actor mumble after 'above-said', much as lawyers often do in reading the preliminaries of a will or the like.

free-will of censure, to like or dislike at their own charge; the author having now departed with his right, it shall be lawful for any man to judge his six penn'orth, his twelve penn'orth, so to his eighteen pence, two shillings, half a crown, to the value of his place—provided always his place get not above his wit. And if he pay for half a dozen, he may censure for all them too, so that he will undertake that they shall be silent. He shall put in for censures here as they do for lots at the lottery; marry, if he drop but sixpence at the door, and will censure a crown's worth, it is thought there is no conscience or justice in that.

It is also agreed that every man here exercise his own judgement, and not censure by contagion, or upon trust, from another's voice or face that sits by him, be he never so first in the Commission of Wit; as also that he be fixed and settled in his censure, that what he approves or not approves today, he will do the same tomorrow, and if tomorrow, the next day, and so the next week, if need be; and not to be brought about by any that sits on the bench with him, though they indict and arraign plays daily. He that will swear *Jeronimo* or *Andronicus* are the best plays yet, shall pass unexcepted at here as a man whose judgement shews it is constant, and hath stood still these five and twenty or

83 *censure* judgement, criticism
charge; ed. (charge, F)
84 *departed with* surrendered, parted with
right, ed. (right: F)
89 *so* provided
95 *contagion* infectious influence
101 *brought about* converted, made to change his mind
bench (i) bench of magistrates (ii) form on the stage occupied by the distinguished and fashionable
104 *unexcepted at* unobjected to

85–7 *six penn'orth . . . half a crown.* The list of prices given here is remarkably high for the time, rather more than double what appears to have been normal. Chambers suggests (ii. 534) that a possible explanation is to be found in the fact that the play was 'not merely a new play, but a new play at a new house'.

91 *the lottery.* A lottery, under the patronage of the King, was opened in 1612 to provide funds for the colonization of Virginia.

97 *the Commission of Wit.* An imaginary body of critics empowered to examine and pass judgement on plays, poems, and the like.

103 *Jeronimo* or *Andronicus.* Thomas Kyd's *The Spanish Tragedy* (*c.* 1587) and Shakespeare's *Titus Andronicus* (1589–90?) had become very old-fashioned by 1614.

thirty years. Though it be an ignorance, it is a virtuous and staid ignorance; and next to truth, a confirmed error does well. Such a one the author knows where to find him.

It is further covenanted, concluded, and agreed that how great soever the expectation be, no person here is to expect more than he knows, or better ware than a Fair will afford; neither to look back to the sword-and-buckler age of Smithfield, but content himself with the present. Instead of a little Davy to take toll o' the bawds, the author doth promise a strutting horse-courser, with a leer drunkard, two or three to attend him, in as good equipage as you would wish. And then for Kindheart, the tooth-drawer, a fine oily pig-woman, with her tapster to bid you welcome, and a consort of roarers for music. A wise Justice of Peace *meditant*, instead of a juggler with an ape. A civil cutpurse *searchant*. A sweet singer of new ballads *allurant*; and as fresh an hypocrite as ever was broached *rampant*. If there be never a servant-monster i' the Fair, who can help it? he says; nor a nest of antics? He is loth to make Nature afraid in his plays, like those that beget Tales, Tempests, and such like drolleries, to mix his head with other men's heels, let the concupiscence of jigs and dances reign as strong as it will amongst you; yet if the puppets will please anybody, they shall be entreated to come in.

115 *leer* sly
116 *equipage* array
117 *pig-woman*, ed. (*Pig-woman* F)
118 *tapster* ed. (*Tapster*, F)
123–4 *nest of antics* group of clowns
125 *drolleries* comic entertainments of a fantastic kind

112–13 *the sword-and-buckler age of Smithfield*. The 'field commonly called West-Smith field, was for many years called *Ruffians hall*, by reason it was the usuall place of Frayes and common fighting, during the time that Sword-and-Bucklers were in use . . . This manner of Fight was frequent with all men, untill the fight of Rapier and Dagger tooke place, and then suddenly the generall quarrell of fighting abated, which began about the 20 yeare of Queen *Elizabeth* . . .' (Stow, *Annals*, 1631, p. 1024 ab, quoted from Nashe, iv. 111).

119–21 *meditant . . . searchant . . . allurant*. A series of mock heraldic terms modelled on such forms as *rampant*.

122–3 *servant-monster*. A patent allusion to Caliban in Shakespeare's *The Tempest*, who is repeatedly addressed as 'servant-monster' by Stephano and Trinculo at the opening of III.ii.

125 *Tales, Tempests*. An obvious reference to *The Winter's Tale* and *The Tempest*.

In consideration of which, it is finally agreed by the foresaid hearers and spectators that they neither in themselves conceal, nor suffer by them to be concealed, any state-decipherer, or politic picklock of the scene, so solemnly ridiculous as to search out who was meant by the gingerbread-woman, who by the hobby-horse-man, who by the costard-monger, nay, who by their wares; or that will pretend to affirm, on his own inspired ignorance, what Mirror of Magistrates is meant by the Justice, what great lady by the pig-woman, what concealed statesman by the seller of mousetraps, and so of the rest. But that such person or persons, so found, be left discovered to the mercy of the author, as a forfeiture to the stage and your laughter aforesaid; as also, such as shall so desperately or ambitiously play the fool by his place aforesaid, to challenge the author of scurrility because the language somewhere savours of Smithfield, the booth, and the pig-broth; or of profaneness because a madman cries, 'God quit you', or 'bless you'. In witness whereof, as you have preposterously put to your seals already, which is your money, you will now add the other part of suffrage, your hands. The play shall presently begin. And though the Fair be not kept in the same region that some here, perhaps, would have it, yet think that therein the author hath observed a special decorum, the place being as dirty as Smithfield, and as stinking every whit.

133 *state-decipherer* professional informer on the look-out for seditious matter
141 *discovered* revealed, exposed
144 *challenge* accuse
148 *preposterously* in reversed order, back to front
put to affixed
150 *suffrage* approval
hands (i) signatures (ii) applause
153 *decorum* sense of fitness

---

133 *politic picklock of the scene*. Informers on the look-out for 'lewd, seditious, or slanderous matter' were, as Jonson knew to his cost, a menace that the playwright had to guard against. He had been imprisoned in 1597 for his share in the lost play *The Isle of Dogs*, and again in 1605 for his share in *Eastward Ho!*

138 *Mirror of Magistrates*. The phrase probably has a double meaning: (i) paragon of magistrates (ii) in allusion to George Whetstone's *A Mirour for Magestrates of Cyties* (1584), in which it is argued that a good magistrate should find out the truth for himself by visiting places of entertainment in disguise.

Howsoever, he prays you to believe his ware is still the same, else you will make him justly suspect that he that is so loth to look on a baby or an hobby-horse here, would be glad to take up a commodity of them, at any laughter or loss, in another place. [*Exeunt*]

158–9 *to take up a commodity of them, at any laughter or loss, in another place.* Jonson refers to a trick, designed to get round the law limiting interest to 10 per cent, which was commonly practised at the time. The money-lender, pleading that he was short of ready cash, would persuade his client to take part or the whole of the loan in the form of goods, such as 'lute-strings and brown paper'. He would then introduce the borrower to another businessman, with whom he was in collusion, prepared to buy these goods at a very large discount. Jonson is saying, in effect, that the spectator who is not willing to pay with laughter for the excellent play he is being offered will be forced into buying very inferior wares elsewhere and will expose himself to derision as a consequence.

BARTHOLMEW FAIR

Act I, Scene i

[*Enter*] LITTLEWIT

LITTLEWIT
A pretty conceit, and worth the finding! I ha' such luck to spin out these fine things still, and like a silk-worm, out of myself. Here's Master Bartholomew Cokes, of Harrow o'th'Hill, i'th'County of Middlesex, Esquire, takes forth his licence to marry Mistress Grace Wellborn of the said place and county. And when does he take it forth? Today! The four-and-twentieth of August! Bartholmew day! Bartholmew upon Bartholmew! There's the device! Who would have marked such a leap-frog chance now? A very less than ames-ace on two dice! Well, go thy ways, John Littlewit, Proctor John Littlewit—one o' the pretty wits o' Paul's, the Little Wit of London, so thou art called, and

3 *Here's* Ed. (Her's F)
8 *device* clever design
9 *leap-frog chance* chance of two interchangeable things appearing together
9–10 *very less* truly slighter (with the word 'chance' understood)
10 *ames-ace* ambs-ace, double ace, lowest possible throw with two dice

---

s.d. *Enter* LITTLEWIT Ed. (LITTLE-WIT {*To him*} WIN. F). Following classical precedent, Jonson lists all the characters taking part in a scene at the opening of that scene, irrespective of when they actually enter, and he does not normally supply stage directions to mark entrances and exits. The character who is first on the list makes the opening speech, which has no speech prefix. In this edition that speech prefix is supplied. A new scene begins when a fresh group of characters appears. It does not necessarily mark a break in the action, which is usually, though not invariably, continuous within the act. Act I of *Bartholmew Fair* is set in Littlewit's house.

3 *Bartholomew*. This is the only occasion on which the full form of this name occurs in the play. Significantly, Littlewit is reading from an official legal document, where the full form should be given.

12 *Paul's*. The middle aisle of St Paul's was, in Jonson's day, the great meeting-place of London. Merchants came there to do business, and the fashionable to exchange news and gossip.

something beside. When a quirk or a quiblin does scape thee, and thou dost not watch, and apprehend it, and bring it afore the constable of conceit—there now, I speak quib too—let 'em carry thee out o' the Archdeacon's court into his kitchen, and make a Jack of thee, instead of a John. There I am again, la!

[*Enter*] *to him* WIN

Win, good morrow, Win. Ay, marry, Win! Now you look finely indeed, Win! This cap does convince! You'd not ha' worn it, Win, nor ha' had it velvet, but a rough country beaver with a copper band, like the coney-skin woman of Budge Row? Sweet Win, let me kiss it! And her fine high shoes, like the Spanish lady! Good Win, go a little; I would fain see thee pace, pretty Win! By this fine cap, I could never leave kissing on't.

WIN

Come, indeed la, you are such a fool, still!

LITTLEWIT

No, but half a one, Win; you are the tother half: man and wife make one fool, Win.—Good!—Is there the proctor, or doctor indeed, i' the diocese, that ever had the fortune to win him such a Win?—There I am again!—I do feel con-

13 *quirk* quip
quiblin quibble, pun
15 *conceit* wit
17 *Jack* mechanical device for turning the spit when roasting meat (*OED*, sb.[1], 7)
20 *does convince* is overwhelming, is a knock-out
22 *beaver* hat made of beaver's fur
coney-skin woman woman who sells rabbit-skins
23 *kiss it* kiss you (baby language)
24 *go* walk
26 *on't* you (literally 'of it')

---

16 *Archdeacon's court*. The court of Arches, where Littlewit is employed.

23 *Budge Row*. A street where the sellers of budge—a kind of fur, consisting of lamb's skin with the wool dressed outwards—had their shops.

24 *the Spanish lady*. The only information we have about this person, who evidently caused quite a stir in the fashionable world, is contained in Jonson's next play *The Devil is an Ass* (1616). There she is described as

An *English* widdow, who hath lately trauell'd,
But shee's call'd the *Spaniard;* 'cause she came
Latest from thence: and keepes the *Spanish* habit.
Such a rare woman! (II.viii, 25–39)

A list of her many accomplishments follows.

ceits coming upon me more than I am able to turn tongue to. A pox o' these pretenders to wit! your Three Cranes, Mitre, and Mermaid men! Not a corn of true salt nor a grain of right mustard amongst them all. They may stand for places or so, again the next witfall, and pay twopence in a quart more for their canary than other men. But gi' me the man can start up a Justice of Wit out of six-shillings beer, and give the law to all the poets and poet-suckers i' town! Because they are the players' gossips? 'Slid, other men have wives as fine as the players', and as well dressed. Come hither, Win. [*Kisses her*]

Act I, Scene ii

[*Enter to them*] WINWIFE

WINWIFE

Why, how now, Master Littlewit? Measuring of lips or moulding of kisses? Which is it?

LITTLEWIT

Troth, I am a little taken with my Win's dressing here! Does't not fine, Master Winwife? How do you apprehend, sir? She would not ha' worn this habit. I challenge all

34 *corn* grain
34–5 *salt . . . mustard* sharp pungent wit
35 *stand for* strive for (*OED*, Stand, *v.*, 71, † b., quoting *The Devil is an Ass*, I.vi, 36)
36 *again* in anticipation of
witfall the letting-fall of a jest or repartee (Horsman)
37 *canary* light sweet wine from the Canary Islands
38 *six-shillings beer* small beer sold at six shillings a barrel
39 *poet-suckers* sucking poets, fledgling poets
39–40 *town*! *Because* ed. (Towne, because F)
40 *gossips* familiar acquaintances
'Slid by God's eyelid
4 *Does't* looks it
How do you apprehend would you believe it

33–4 *Three Cranes, Mitre, and Mermaid.* London taverns, much frequented by playwrights and poets. The Mermaid, Jonson's favourite haunt, was, according to Thomas Fuller, the scene of many 'wit-combats' between him and Shakespeare (H & S, i. 50. n.3).
40 *Because . . . gossips*? Littlewit's mind suddenly reverts to the 'pretenders to wit', who, he thinks, give themselves airs.

Cheapside to shew such another—Moorfields, Pimlico Path, or the Exchange, in a summer evening—with a lace to boot, as this has. Dear Win, let Master Winwife kiss you. He comes a-wooing to our mother, Win, and may be our father perhaps, Win. There's no harm in him, Win.

WINWIFE

None i' the earth, Master Littlewit. [*Kisses her*]

LITTLEWIT

I envy no man my delicates, sir.

WINWIFE

Alas, you ha' the garden where they grow still! A wife here with a strawberry-breath, cherry-lips, apricot-cheeks, and a soft velvet head, like a melicotton.

LITTLEWIT

Good i'faith!—Now dullness upon me, that I had not that before him, that I should not light on't as well as he! Velvet head!

WINWIFE

But my taste, Master Littlewit, tends to fruit of a later kind: the sober matron, your wife's mother.

LITTLEWIT

Ay! We know you are a suitor, sir. Win and I both wish you well. By this licence here, would you had her, that your two names were as fast in it as here are a couple. Win would fain have a fine young father-i'-law with a feather, that her mother might hood it and chain it with Mistress Overdo. But you do not take the right course, Master Winwife.

WINWIFE

No? Master Littlewit, why?

LITTLEWIT

You are not mad enough.

WINWIFE

How? Is madness a right course?

12 *delicates* delights, delicacies
15 *melicotton* peach grafted on a quince
25 *hood it and chain it* shew an ostentatious pride in her husband's hood and chain (the marks of his office)

---

6 *Cheapside.* The mercers and haberdashers had their shops in this street.

6–7 *Moorfields, Pimlico Path, or the Exchange.* All places of resort for the citizens of London. Moorfields, to the north-east of the City walls, had been laid out as a park in 1606. Pimlico in the village of Hoxton was a house famous for its cakes and ale; and the New Exchange in the Strand, built in 1608–09, had milliners' and sempstresses' shops which made it attractive to women.

LITTLEWIT

I say nothing, but I wink upon Win. You have a friend, one Master Quarlous, comes here sometimes?

WINWIFE

Why, he makes no love to her, does he?

LITTLEWIT

Not a tokenworth that ever I saw, I assure you. But—

WINWIFE

What?

LITTLEWIT

He is the more madcap o' the two. You do not apprehend me.

WIN

You have a hot coal i' your mouth now, you cannot hold.

LITTLEWIT

Let me out with it, dear Win.

WIN

I'll tell him myself.

LITTLEWIT

Do, and take all the thanks, and much good do thy pretty heart, Win.

WIN

Sir, my mother has had her nativity-water cast lately by the cunning men in Cow-lane, and they ha' told her her fortune, and do ensure her she shall never have happy hour, unless she marry within this sennight; and when it is, it must be a madman, they say.

LITTLEWIT

Ay, but it must be a gentleman madman.

WIN

Yes, so the tother man of Moorfields says.

WINWIFE

But does she believe 'em?

39 *good do* Ed. (do good F) good may it do
42 *cunning men* fortune-tellers
43 *ensure* assure
44 *sennight* period of seven nights, week

---

33 *tokenworth.* Tokens were pieces of metal issued by tradesmen to overcome the shortage of small change. As they had no general currency, a 'tokenworth' signified 'the least possible amount'.

41 *nativity-water cast.* Win seems to be confusing the casting (calculation) of a horoscope with the casting (inspection) of urine for the diagnosis of disease.

42 *Cow-lane.* The modern King Street.

LITTLEWIT

Yes, and has been at Bedlam twice since, every day, to enquire if any gentleman be there, or to come there, mad!

WINWIFE

Why, this is a confederacy, a mere piece of practice upon her, by these impostors!

LITTLEWIT

I tell her so; or else say I that they mean some young madcap gentleman, for the devil can equivocate as well as a shopkeeper, and therefore would I advise you to be a little madder than Master Quarlous, hereafter.

WINWIFE

Where is she? Stirring yet?

LITTLEWIT

Stirring! Yes, and studying an old elder, come from Banbury, a suitor that puts in here at meal-tide, to praise the painful brethren, or pray that the sweet singers may be restored; says a grace as long as his breath lasts him! Sometime the spirit is so strong with him it gets quite out of him, and then my mother, or Win, are fain to fetch it again with malmsey, or *aqua coelestis*.

WIN

Yes indeed, we have such a tedious life with him for his diet,

51 *confederacy* conspiracy
mere sheer, downright
practice trickery or imposture practised (*OED*, Practice, 7., citing this passage)
54 *equivocate* deal in ambiguities
60 *painful* diligent
63 *fetch it again* bring it back, i.e., revive him
64 *aqua coelestis* spirit distilled from wine, kind of brandy
65 *tedious* irksome

---

49 *Bedlam*. The hospital of St Mary of Bethlehem in Bishopsgate was a lunatic asylum. Citizens would go to visit it, much as they go to the Zoo today.

59 *meal-tide*. Littlewit is jeering at the Puritan habit of replacing 'mass', in words such as 'Christmas', with 'tide' meaning 'time'. Cf. *The Alchemist*, III.ii, 43, where, when Subtle mentions 'Christ-masse', Ananias interjects: '*Christ-tide*, I pray you'.

60–1 *sweet singers . . . restored*. In the Geneva version of the Bible (1560) David is called 'the sweet singer of Israel' (2 Samuel, xxiii. 1). The reference here is, however, to the Puritan ministers who had been deprived of their livings because they refused to conform to the constitution of the Church of England as set out in 1604.

and his clothes too; he breaks his buttons and cracks seams at every saying he sobs out.

LITTLEWIT

He cannot abide my vocation, he says.

WIN

No, he told my mother a proctor was a claw of the Beast, and that she had little less than committed abomination in marrying me so as she has done.

LITTLEWIT

Every line, he says, that a proctor writes, when it comes to be read in the Bishop's court, is a long black hair, kembed out of the tail of Antichrist.

WINWIFE

When came this proselyte?

LITTLEWIT

Some three days since.

Act I, Scene iii

[*Enter to them*] QUARLOUS

QUARLOUS

O sir, ha' you ta'en soil here? It's well a man may reach you after three hours running, yet! What an unmerciful companion art thou, to quit thy lodging at such ungentlemanly hours! None but a scattered covey of fiddlers, or one of these rag-rakers in dunghills, or some marrow-bone man at most, would have been up when thou wert gone abroad, by all description. I pray thee what ailest thou, thou canst not sleep? Hast thou thorns i' thy eyelids, or thistles i' thy bed?

WINWIFE

I cannot tell. It seems you had neither i' your feet, that took this pain to find me.

QUARLOUS

No, an I had, all the lime-hounds o' the City should have

73 *kembed* combed
1 *ta'en soil* taken refuge (technical term used in deer-hunting)
5 *rag-rakers . . . marrow-bone man* equivalents of the modern rag-and-bone man
11 *lime-hounds* lyam-hounds, bloodhounds held on a lyam (leash)

69 *the Beast.* The Beast of the Apocalypse (Revelation, xiii) was equated by the Protestants generally, and especially by the Puritans, with Antichrist, identified as the Pope and the Church of Rome.

drawn after you by the scent rather. Master John Littlewit! God save you, sir. 'Twas a hot night with some of us, last night, John. Shall we pluck a hair o' the same wolf today, Proctor John?

LITTLEWIT

Do you remember, Master Quarlous, what we discoursed on last night?

QUARLOUS

Not I, John: nothing that I either discourse or do at those times. I forfeit all to forgetfulness.

LITTLEWIT

No? Not concerning Win? Look you, there she is, and dressed as I told you she should be. Hark you, sir, had you forgot?

QUARLOUS

By this head, I'll beware how I keep you company, John, when I drink, an you have this dangerous memory! That's certain.

LITTLEWIT

Why, sir?

QUARLOUS

Why? [*To the rest*] We were all a little stained last night, sprinkled with a cup or two, and I agreed with Proctor John here to come and do somewhat with Win—I know not what 'twas—today; and he puts me in mind on't now; he says he was coming to fetch me.—Before truth, if you have that fearful quality, John, to remember when you are sober, John, what you promise drunk, John, I shall take heed of you, John. For this once, I am content to wink at you. Where's your wife? Come hither, Win. *He kisseth her*

WIN

Why, John! Do you see this, John? Look you! Help me, John.

12 *drawn after* tracked
13 *hot* hectic
14 *hair o' the same wolf* cf. 'hair of the dog that bit you'
18 *do* ed. (doe, F)
19 *times.* ed. (times F)
20 *Win?* Ed. (*Win*, F)
24 *drink* Ed. (drunke F)
27 *stained* the worse for drink
34 *wink at you* overlook your indiscretion

---

27 s.d. *To the rest* ed. (not in F). This direction seems necessary in view of Quarlous's reference to 'Proctor John here' (ll. 28–9).

LITTLEWIT

O Win, fie, what do you mean, Win? Be womanly, Win. Make an outcry to your mother, Win? Master Quarlous is an honest gentleman, and our worshipful good friend, Win; and he is Master Winwife's friend, too. And Master Winwife comes a suitor to your mother, Win, as I told you before, Win, and may perhaps be our father, Win. They'll do you no harm, Win, they are both our worshipful good friends. Master Quarlous! You must know Master Quarlous, Win; you must not quarrel with Master Quarlous, Win.

QUARLOUS

No, we'll kiss again and fall in.

LITTLEWIT

Yes, do, good Win.

WIN

I'faith you are a fool, John.

LITTLEWIT

A fool-John she calls me, do you mark that, gentlemen? Pretty littlewit of velvet! A fool-John!

QUARLOUS

She may call you an apple-John, if you use this.

WINWIFE

Pray thee forbear, for my respect somewhat.

QUARLOUS

Hoy-day! How respective you are become o' the sudden! I fear this family will turn you reformed too; pray you come about again. Because she is in possibility to be your daughter-in-law, and may ask you blessing hereafter, when she courts

41 *friend* Ed. (friends F)

47 *fall in* (i) be reconciled (ii) copulate (cf. *Troilus and Cressida*, III.i, 96–7)

52 *use this* behave thus

54 *respective* concerned about good manners

57 *ask you blessing* ask you for your blessing

57–8 *courts it* plays the courtier

---

50 *fool-John.* As Littlewit seems pleased with this appellation, he is probably taking 'fool' as the term of endearment that it could be in the early seventeenth century (cf. *King Lear*, V.iii, 305).

52 *apple-John.* A kind of apple that was thought to be at its best when shrivelled and withered. It seems to have been regarded as symbolic of impotence (cf. *2 Henry IV*, II.iv, 3–10), and this sense fits well with Quarlous's jeer.

it to Tottenham to eat cream—well, I will forbear, sir; but i'faith, would thou wouldst leave thy exercise of widow-hunting once, this drawing after an old reverend smock by the splay-foot! There cannot be an ancient tripe or trillibub i' the town, but thou art straight nosing it; and 'tis a fine occupation thou'lt confine thyself to when thou hast got one —scrubbing a piece of buff, as if thou hadst the perpetuity of Pannier-alley to stink in; or perhaps, worse, currying a carcass that thou hast bound thyself to alive. I'll be sworn, some of them, that thou art or hast been a suitor to, are so old as no chaste or married pleasure can ever become 'em. The honest instrument of procreation has, forty years since, left to belong to 'em. Thou must visit 'em, as thou wouldst do a tomb, with a torch, or three handfuls of link, flaming hot, and so thou mayst hap to make 'em feel thee, and after, come to inherit according to thy inches. A sweet course for a man to waste the brand of life for, to be still raking himself a fortune in an old woman's embers. We shall ha' thee, after thou hast been but a month married to one of 'em, look like the quartan ague and the black jaundice met in a face, and walk as if thou hadst borrowed legs of a spinner and voice of a cricket. I would endure to hear fifteen sermons a week for her, and such coarse and loud ones as some of 'em must be;

58 *cream—well* Ed. (creame. Well F)
59 *exercise* regular occupation
60 *once* once for all
drawing after tracking
smock woman (derogatory)
61 *splay-foot* flat foot that turns outwards
tripe or trillibub bag of guts (literally 'entrails')
64 *buff* (i) tough leather (ii) bare skin
perpetuity perpetual tenure
65 *currying* (i) rubbing down (as with a horse) (ii) flattering
69–70 *left to belong* ceased to be of interest (*OED*, Belong, *v*., 2.)
71 *link* tow and pitch used for torches
73 *inherit* possess your share (of the old woman's fortune)
inches size, length (of penis)
74 *brand* fire
77 *quartan ague* fever in which the paroxysm occurs every fourth day
78 *spinner* spider
79 *for* instead of

58 *to Tottenham to eat cream.* Tottenham Court was famed for its cream, cakes, and ale.

65 *Pannier-alley.* A passage opening out of Pater Noster Row, where tripe and skins were sold.

I would e'en desire of Fate I might dwell in a drum, and take in my sustenance with an old broken tobacco-pipe and a straw. Dost thou ever think to bring thine ears or stomach to the patience of a dry grace as long as thy tablecloth, and droned out by thy son here, that might be thy father, till all the meat o' thy board has forgot it was that day i' the kitchen? Or to brook the noise made in a question of predestination, by the good labourers and painful eaters assembled together, put to 'em by the matron, your spouse, who moderates with a cup of wine, ever and anon, and a sentence out of Knox between? Or the perpetual spitting before and after a sober drawn exhortation of six hours, whose better part was the 'hum-ha-hum'? Or to hear prayers groaned out over thy iron chests, as if they were charms to break 'em? And all this, for the hope of two apostle-spoons, to suffer! And a cup to eat a caudle in! For that will be thy legacy. She'll ha' conveyed her state, safe enough from thee, an she be a right widow.

WINWIFE

Alas, I am quite off that scent now.

QUARLOUS

How so?

WINWIFE

Put off by a brother of Banbury, one that, they say, is come here, and governs all already.

QUARLOUS

What do you call him? I knew divers of those Banburians when I was in Oxford.

WINWIFE

Master Littlewit can tell us.

LITTLEWIT

Sir!—Good Win, go in, and if Master Bartholmew Cokes

84 *patience* enduring, suffering
dry (i) boring (ii) thirst-inducing (because of its length)
90 *moderates* acts as moderator, arbitrates
91 *sentence* maxim, well-known quotation
96 *caudle* warm concoction given to invalids
97 *conveyed her state* made a legal conveyance of her estate to another

---

91 *Knox*. The works of John Knox (*c*. 1505–1572) the Scottish reformer were popular among the Puritans.

96 *apostle-spoons*. It was customary for the sponsors at a baptism to give the infant a set of silver spoons with the figure of an apostle on the handle of each.

his man come for the licence—the little old fellow—let him speak with me. [*Exit* WIN]
What say you, gentlemen?

WINWIFE
What call you the reverend elder you told me of—your Banbury man?

LITTLEWIT
Rabbi Busy, sir. He is more than an elder, he is a prophet, sir.

QUARLOUS
O, I know him! A baker, is he not?

LITTLEWIT
He was a baker, sir, but he does dream now, and see visions; he has given over his trade.

QUARLOUS
I remember that too—out of a scruple he took that, in spiced conscience, those cakes he made were served to bridales, maypoles, morrises, and such profane feasts and meetings. His Christen name is Zeal-of-the-land.

LITTLEWIT
Yes, sir, Zeal-of-the-land Busy.

WINWIFE
How! what a name's there!

LITTLEWIT
O, they have all such names, sir. He was witness for Win here—they will not be called godfathers—and named her Win-the-fight. You thought her name had been Winifred, did you not?

WINWIFE
I did indeed.

LITTLEWIT
He would ha' thought himself a stark reprobate, if it had.

QUARLOUS
Ay, for there was a blue-starch-woman o' the name, at the same time. A notable hypocritical vermin it is; I know him.

117 *spiced* tender, scrupulous
118 *bridales* wedding feasts
119 *morrises* morris dances

---

119 *maypoles . . . meetings.* The more rigid Protestants, not merely the Puritans, were strongly opposed to popular merry-makings such as these, because they saw them, quite rightly, as survivals of paganism.

129 *blue-starch-woman.* Laundress who used blue starch to whiten and set ruffs, which were associated with the sin of pride.

One that stands upon his face more than his faith, at all times; ever in seditious motion, and reproving for vain-glory; of a most lunatic conscience and spleen, and affects the violence of singularity in all he does.—He has undone a grocer here, in Newgate-market, that broked with him, trusted him with currants, as arrant a zeal as he; that's by the way.—By his profession, he will ever be i' the state of innocence, though, and childhood; derides all antiquity; defies any other learning than inspiration; and what discretion soever years should afford him, it is all prevented in his original ignorance. Ha' not to do with him, for he is a fellow of a most arrogant and invincible dullness, I assure you. Who is this?

Act I, Scene iv

[*Enter to them*] WASP, [WIN]

WASP

By your leave, gentlemen, with all my heart to you, and God you good morrow. Master Littlewit, my business is to you. Is this licence ready?

LITTLEWIT

Here, I ha' it for you in my hand, Master Humphrey.

WASP

That's well. Nay, never open or read it to me; it's labour in vain, you know. I am no clerk, I scorn to be saved by my book; i'faith I'll hang first. Fold it up o' your word and gi' it me. What must you ha' for't?

131 *stands upon his face* relies on his effrontery
132 *in seditious motion* causing trouble
136 *zeal* zealot
140 *prevented* balked, precluded
1–2 *God you* God give you

---

135 *Newgate-market.* Established for the sale of corn and meal, this market was, by Jonson's time, dealing in other kinds of foodstuff as well. *broked* ed. (broke F) did business. All other editors retain 'broke', but then have difficulty in explaining it. This editor thinks that Jonson wrote 'brokd', which the compositor turned into 'broke'.

6–7 *to be saved by my book.* Wasp is referring to the 'neck-verse', as it was called. Until 1827 anyone who could read a Latin verse (usually the beginning of the fifty-first psalm) printed in black-letter was exempted from sentence on his first conviction. Also known as 'benefit of clergy', since it was originally the privilege of exemption from trial before a secular court claimed by clergymen arraigned for felony, the neck-verse had saved Jonson's life in October 1598, when he was tried at the Old Bailey for killing the actor Gabriel Spencer in a duel.

LITTLEWIT

We'll talk of that anon, Master Humphrey.

WASP

Now, or not at all, good Master Proctor; I am for no anons, I assure you.

LITTLEWIT

Sweet Win, bid Solomon send me the little black box within, in my study.

WASP

Ay, quickly, good mistress, I pray you, for I have both eggs o' the spit, and iron i' the fire. [*Exit* WIN]
Say what you must have, good Master Littlewit.

LITTLEWIT

Why, you know the price, Master Numps.

WASP

I know? I know nothing, I. What tell you me of knowing, now I am in haste? Sir, I do not know, and I will not know, and I scorn to know; and yet, now I think on't, I will and do know as well as another: you must have a mark for your thing here, and eightpence for the box. I could ha' saved twopence i' that, an I had bought it myself, but here's fourteen shillings for you. Good Lord! How long your little wife stays! Pray God, Solomon, your clerk, be not looking i' the wrong box, Master Proctor.

LITTLEWIT

Good i'faith! No, I warrant you, Solomon is wiser than so, sir.

WASP

Fie, fie, fie, by your leave, Master Littlewit, this is scurvy, idle, foolish, and abominable, with all my heart; I do not like it.

WINWIFE

Do you hear? Jack Littlewit, what business does thy pretty head think this fellow may have, that he keeps such a coil with?

18 *nothing, I.* Ed. (nothing. I, F)

18–19 *knowing, now I am in haste? Sir,* Ed. (knowing? (now I am in hast) Sir, F)

21 *mark* thirteen shillings and fourpence (two-thirds of a pound sterling)

33–4 *keeps such a coil with* makes such a fuss about

14–15 *eggs o' the spit, and iron i' the fire.* Two proverbial expressions (Tilley, E86 and I99) denoting haste.

QUARLOUS

More than buying of gingerbread i' the Cloister here, for that we allow him, or a gilt pouch i' the Fair?

LITTLEWIT

Master Quarlous, do not mistake him. He is his master's both-hands, I assure you.

QUARLOUS

What? To pull on his boots, a-mornings, or his stockings? Does he?

LITTLEWIT

Sir, if you have a mind to mock him, mock him softly, and look tother way; for if he apprehend you flout him once, he will fly at you presently. A terrible testy old fellow, and his name is Wasp too.

QUARLOUS

Pretty insect! Make much on him.

WASP

A plague o' this box, and the pox too, and on him that made it, and her that went for't, and all that should ha' sought it, sent it, or brought it! Do you see, sir?

LITTLEWIT

Nay, good Master Wasp.

WASP

Good Master Hornet, turd i' your teeth, hold you your tongue! Do not I know you? Your father was a pothecary, and sold glisters, more than he gave, I wusse.

[*Enter* WIN, *with the box*]

And turd i' your little wife's teeth too—here she comes—'twill make her spit, as fine as she is, for all her velvet-custard on her head, sir.

LITTLEWIT

O! be civil, Master Numps.

WASP

Why, say I have a humour not to be civil; how then? Who shall compel me? You?

38 *both-hands* factotum
43 *presently* immediately
52 *glisters* clysters, enemas
I wusse iwis, certainly, truly
54 *velvet-custard* velvet hat in the shape of a pie (custard)
57 *humour* inclination

35 *the Cloister.* The Cloisters of Christ Church, near to Smithfield, were used as a mart for various wares at the time of the Fair.

LITTLEWIT

Here is the box now.

WASP

Why, a pox o' your box, once again! Let your little wife stale in it, an she will. Sir, I would have you to understand, and these gentlemen too, if they please—

WINWIFE

With all our hearts, sir.

WASP

That I have a charge, gentlemen.

LITTLEWIT

They do apprehend, sir.

WASP

Pardon me, sir, neither they nor you can apprehend me yet.—You are an ass.—I have a young master; he is now upon his making and marring. The whole care of his well-doing is now mine. His foolish schoolmasters have done nothing but run up and down the country with him to beg puddings and cake-bread of his tenants, and almost spoiled him; he has learned nothing but to sing catches and repeat *Rattle bladder rattle* and *O, Madge*. I dare not let him walk alone, for fear of learning of vile tunes, which he will sing at supper and in the sermon-times! If he meet but a carman i' the street, and I find him not talk to keep him off on him, he will whistle him and all his tunes over at night in his sleep! He has a head full of bees! I am fain now, for this little time I am absent, to leave him in charge with a gentlewoman. 'Tis true she is a Justice of Peace his wife, and a gentlewoman o' the hood, and his natural sister; but what may happen under a woman's government, there's the doubt. Gentlemen, you do not know him; he is another manner of piece than you think for! But nineteen year old,

61 *stale* piss (usually said of horses and cattle)
71 *puddings* sausages
cake-bread bread of a fine cake-like quality
75 *carman* carter, carrier
81 *o' the hood* of consequence
83–4 *another manner of piece* a different sort of person

73 *Rattle bladder rattle*. Part of a proverbial piece of nonsense which ran: 'Three blue beans in a blue bladder, rattle, bladder, rattle' (Tilley, B124). *O, Madge*. A ballad about the barn-owl, which was known as Madge or Madge-howlet.

78 *He has a head full of bees*. Proverbial (Tilley, H255) for 'he is full of crazy notions' (cf. 'He has bees in his bonnet').

and yet he is taller than either of you, by the head, God bless him!

QUARLOUS

Well, methinks this is a fine fellow!

WINWIFE

He has made his master a finer by this description, I should think.

QUARLOUS

'Faith, much about one; it's cross and pile; whether for a new farthing.

WASP

I'll tell you, gentlemen—

LITTLEWIT

Will't please you drink, Master Wasp?

WASP

Why, I ha' not talked so long to be dry, sir. You see no dust or cobwebs come out o' my mouth, do you? You'd ha' me gone, would you?

LITTLEWIT

No, but you were in haste e'en now, Master Numps.

WASP

What an I were? So I am still, and yet I will stay too. Meddle you with your match, your Win there; she has as little wit as her husband it seems. I have others to talk to.

LITTLEWIT

She's my match indeed, and as little wit as I. Good!

WASP

We ha' been but a day and a half in town, gentlemen, 'tis true. And yesterday i' the afternoon we walked London to shew the city to the gentlewoman he shall marry, Mistress Grace. But afore I will endure such another half day with him I'll be drawn with a good gib-cat through the great pond at home, as his uncle Hodge was! Why, we could not meet that heathen thing all day but stayed him. He would name

90 *cross and pile* heads and tails. Proverbial (Tilley, C835), French *croix et pile* (the two sides of a coin)

90–1 *whether for a new farthing* nothing in it, there is not a farthings-worth of difference ('whether' = 'no matter which of the two')

108 *stayed him* stopped him in his tracks

106–7 *drawn . . . home.* The reference is to a rather primitive rustic joke. A bet is made with a foolish person that a gib-cat (tom-cat) will draw him through a pond. A rope is tied round him; the loose end is thrown across the pond; and the cat fastened to it with packthread. Those appointed to guide the cat then haul the victim through the water.

you all the signs over, as he went, aloud; and where he spied a parrot or a monkey, there he was pitched with all the little long-coats about him, male and female. No getting him away! I thought he would ha' run mad o' the black boy in Bucklersbury that takes the scurvy, roguy tobacco there.

LITTLEWIT

You say true, Master Numps: there's such a one indeed.

WASP

It's no matter whether there be or no. What's that to you?

QUARLOUS

He will not allow of John's reading at any hand.

Act I, Scene v

[*Enter to them*] COKES, MISTRESS OVERDO, GRACE

COKES

O Numps! are you here, Numps? Look where I am, Numps! And Mistress Grace, too! Nay, do not look angerly, Numps. My sister is here, and all. I do not come without her.

WASP

What the mischief! Do you come with her? Or she with you?

COKES

We came all to seek you, Numps.

WASP

To seek me? Why, did you all think I was lost? Or run away with your fourteen shillingsworth of small ware here? Or that I had changed it i' the Fair for hobby-horses? 'Sprecious—to seek me!

MISTRESS OVERDO

Nay, good Master Numps, do you shew discretion, though he be exorbitant, as Master Overdo says, an't be but for conservation of the peace.

110 *pitched* fixed
111 *long-coats* children
117 *reading* comment
at any hand on any account
4 *mischief!* ed. (mischiefe, F)
8 *changed* exchanged
8–9 *'Sprecious* by God's precious blood
11 *exorbitant* out of hand (like something that has gone out of orbit)

113 *Bucklersbury.* A street in London where herbalists, who also sold tobacco, had their shops. Cf. *The Merry Wives of Windsor*, III.iii, 63.

WASP

Marry gip, goody she-Justice, Mistress French-hood! Turd i' your teeth; and turd i' your French-hood's teeth, too, to do you service, do you see? Must you quote your Adam to me? You think you are Madam Regent still, Mistress Overdo, when I am in place? No such matter, I assure you; your reign is out when I am in, dame.

MISTRESS OVERDO

I am content to be in abeyance, sir, and be governed by you. So should he too, if he did well. But 'twill be expected you should also govern your passions.

WASP

Will't so forsooth? Good Lord! How sharp you are! With being at Bedlam yesterday? Whetstone has set an edge upon you, has he?

MISTRESS OVERDO

Nay, if you know not what belongs to your dignity, I do, yet, to mine.

WASP

Very well, then.

COKES

Is this the licence, Numps? For love's sake, let me see't. I never saw a licence.

WASP

Did you not so? Why, you shall not see't, then.

COKES

An you love me, good Numps.

WASP

Sir, I love you, and yet I do not love you i' these fooleries. Set your heart at rest; there's nothing in't but hard words. And what would you see't for?

13 *French-hood* kind of hood fashionable among citizens' wives

---

13 *Marry gip*. An exclamatory oath which probably originated from 'By Mary Gipcy' ('by St Mary of Egypt'), but then became confused with 'Gip' meaning (i) gee-up (to a horse) and (ii) 'go along with you' (to a person).

23 *Whetstone*. 'A whetstone cannot cut but yet it makes tools cut' was a proverbial saying (Tilley, W299), but there is also a reference here to a specific person. H & S suggest that Whetstone was probably 'the name of a keeper at the Bethlehem Hospital', but, in view of the context, it would seem far more likely that it was the name of a well-known inmate. Cf. 'the dullness of the fool is the whetstone of the wits' (*As You Like It*, I.ii, 49–50).

COKES

I would see the length and the breadth on't, that's all; and I will see't now, so I will.

WASP

You sha' not see it here.

COKES

Then I'll see't at home, and I'll look upo' the case here.

WASP

Why, do so. [*Holds up the box*] A man must give way to him a little in trifles, gentlemen. These are errors, diseases of youth, which he will mend when he comes to judgement and knowledge of matters. I pray you conceive so, and I thank you. And I pray you pardon him, and I thank you again.

QUARLOUS

Well, this dry nurse, I say still, is a delicate man.

WINWIFE

And I am for the cosset, his charge! Did you ever see a fellow's face more accuse him for an ass?

QUARLOUS

Accuse him? It confesses him one without accusing. What pity 'tis yonder wench should marry such a cokes!

WINWIFE

'Tis true.

QUARLOUS

She seems to be discreet, and as sober as she is handsome.

WINWIFE

Ay, and if you mark her, what a restrained scorn she casts upon all his behaviour and speeches!

COKES

Well, Numps, I am now for another piece of business more, the Fair, Numps, and then—

WASP

Bless me! deliver me! help! hold me! the Fair!

COKES

Nay, never fidge up and down, Numps, and vex itself. I am resolute Bartholmew in this. I'll make no suit on't to you. 'Twas all the end of my journey, indeed, to shew Mistress

40 *trifles, gentlemen* Ed. (trifles: Gentlemen F)
46 *cosset* spoilt child (literally 'lamb brought up by hand')
49 *cokes* ninny
57 *fidge* move restlessly, fidget
itself yourself

Grace my Fair. I call't my Fair because of Bartholmew: you know my name is Bartholmew, and Bartholmew Fair.

LITTLEWIT

That was mine afore, gentlemen—this morning. I had that i'faith, upon his licence; believe me, there he comes after me.

QUARLOUS

Come, John, this ambitious wit of yours, I am afraid, will do you no good i' the end.

LITTLEWIT

No? Why sir?

QUARLOUS

You grow so insolent with it, and overdoing, John, that if you look not to it, and tie it up, it will bring you to some obscure place in time, and there 'twill leave you.

WINWIFE

Do not trust it too much, John; be more sparing, and use it but now and then. A wit is a dangerous thing in this age; do not overbuy it.

LITTLEWIT

Think you so, gentlemen? I'll take heed on't hereafter.

WIN

Yes, do, John.

COKES

A pretty little soul, this same Mistress Littlewit! Would I might marry her.

GRACE

[*Aside*] So would I, or anybody else, so I might scape you.

COKES

Numps, I will see it, Numps, 'tis decreed. Never be melancholy for the matter.

WASP

Why, see it, sir, see it, do see it! Who hinders you? Why do you not go see it? 'Slid, see it.

COKES

The Fair, Numps, the Fair.

WASP

Would the Fair and all the drums and rattles in't were i' your belly for me; they are already i' your brain. He that had the means to travel your head, now, should meet finer sights than any are i' the Fair, and make a finer voyage on't, to see it all hung with cockle-shells, pebbles, fine wheat-straws, and here and there a chicken's feather and a cobweb.

67 *insolent* extravagant

72 *overbuy* pay too much for (by allowing it to get you into trouble)

QUARLOUS

Good faith, he looks, methinks, an you mark him, like one that were made to catch flies, with his Sir Cranion legs.

WINWIFE

And his Numps, to flap 'em away.

WASP

God be w'you, sir. There's your bee in a box, and much good do't you. [*Gives him the box, and offers to leave*]

COKES

Why, 'your friend and Bartholmew', an you be so contumacious.

QUARLOUS

What mean you, Numps?

WASP

I'll not be guilty, I, gentlemen.

MISTRESS OVERDO

You will not let him go, brother, and lose him?

COKES

Who can hold that will away? I had rather lose him than the Fair, I wusse.

WASP

You do not know the inconvenience, gentlemen, you persuade to; nor what trouble I have with him in these humours. If he go to the Fair, he will buy of everything to a baby there; and household-stuff for that too. If a leg or an arm on him did not grow on, he would lose it i' the press. Pray heaven I bring him off with one stone! And then he is such a ravener after fruit! You will not believe what a coil I had t'other day to compound a business between a Catherine-pear-woman and him about snatching! 'Tis intolerable, gentlemen.

WINWIFE

O! but you must not leave him now to these hazards, Numps.

90 *Sir Cranion* daddy-long-legs

92 *God be w'you* God be with you (original form of 'good-bye')

94 '*your . . . Bartholmew*' ed. (your . . . *Bartholmew* F) farewell. Cokes is using a common form of subscribing a letter.

98 *lose* Ed. (loose F)

99 *Who can hold that will away*? Proverbial (Tilley, H515); *that* = him who.
lose Ed. (loose F)

103–4 *buy of everything to a baby there* buy some of everything there, down to and including a doll

106 *stone* testicle

107 *coil* trouble, fuss

WASP

Nay, he knows too well I will not leave him, and that makes him presume. Well, sir, will you go now? If you have such an itch i' your feet to foot it to the Fair, why do you stop? Am I your tarriers? Go, will you go! Sir, why do you not go?

COKES

O Numps! have I brought you about? Come, Mistress Grace, and sister, I am resolute Bat, i'faith, still.

GRACE

Truly, I have no such fancy to the Fair, nor ambition to see it; there's none goes thither of any quality or fashion.

COKES

O Lord, sir! You shall pardon me, Mistress Grace, we are enow of ourselves to make it a fashion; and for qualities, let Numps alone, he'll find qualities.

[*Exeunt* COKES, WASP, GRACE, MISTRESS OVERDO]

QUARLOUS

What a rogue in apprehension is this! To understand her language no better!

WINWIFE

Ay, and offer to marry to her! Well, I will leave the chase of my widow for today, and directly to the Fair. These flies cannot, this hot season, but engender us excellent creeping sport.

QUARLOUS

A man that has but a spoonful of brain would think so. Farewell, John. [*Exeunt* QUARLOUS, WINWIFE]

LITTLEWIT

Win, you see 'tis in fashion to go to the Fair, Win. We must to the Fair too, you and I, Win. I have an affair i' the Fair, Win, a puppet-play of mine own making—say nothing—that I writ for the motion-man, which you must see, Win.

WIN

I would I might, John, but my mother will never consent to such a—'profane motion' she will call it.

115 *tarriers* hinderers
will you go! ed. (will you goe? F) if you want to go
116 *about* round
119 *quality* social standing
121 *qualities* features of character
121–2 *let Numps alone* leave it to Numps
123 *rogue in apprehension* lack-brain, unintelligent beggar
134 *motion-man* puppet-master
136 *a—'profane motion' she* ed. (a *prophane motion:* she F)

LITTLEWIT

Tut, we'll have a device, a dainty one.—Now, Wit, help at a pinch; good Wit, come; come, good Wit, an't be thy will.—I have it, Win, I have it i'faith, and 'tis a fine one. Win, long to eat of a pig, sweet Win, i' the Fair, do you see? I' the heart o' the Fair; not at Pie-corner. Your mother will do anything, Win, to satisfy your longing, you know; pray thee long presently, and be sick o' the sudden, good Win. I'll go in and tell her. Cut thy lace i' the mean time, and play the hypocrite, sweet Win.

WIN

No, I'll not make me unready for it. I can be hypocrite enough, though I were never so strait-laced.

LITTLEWIT

You say true. You have been bred i' the family, and brought up to't. Our mother is a most elect hypocrite, and has maintained us all this seven year with it, like gentlefolks.

WIN

Ay, let her alone, John; she is not a wise wilful widow for nothing, nor a sanctified sister for a song. And let me alone too; I ha' somewhat o' the mother in me; you shall see. Fetch her, fetch her! Ah, ah! [*Exit* LITTLEWIT]

Act I, Scene vi

[*Enter to her*] PURECRAFT, LITTLEWIT

PURECRAFT

Now the blaze of the beauteous discipline fright away this evil from our house! How now, Win-the-fight, child, how do you? Sweet child, speak to me.

WIN

Yes, forsooth.

146 *make me unready* undress
147 *strait-laced* (i) wearing a tightly laced bodice (ii) rigidly moral
153 *mother* (i) female parent (ii) hysteria
1 *discipline* religious practice (of the Puritans)

141 *Pie-corner*. The site of an old tavern, whose sign was a magpie, this place in West Smithfield was given over to cook-shops. It was at Pie-corner that Face first met Subtle 'Taking his meale of steeme in, from cookes stalls' (*The Alchemist*, I.i, 26).

150 *this seven year*. The statement is endorsed by Purecraft's confession at V.ii, 50–60.

PURECRAFT

Look up, sweet Win-the-fight, and suffer not the enemy to enter you at this door; remember that your education has been with the purest. What polluted one was it that named first the unclean beast, pig, to you, child?

WIN

Uh, Uh!

LITTLEWIT

Not I, o' my sincerity, mother. She longed above three hours ere she would let me know it. Who was it, Win?

WIN

A profane black thing with a beard, John.

PURECRAFT

O! resist it, Win-the-fight, it is the Tempter, the wicked Tempter; you may know it by the fleshly motion of pig. Be strong against it and its foul temptations in these assaults, whereby it broacheth flesh and blood, as it were, on the weaker side; and pray against its carnal provocations, good child, sweet child, pray.

LITTLEWIT

Good mother, I pray you that she may eat some pig, and her belly-ful, too; and do not you cast away your own child, and perhaps one of mine, with your tale of the Tempter. How do you, Win? Are you not sick?

WIN

Yes, a great deal, John. Uh, uh!

PURECRAFT

What shall we do? Call our zealous brother Busy hither, for his faithful fortification in this charge of the adversary. [*Exit* LITTLEWIT]

Child, my dear child, you shall eat pig, be comforted, my sweet child.

WIN

Ay, but i' the Fair, mother.

PURECRAFT

I mean i' the Fair, if it can be any way made or found lawful.

[*Enter* LITTLEWIT]

Where is our brother Busy? Will he not come? Look up, child.

LITTLEWIT

Presently, mother, as soon as he has cleansed his beard. I found him, fast by the teeth i' the cold turkey-pie i' the

14 *motion* prompting

cupboard, with a great white loaf on his left hand, and a glass of malmsey on his right.

PURECRAFT

Slander not the brethren, wicked one.

[*Enter to them*] BUSY

LITTLEWIT

Here he is now, purified, mother.

PURECRAFT

O Brother Busy! your help here to edify and raise us up in a scruple. My daughter Win-the-fight is visited with a natural disease of women, called 'A longing to eat pig'.

LITTLEWIT

Ay sir, a Bartholmew pig, and in the Fair.

PURECRAFT

And I would be satisfied from you, religiously-wise, whether a widow of the sanctified assembly, or a widow's daughter, may commit the act without offence to the weaker sisters.

BUSY

Verily, for the disease of longing, it is a disease, a carnal disease, or appetite, incident to women; and as it is carnal, and incident, it is natural, very natural. Now pig, it is a meat, and a meat that is nourishing, and may be longed for, and so consequently eaten; it may be eaten; very exceeding well eaten. But in the Fair, and as a Bartholmew-pig, it cannot be eaten, for the very calling it a Bartholmew-pig, and to eat it so, is a spice of idolatry, and you make the Fair no better than one of the high places. This, I take it, is the state of the question. A high place.

LITTLEWIT

Ay, but in state of necessity, place should give place, Master Busy.—I have a conceit left, yet.

PURECRAFT

Good Brother Zeal-of-the-land, think to make it as lawful as you can.

37–8 *raise us up in a scruple* assist us in a question of conscience
51 *spice* kind, species

54 *place should give place.* Littlewit is quibbling, taking Busy's 'high place' (in the Scriptural sense of a place of idolatrous worship and sacrifice) as 'high rank or position' and saying that a man in high place must yield precedence to a better man—a version of *noblesse oblige*. Cf. the proverb (Tilley, M238) 'Man honours the place, not the place the man'.

LITTLEWIT

Yes sir, and as soon as you can; for it must be, sir. You see the danger my little wife is in, sir.

PURECRAFT

Truly, I do love my child dearly, and I would not have her miscarry, or hazard her first fruits, if it might be otherwise.

BUSY

Surely, it may be otherwise, but it is subject to construction, subject, and hath a face of offence with the weak, a great face, a foul face, but that face may have a veil put over it, and be shadowed, as it were; it may be eaten, and in the Fair, I take it, in a booth, the tents of the wicked. The place is not much, not very much; we may be religious in midst of the profane, so it be eaten with a reformed mouth, with sobriety, and humbleness; not gorged in with gluttony, or greediness; there's the fear; for, should she go there as taking pride in the place, or delight in the unclean dressing, to feed the vanity of the eye, or the lust of the palate, it were not well, it were not fit, it were abominable, and not good.

LITTLEWIT

Nay, I knew that afore, and told her on't. But courage, Win, we'll be humble enough; we'll seek out the homeliest booth i' the Fair, that's certain; rather than fail, we'll eat it o' the ground.

PURECRAFT

Ay, and I'll go with you myself, Win-the-fight, and my brother, Zeal-of-the-land, shall go with us too, for our better consolation.

WIN

Uh, uh!

LITTLEWIT

Ay, and Solomon too, Win; the more the merrier, Win. [*Aside to* WIN] We'll leave Rabbi Busy in a booth.— Solomon, my cloak.

[*Enter to them*] SOLOMON

SOLOMON

Here, sir.

BUSY

In the way of comfort to the weak, I will go and eat. I will eat exceedingly, and prophesy. There may be a good use made

63 *face of offence* look of a stumbling-block
70 *fear* thing to be feared

of it, too, now I think on't: by the public eating of swine's flesh, to profess our hate and loathing of Judaism, whereof the brethren stand taxed. I will therefore eat, yea, I will eat exceedingly.

LITTLEWIT

Good i'faith, I will eat heartily too, because I will be no Jew; I could never away with that stiff-necked generation. And truly, I hope my little one will be like me, that cries for pig so, i' the mother's belly.

BUSY

Very likely, exceeding likely, very exceeding likely.

[*Exeunt*]

Act II, Scene i

[*Enter*] JUSTICE OVERDO, [*disguised as Mad Arthur of Bradley*]

OVERDO

Well, in Justice' name, and the King's, and for the Commonwealth! Defy all the world, Adam Overdo, for a disguise, and all story; for thou hast fitted thyself, I swear. Fain would I meet the Lynceus now, that eagle's eye, that piercing Epidaurian serpent, as my Quintus Horace calls him, that

93 *away with* tolerate, put up with
stiff-necked generation stubborn race (cf. Deuteronomy, ix. 13, Acts, vii, 51, etc.)
1–2 *Commonwealth* common weal, general good
3 *fitted* perfectly furnished

89–90 *Judaism, whereof the brethren stand taxed.* The Puritans were accused (taxed) of Judaism not only because of the emphasis they placed on the Old Testament but also because, very much to their credit, they were, first in Holland and then in England, more tolerant in their attitude towards the Jews than other Christian sects were. It was Oliver Cromwell who allowed the Jews to return to England from which they had been expelled by Edward I.

4 *Lynceus.* One of the Argonauts, famous for his extraordinarily keen eyesight.

4–5 *piercing Epidaurian serpent . . . him.* Horace writes:

cur in amicorum vitiis tam cernis acutum
quam aut aquila aut serpens Epidaurius? (*Satires*, I.iii. 26–7):

'Why, when you look into the failings of your friends, are you as sharp-sighted as an eagle or a serpent of Epidaurus?' Serpents, which were supposed to have very keen eyes, were sacred to Aesculapius, the god of medicine, who was worshipped in the form of a serpent at Epidaurus in Greece.

could discover a Justice of Peace, and lately of the Quorum, under this covering. They may have seen many a fool in the habit of a Justice; but never till now a Justice in the habit of a fool. Thus must we do, though, that wake for the public good; and thus hath the wise magistrate done in all ages. There is a doing of right out of wrong, if the way be found. Never shall I enough commend a worthy worshipful man, sometime a capital member of this city, for his high wisdom in this point, who would take you, now the habit of a porter, now of a carman, now of the dog-killer in this month of August, and in the winter of a seller of tinder-boxes. And what would he do in all these shapes? Marry, go you into every alehouse, and down into every cellar; measure the length of puddings, take the gauge of black pots and cans, ay, and custards, with a stick; and their circumference, with a thread; weigh the loaves of bread on his middle finger. Then would he send for 'em, home; give the puddings to the poor, the bread to the hungry, the custards to his children; break the pots, and burn the cans, himself; he would not trust his corrupt officers; he would do't himself. Would all men in authority would follow this worthy precedent! For, alas, as we are public persons, what do we know? Nay, what can we know? We hear with other men's ears; we see with other men's eyes; a foolish constable or a sleepy watchman is all our information. He slanders a gentleman, by the virtue of his place, as he calls it, and we, by the vice of ours, must believe him; as, a while agone, they made me, yea me, to mistake an honest zealous pursuivant for a seminary, and a

9 *wake* are vigilant, keep watch and ward

13 *capital* leading

29 *eyes;* Ed. (eyes? F)

33 *pursuivant* state official having power to execute warrants for arrest *seminary* Roman Catholic priest trained at one of the seminaries in Europe

---

6 *Quorum*. Certain justices, selected for their learning and ability, whose presence was necessary to constitute a bench of magistrates.

12–13 *a worthy . . . city*. C. S. Alden thinks the individual in question was Sir Thomas Hayes, Lord Mayor of London in 1614, who disguised himself in order to visit and find out the truth about 'lewd houses' and the malpractices of those who kept 'victualling houses and ale-houses' (see H & S, x. 185).

15 *dog-killer*. Acting under the mistaken impression that dogs carried the infection, the city fathers hired a dog-killer to exterminate all stray dogs in times of plague, thus freeing the black rat, whose fleas were the true source of the infection, from its chief enemy.

proper young Bachelor of Music for a bawd. This we are subject to, that live in high place: all our intelligence is idle, and most of our intelligencers knaves; and, by your leave, ourselves thought little better, if not arrant fools, for believing 'em. I, Adam Overdo, am resolved therefore to spare spy-money hereafter, and make mine own discoveries. Many are the yearly enormities of this Fair, in whose courts of Pie-powders I have had the honour, during the three days sometimes, to sit as judge. But this is the special day for detection of those foresaid enormities. Here is my black book for the purpose; this the cloud that hides me; under this covert I shall see and not be seen. On, Junius Brutus! And as I began, so I'll end: in Justice' name, and the King's, and for the Commonwealth! [*Stands aside*]

Act II, Scene ii

[*Enter*] LEATHERHEAD [*and*] TRASH

LEATHERHEAD

The Fair's pestilence dead, methinks. People come not abroad today, whatever the matter is. Do you hear, Sister Trash, Lady o' the Basket? Sit farther with your gingerbread-progeny there, and hinder not the prospect of my shop, or I'll ha' it proclaimed i' the Fair what stuff they are made on.

TRASH

Why, what stuff are they made on, Brother Leatherhead? Nothing but what's wholesome, I assure you.

35 *intelligence* information
idle unreliable
36 *intelligencers* spies, informers
40 *enormities* monstrous offences and irregularities
of Ed. (of of F)
45 *covert* disguise
1 *pestilence plaguily*

40–1 *courts of Pie-powders*. Summary courts held at fairs and markets to administer justice among the itinerant dealers and their customers. 'Pie-powders' (French *pied-poudreux*) = 'dustyfoot', 'wayfarer'.

45 *Junius Brutus*. Lucius Junius Brutus, who drove the Tarquins out of Rome and founded the Roman Republic, is invoked by Overdo for two reasons: he disguised himself as an idiot in order to escape the vigilance of Tarquinius Superbus, and he sentenced his own sons to death when they conspired to restore the Tarquins, thus winning a reputation as an inflexible judge.

LEATHERHEAD

Yes, stale bread, rotten eggs, musty ginger, and dead honey, you know.

OVERDO

[*Aside*] Ay! have I met with enormity so soon?

LEATHERHEAD

I shall mar your market, old Joan.

TRASH

Mar my market, thou too-proud pedlar? Do thy worst. I defy thee; ay, and thy stable of hobby-horses. I pay for my ground as well as thou dost. An thou wrong'st me, for all thou art parcel-poet and an inginer, I'll find a friend shall right me, and make a ballad of thee and thy cattle all over. Are you puffed up with the pride of your wares? Your arsedine?

LEATHERHEAD

Go to, old Joan, I'll talk with you anon; and take you down too afore Justice Overdo. He is the man must charm you; I'll ha' you i' the Pie-powders.

TRASH

Charm me? I'll meet thee face to face afore his worship when thou dar'st; and though I be a little crooked o' my body, I'll be found as upright in my dealing as any woman in Smithfield, I. Charm me!

OVERDO

[*Aside*] I am glad to hear my name is their terror yet; this is doing of justice.

[*Enter to them*] PASSENGERS

LEATHERHEAD

What do you lack? What is't you buy? What do you lack? Rattles, drums, halberts, horses, babies o' the best? Fiddles o'th'finest?

Enter COSTARDMONGER [*followed by*] NIGHTINGALE

COSTARDMONGER

Buy any pears, pears, fine, very fine pears!

10 s.p. OVERDO Ed. (IVS. F)
14 *dost. An* Ed. (dost, and F)
15 *parcel-poet* a bit of a poet, part-time poet
inginer, I'll Ed. (Inginer. I'll F); *inginer* designer, contriver of shows
16 *cattle* wares
18 *arsedine* gold-coloured alloy used for ornamenting toys
20 *charm you* subdue your tongue (as though by magic)

TRASH

Buy any gingerbread, gilt gingerbread!

NIGHTINGALE [*Sings*]

Hey, now the Fair's a filling!
O, for a tune to startle
The birds o' the booths here billing
Yearly with old Saint Bartle!
The drunkards they are wading,
The punks and chapmen trading;
Who'd see the Fair without his lading?

Buy any ballads, new ballads?

[*Enter*] URSLA

URSLA

Fie upon't! Who would wear out their youth and prime thus in roasting of pigs, that had any cooler vocation? Hell's a kind of cold cellar to't, a very fine vault, o' my conscience! What, Mooncalf!

MOONCALF

[*Within*] Here, Mistress.

NIGHTINGALE

How now, Ursla? In a heat, in a heat?

URSLA

[*To* MOONCALF] My chair, you false faucet you; and my morning's draught, quickly, a bottle of ale to quench me, rascal.—I am all fire and fat, Nightingale, I shall e'en melt away to the first woman, a rib, again, I am afraid. I do water the ground in knots as I go, like a great garden-pot; you may follow me by the S's I make.

NIGHTINGALE

Alas, good Urs! Was Zekiel here this morning?

URSLA

Zekiel? What Zekiel?

NIGHTINGALE

Zekiel Edgworth, the civil cutpurse—you know him well enough—he that talks bawdy to you still. I call him my secretary.

32 *gilt* given a golden appearance (cf. 'to take the gilt off the gingerbread')
37 *wading* half seas over
39 *lading* freight (of fairings)
47 *faucet* tap for a barrel
51 *knots* intricate figures of criss-cross lines
57 *secretary* confidant

URSLA

He promised to be here this morning, I remember.

NIGHTINGALE

When he comes, bid him stay. I'll be back again presently.

URSLA

Best take your morning's dew in your belly, Nightingale.

MOONCALF *brings in the chair*

Come, sir, set it here. Did not I bid you should get this chair let out o' the sides for me, that my hips might play? You'll never think of anything till your dame be rump-galled. 'Tis well, changeling; because it can take in your grasshopper's thighs, you care for no more. Now you look as you had been i' the corner o' the booth, fleaing your breech with a candle's end, and set fire o' the Fair. Fill, stote, fill.

OVERDO

[*Aside*] This pig-woman do I know, and I will put her in for my second enormity. She hath been before me, punk, pinnace, and bawd, any time these two and twenty years, upon record i' the Pie-powders.

URSLA

Fill again, you unlucky vermin.

MOONCALF

'Pray you be not angry, mistress; I'll ha' it widened anon.

URSLA

No, no, I shall e'en dwindle away to't ere the Fair be done, you think, now you ha' heated me! A poor vexed thing I am. I feel myself dropping already as fast as I can; two stone o' suet a day is my proportion. I can but hold life and soul together with this—here's to you, Nightingale—and a whiff of tobacco at most. Where's my pipe now? Not filled? Thou arrant incubee!

NIGHTINGALE

Nay, Ursla, thou'lt gall between the tongue and the teeth with fretting now.

URSLA

How can I hope that ever he'll discharge his place of trust—

64 *changeling* stupid or ugly child left by the fairies in place of one they have stolen
66 *fleaing* removing fleas from
67 *stote* (i) stoat (ii) stot (clumsy stupid person)
70 *pinnace* go-between
77 *proportion* estimate
80 *incubee* offspring of a woman and an incubus

tapster, a man of reckoning under me—that remembers nothing I say to him? [*Exit* NIGHTINGALE] But look to't, sirrah, you were best. Threepence a pipeful I will ha' made of all my whole half-pound of tobacco, and a quarter of a pound of coltsfoot mixed with it too, to itch it out. I that have dealt so long in the fire will not be to seek in smoke now. Then, six and twenty shillings a barrel I will advance o' my beer, and fifty shillings a hundred o' my bottle-ale; I ha' told you the ways how to raise it. Froth your cans well i' the filling at length, rogue, and jog your bottles o' the buttock, sirrah; then skink out the first glass, ever, and drink with all companies, though you be sure to be drunk; you'll misreckon the better, and be less ashamed on't. But your true trick, rascal, must be to be ever busy, and mis-take away the bottles and cans in haste before they be half drunk off, and never hear anybody call, if they should chance to mark you, till you ha' brought fresh, and be able to forswear 'em. Give me a drink of ale.

OVERDO

[*Aside*] This is the very womb and bed of enormity gross as herself! This must all down for enormity, all, every whit on't.
One knocks

URSLA

Look who's there, sirrah! Five shillings a pig is my price—at least. If it be a sow-pig, sixpence more. If she be a great-bellied wife, and long for't, sixpence more for that.

OVERDO

[*Aside*] *O tempora! O mores!* I would not ha' lost my discovery of this one grievance for my place and worship o' the bench. How is the poor subject abused here! Well, I will fall in with her, and with her Mooncalf, and wind out wonders of enormity. [*Comes forward*]

88 *itch* eke
89 *to seek in* short of
91 *advance* raise the price
93 *at length* i.e., with the can held as far below the spigot as possible
94 *skink* pour
107 *O tempora*! *O mores*! (Cicero, *In Catilinam,* I.i. 2) What an age! What manners!

---

110 *wind* ed. (winne F) smell, scent (*OED*, Wind, *v.*[2], c.). It is difficult to find any parallel for 'win out' in the sense it should have here, whereas the hunting term 'wind out' fits what Overdo sees himself as doing and is consonant with the use of animal imagery in the play. Cf. Barry's *Ram Alley* (1607–08): 'No nose to smell, and winde out all your tricks' (II.i).

By thy leave, goodly woman and the fatness of the Fair, oily as the King's constable's lamp, and shining as his shoeing-horn! Hath thy ale virtue, or thy beer strength, that the tongue of man may be tickled, and his palate pleased in the morning? Let thy pretty nephew here go search and see.

URSLA

What new roarer is this?

MOONCALF

O Lord, do you not know him, mistress? 'Tis mad Arthur of Bradley, that makes the orations.—Brave master, old Arthur of Bradley, how do you? Welcome to the Fair! When shall we hear you again to handle your matters, with your back again a booth, ha? I ha' been one o' your little disciples, i' my days!

OVERDO

Let me drink, boy, with my love, thy aunt here, that I may be eloquent; but of thy best, lest it be bitter in my mouth, and my words fall foul on the Fair.

URSLA

Why dost thou not fetch him drink? And offer him to sit?

MOONCALF

Is't ale or beer, Master Arthur?

OVERDO

Thy best, pretty stripling, thy best; the same thy dove drinketh, and thou drawest on holy-days.

URSLA

Bring him a sixpenny bottle of ale; they say a fool's handsel is lucky.

OVERDO

Bring both, child. Ale for Arthur, and beer for Bradley. Ale for thine aunt, boy. [*Exit* MOONCALF]
[*Aside*] My disguise takes to the very wish and reach of it. I shall, by the benefit of this, discover enough and more, and

122 *again* against
124 *aunt* gossip
129 *dove* darling
135 *takes* works, succeeds

118–19 *mad Arthur of Bradley*. The hero of an old song, going back at least as far as the mid-sixteenth century, called 'The Ballad of the Wedding of Arthur of Bradley'. Jonson endows him with a fondness for making orations in order to fit him for the role Overdo takes on.

131–2 *a fool's handsel is lucky*. A well-known proverb (Tilley, F517); 'handsel' is the first money taken in a day.

yet get off with the reputation of what I would be—a certain middling thing between a fool and a madman.

Act II, Scene iii

[*Enter*] KNOCKEM *to them*

KNOCKEM
What! my little lean Ursla! my she-bear! art thou alive yet? With thy litter of pigs to grunt out another Bartholmew Fair, ha?

URSLA
Yes, and to amble afoot, when the Fair is done, to hear you groan out of a cart, up the heavy hill.

KNOCKEM
Of Holborn, Ursla, meanst thou so? For what? For what, pretty Urs?

URSLA
For cutting halfpenny purses, or stealing little penny dogs out o' the Fair.

KNOCKEM
O! good words, good words, Urs.

OVERDO
[*Aside*] Another special enormity. A cutpurse of the sword, the boot, and the feather! Those are his marks.

[*Enter* MOONCALF]

URSLA
You are one of those horse-leeches that gave out I was dead, in Turnbull Street, of a surfeit of bottle-ale and tripes?

KNOCKEM
No, 'twas better meat, Urs: cows' udders, cows' udders!

URSLA
Well, I shall be meet with your mumbling mouth one day.

KNOCKEM
What? Thou'lt poison me with a neuft in a bottle of ale, wilt

11 *sword*, Ed. (sword! F)
13 *horse-leeches* (i) farriers (ii) large blood-sucking leeches (iii) rapacious predators
16 *meet with* quits with, revenged on
17 *neuft* newt

5 *groan . . . heavy hill.* Criminals sentenced to hanging were conveyed by cart from Newgate Gaol, up Holborn Hill, to the gallows at Tyburn; 'heavy' = 'grievous', 'distressing'.

thou? Or a spider in a tobacco-pipe, Urs? Come, there's no malice in these fat folks. I never fear thee, an I can scape thy lean Mooncalf here. Let's drink it out, good Urs, and no vapours! [*Exit* URSLA]

OVERDO

Dost thou hear, boy?—There's for thy ale, and the remnant for thee.—Speak in thy faith of a faucet, now. Is this goodly person before us here, this 'vapours', a knight of the knife?

MOONCALF

What mean you by that, Master Arthur?

OVERDO

I mean a child of the horn-thumb, a babe of booty, boy, a cutpurse.

MOONCALF

O Lord, sir! far from it. This is Master Dan Knockem—Jordan, the ranger of Turnbull. He is a horse-courser, sir.

OVERDO

Thy dainty dame, though, called him cutpurse.

MOONCALF

Like enough, sir. She'll do forty such things in an hour, an you listen to her, for her recreation, if the toy take her i' the greasy kerchief. It makes her fat, you see. She battens with it.

OVERDO

[*Aside*] Here might I ha' been deceived now, and ha' put a fool's blot upon myself, if I had not played an after-game o' discretion.

URSLA *comes in again dropping*

29 *Jordan* chamber-pot
32 *toy* whim
33 *kerchief* cloth used as head-cover, but here the head itself
36 *after-game* second game played to reverse the outcome of the first
37 s.d. *dropping* exhausted and dripping with sweat

18–19 *there's no malice in these fat folks.* A version of the proverb 'Fat folks are good-natured' (Tilley, F419).

21 *vapours.* This word which is used extensively in the play, is defined by Jonson himself in the s.d. at IV.iv, 26 as 'nonsense'. For Knockem, who employs it incessantly, it means whatever he wants it to mean—usually little or nothing. It seems, however, to have two main connotations: (i) fantastic notions (ii) a ridiculous urge to brag and quarrel.

26 *horn-thumb.* Cutpurses protected their thumbs with a piece of horn, so that they did not cut themselves in the act of cutting a purse.

KNOCKEM

Alas, poor Urs, this's an ill season for thee.

URSLA

Hang yourself, hackney-man.

KNOCKEM

How, how, Urs? Vapours? Motion breed vapours?

URSLA

Vapours! Never tusk, nor twirl your dibble, good Jordan, I know what you'll take to a very drop. Though you be captain o' the roarers, and fight well at the case of piss-pots, you shall not fright me with your lion-chap, sir, nor your tusks. You angry? You are hungry. Come, a pig's head will stop your mouth and stay your stomach at all times.

KNOCKEM

Thou art such another mad merry Urs still! Troth, I do make conscience of vexing thee now i' the dog-days, this hot weather, for fear of foundering thee i' the body, and melting down a pillar of the Fair. Pray thee take thy chair again, and keep state; and let's have a fresh bottle of ale, and a pipe of tobacco; and no vapours. I'll ha' this belly o' thine taken up, and thy grass scoured, wench. Look! here's Ezekiel Edgworth, a fine boy of his inches as any is i' the Fair! Has still money in his purse, and will pay all with a kind heart, and good vapours.

40 *How, how, Urs? Vapours*? Ed. (How? how? *Vrs*, vapours! F)
Motion breed vapours? Does activity give rise to tantrums?
44 *lion-chap* lion's jaw
49 *foundering* causing a horse to break down by overworking it
51 *keep state* act like a queen
52 *taken up* reduced (farriers' terminology)
53 *scoured* purged out

---

41 *Never tusk, nor twirl your dibble*. An obscure and disputed passage; *OED* suggests that 'tusk' means 'show your teeth', and 'twirl your dibble' = 'twist your moustache'. It seems more likely, however, since Ursla goes on to refer to Jordan's 'lion-chap' and his 'tusks', that 'tusks' are the ends of the moustache and the 'dibble' a little spade beard; 'tusk' would then mean 'twist up the ends of your moustache', and 'twirl your dibble', 'twist your little beard around'.

43 *at the case of piss-pots*. To 'fight at the case of pistols' was to fight with a pair of pistols; but Ursla cleverly replaces the expected 'pistols' with 'piss-pots'.

53–6 *Look! . . . vapours*. While Knockem is saying these words, Edgworth makes his way from the rear of the stage to the front, where Knockem and Ursla are. He is not regarded as being fully on stage until he joins them.

Act II, Scene iv

[*Enter*] *to them* EDGWORTH, NIGHTINGALE, CORNCUTTER, TINDERBOX-MAN, PASSENGERS

EDGWORTH

That I will, indeed, willingly, Master Knockem. [*To* MOONCALF] Fetch some ale and tobacco. [*Exit* MOONCALF]

LEATHERHEAD

What do you lack, gentlemen? Maid, see a fine hobby-horse for your young master; cost you but a token a week his provender.

CORNCUTTER

Ha' you any corns i' your feet and toes?

TINDERBOX-MAN

Buy a mousetrap, a mousetrap, or a tormentor for a flea.

TRASH

Buy some gingerbread.

NIGHTINGALE

Ballads, ballads! fine new ballads!
Hear for your love, and buy for your money!
A delicate ballad o' 'The Ferret and the Coney';
'A Preservative again the Punk's Evil';
Another of 'Goose-green Starch and the Devil';

1 *Knockem*. Ed. (*Knockhum*, F)
7 *tormentor* trap
12 *Punk's Evil* venereal disease
13 *Goose-green* (more usually 'gooseturd-green') yellowish green

s.d. TINDERBOX-MAN. Here, and in the s.p. of the one speech assigned to him (l. 7), the Tinderbox-man takes the place of the Mousetrap-man listed among the Persons of the Play, though mousetraps still appear to be his main stock in trade.

10 *Hear . . . money*. Cf. the proverbial 'not to be had for love or money' (Tilley, L484).

11 *The Ferret and the Coney*. The swindler and the dupe (thieves' cant)

13 *Goose-green Starch and the Devil*. The story on which this 'goodly Ballad against Pride' was based is told by Philip Stubbes in his *Anatomie of Abuses* (1583). It concerns a proud young woman of Antwerp who, dissatisfied with the way in which her ruffs were starched, wished that the Devil might take her 'when she weare any of those Neckerchers again'. Thereupon, the Devil came to her in the likeness of a young man, set her ruffs beautifully, so that she fell in love with him, and then, in the act of kissing her, broke her neck (*The Anatomie of Abuses*, ed. Furnivall, 1877, i. 71–2).

'A Dozen of Divine Points' and 'The Godly Garters';
'The Fairing of Good Counsel', of an ell and three quarters.
What is't you buy?
'The Windmill blown down by the witch's fart!',
Or 'Saint George, that O! did break the dragon's heart!'

[*Enter* MOONCALF]

EDGWORTH
Master Nightingale, come hither, leave your mart a little.

NIGHTINGALE
O my secretary! What says my secretary?

OVERDO
Child o' the bottles, what's he? What's he?

MOONCALF
A civil young gentleman, Master Arthur, that keeps company with the roarers, and disburses all still. He has ever money in his purse. He pays for them, and they roar for him: one does good offices for another. They call him the secretary, but he serves nobody. A great friend of the ballad-man's, they are never asunder.

OVERDO
What pity 'tis so civil a young man should haunt this debauched company! Here's the bane of the youth of our time apparent. A proper penman, I see't in his countenance; he has a good clerk's look with him, and I warrant him a quick hand.

MOONCALF
A very quick hand, sir. [*Exit*]

EDGWORTH
(*This they whisper that* OVERDO *hears it not*)
All the purses and purchase I give you today by conveyance, bring hither to Ursla's presently. Here we

15 *ell* forty-five inches
19 *mart* trade
21 *What's* Ed. (what F)
24 *roar* behave noisily and riotously (to help the cutpurse)
34 *purchase* booty, stolen goods
34–5 *conveyance* sleight of hand

---

14 *A Dozen of Divine Points.* Twelve moral maxims, in the form of a ballad, 'sent by a gentlewoman to her lover for a new yeares gift'.
The Godly Garters. Probably the ballad which John Charlwood entered on the Stationers' Register on 20 October 1578 under the title 'A paire of garters for yonge men to weare that serve the Lord God and Lyve in his feare'.

will meet at night in her lodge, and share. Look you choose good places for your standing i' the Fair, when you sing, Nightingale.

URSLA

Ay, near the fullest passages; and shift 'em often.

EDGWORTH

And i' your singing you must use your hawk's eye nimbly, and fly the purse to a mark still—where 'tis worn and o' which side—that you may gi' me the sign with your beak, or hang your head that way i' the tune.

URSLA

Enough, talk no more on't. Your friendship, masters, is not now to begin. Drink your draught of indenture, your sup of covenant, and away. The Fair fills apace, company begins to come in, and I ha' ne'er a pig ready yet.

KNOCKEM

Well said! Fill the cups and light the tobacco. Let's give fire i'th'works, and noble vapours.

EDGWORTH

And shall we ha' smocks, Ursla, and good whimsies, ha?

URSLA

Come, you are i' your bawdy vein! The best the Fair will afford, Zekiel, if bawd Whit keep his word.

[*Enter* MOONCALF]

How do the pigs, Mooncalf?

MOONCALF

Very passionate, mistress; one on 'em has wept out an eye. Master Arthur o' Bradley is melancholy here; nobody talks to him. Will you any tobacco, Master Arthur?

39 *fullest passages* most crowded thoroughfares
45 *draught of indenture* pledge drunk on the signing of an agreement, with a pun on 'draft'
50 *smocks* wenches
54 *passionate* sorrowful, sorry for themselves

---

41 *fly the purse to a mark.* Indicate precisely where the purse is—an image taken from hawking.

44–5 *Your friendship . . . begin.* A significant reminiscence of Chaucer's remark about the collusion between the Doctor and the apothecaries:

For ech of hem made other for to winne;
Hir frendschipe nas nat newe to beginne. (Prologue to *The Canterbury Tales*, 427–8)

50 *whimsies.* Also occurring in the form 'whimsbies', this is a variant on the vulgar 'quims', i.e., 'female genitalia', used as a synonym for 'whores'.

OVERDO
No, boy, let my meditations alone.

MOONCALF
He's studying for an oration now.

OVERDO
[*Aside*] If I can, with this day's travail and all my policy, but rescue this youth here out of the hands of the lewd man and the strange woman, I will sit down at night and say with my friend Ovid, *Iamque opus exegi, quod nec Iovis ira, nec ignis, etc.*

KNOCKEM
Here, Zekiel; here's a health to Ursla, and a kind vapour! Thou hast money i' thy purse still, and store! How dost thou come by it? Pray thee vapour thy friends some in a courteous vapour.

EDGWORTH
Half I have, Master Dan Knockem, is always at your service.

OVERDO
[*Aside*] Ha, sweet nature! What goshawk would prey upon such a lamb?

KNOCKEM
Let's see what 'tis, Zekiel, count it! [*To* MOONCALF] Come, fill him to pledge me.

Act II, Scene v

[*Enter*] WINWIFE, QUARLOUS, *to them*

WINWIFE
We are here before 'em, methinks.

QUARLOUS
All the better; we shall see 'em come in now.

LEATHERHEAD
What do you lack, gentlemen, what is't you lack? A fine

59 *policy* shrewd contriving
61 *strange woman*, Ed. (strange woman. F) harlot
65 *store* plenty

62–3 *Iamque . . . ignis, etc.* Having completed his *Metamorphoses*, Ovid expresses, in the last nine lines of that work, his conviction that it will bring him immortal fame. The passage opens thus:

Iamque opus exegi, quod nec Iovis ira, nec ignis,
Nec poterit ferrum, nec edax abolere vetustas (xv. 871–2):

'And now I have finished a work, which neither the anger of Jove, nor fire, nor sword, nor devouring time will ever destroy'.

horse? A lion? A bull? A bear? A dog or a cat? An excellent fine Bartholmew-bird? Or an instrument? What is't you lack?

QUARLOUS

'Slid! here's Orpheus among the beasts, with his fiddle and all!

TRASH

Will you buy any comfortable bread, gentlemen?

QUARLOUS

And Ceres selling her daughter's picture in gingerwork!

WINWIFE

That these people should be so ignorant to think us chapmen for 'em! Do we look as if we would buy gingerbread? Or hobby-horses?

QUARLOUS

Why, they know no better ware than they have, nor better customers than come. And our very being here makes us fit to be demanded, as well as others. Would Cokes would come! There were a true customer for 'em.

KNOCKEM

[*To* EDGWORTH] How much is't? Thirty shillings? Who's yonder? Ned Winwife? And Tom Quarlous, I think! Yes.—Gi' me it all, gi' me it all.—Master Winwife! Master Quarlous! Will you take a pipe of tobacco with us?—Do not discredit me now, Zekiel.

WINWIFE

Do not see him! He is the roaring horse-courser. Pray thee let's avoid him; turn down this way.

QUARLOUS

'Slud, I'll see him, and roar with him too, an he roared as loud as Neptune. Pray thee go with me.

9 *comfortable bread* bread that does the stomach good
11 *chapmen* customers
25 *'Slud* by God's blood

7 *Orpheus among the beasts.* According to Greek myth, Orpheus, the greatest poet and musician who ever lived, could charm beasts with the sound of his lyre.

10 *Ceres selling . . . gingerwork!* Ceres, goddess of the cornfield, was the mother of Proserpina. When her daughter was carried off to Hades by Pluto, Ceres wandered about for nine days seeking news of her before she discovered what had happened.

WINWIFE
You may draw me to as likely an inconvenience, when you please, as this.

QUARLOUS
Go to then, come along. We ha' nothing to do, man, but to see sights now.

KNOCKEM
Welcome, Master Quarlous, and Master Winwife! Will you take any froth and smoke with us?

QUARLOUS
Yes, sir; but you'll pardon us if we knew not of so much familiarity between us afore.

KNOCKEM
As what, sir?

QUARLOUS
To be so lightly invited to smoke and froth.

KNOCKEM
A good vapour! Will you sit down, sir? This is old Ursla's mansion; how like you her bower? Here you may ha' your punk and your pig in state, sir, both piping hot.

QUARLOUS
I had rather ha' my punk cold, sir.

OVERDO
[*Aside*] There's for me: punk! and pig!

URSLA *She calls within*
What, Mooncalf, you rogue!

MOONCALF
By and by; the bottle is almost off, mistress. Here, Master Arthur.

URSLA
[*Within*] I'll part you and your play-fellow there i' the guarded coat, an you sunder not the sooner.

KNOCKEM
Master Winwife, you are proud, methinks; you do not talk, nor drink. Are you proud?

WINWIFE
Not of the company I am in, sir, nor the place, I assure you.

KNOCKEM
You do not except at the company, do you? Are you in vapours, sir?

27 *as likely an inconvenience* as promising a piece of mischief (Spencer)
40 *cold* because a 'hot' punk would be one with venereal disease
43 *off* finished
46 *guarded* trimmed (with lace or braid)

MOONCALF

Nay, good Master Dan Knockem, respect my mistress' bower, as you call it. For the honour of our booth, none o' your vapours here.

URSLA *She comes out with a fire-brand*

Why, you thin lean polecat you, an they have a mind to be i' their vapours, must you hinder 'em? What did you know, vermin, if they would ha' lost a cloak, or such a trifle? Must you be drawing the air of pacification here, while I am tormented within, i' the fire, you weasel?

MOONCALF

Good mistress, 'twas in the behalf of your booth's credit that I spoke.

URSLA

Why, would my booth ha' broke if they had fallen out in't, sir? Or would their heat ha' fired it? In, you rogue, and wipe the pigs, and mend the fire, that they fall not, or I'll both baste and roast you till your eyes drop out, like 'em. Leave the bottle behind you, and be curst a while.

[*Exit* MOONCALF]

QUARLOUS

Body o' the Fair! what's this? Mother o' the bawds?

KNOCKEM

No, she's mother o' the pigs, sir, mother o' the pigs!

WINWIFE

Mother o' the Furies, I think, by her fire-brand.

QUARLOUS

Nay, she is too fat to be a Fury, sure; some walking sow of tallow!

WINWIFE

An inspired vessel of kitchen-stuff! *She drinks this while*

QUARLOUS

She'll make excellent gear for the coach-makers here in Smithfield to anoint wheels and axle-trees with.

62 *broke* (i) fallen to pieces (ii) gone bankrupt (punning on 'credit')
65 *baste . . . roast* beat (in addition to normal culinary meanings)
70 *sure;* ed. (sure, F)
73 *gear* material, stuff

70 *too fat to be a Fury*. Because 'Fat folks are good-natured' (Tilley, F419).
70–1 *walking sow of tallow*. Large oblong mass of tallow endowed with the power of movement; cf. 'sow of lead', 'sow of iron' (*OED*, Sow, *sb.*[1] 6. a. and b.); a sow of lead weighed about 300 lb.
72 *An inspired vessel of kitchen-stuff*. A container full of dripping that has been given the breath of life, with an allusion to Genesis, ii. 7.

URSLA

Ay, ay, gamesters, mock a plain plump soft wench o' the suburbs, do, because she's juicy and wholesome. You must ha' your thin pinched ware, pent up i' the compass of a dog-collar—or 'twill not do—that looks like a long laced conger set upright; and a green feather, like fennel i' the joll on't.

KNOCKEM

Well said, Urs, my good Urs! To 'em, Urs!

QUARLOUS

Is she your quagmire, Dan Knockem? Is this your bog?

NIGHTINGALE

We shall have a quarrel presently.

KNOCKEM

How? Bog? Quagmire? Foul vapours! Hum'h!

QUARLOUS

Yes, he that would venture for't, I assure him, might sink into her, and be drowned a week ere any friend he had could find where he were.

WINWIFE

And then he would be a fortnight weighing up again.

QUARLOUS

'Twere like falling into a whole shire of butter. They had need be a team of Dutchmen, should draw him out.

KNOCKEM

Answer 'em, Urs. Where's thy Bartholmew-wit now? Urs, thy Bartholmew-wit?

URSLA

Hang 'em, rotten, roguy cheaters! I hope to see 'em plagued one day—poxed they are already, I am sure—with lean playhouse poultry, that has the bony rump sticking out,

---

78 *laced* (i) streaked (ii) slashed (ready for cooking)
79 *joll* head (of a fish)
88 *weighing up* raising up (of an anchor or sunken ship)
95 *playhouse poultry* whores (cf. French *poules*) who frequented theatres

---

76 *suburbs*. The suburbs of London, especially those on the South Bank, were notorious for their brothels; in the City itself prostitution was more strictly regulated.

82 *quagmire . . . bog*. Horse-dealers kept a part of their yards in a very soft wet condition, so that horses with unsound legs could stand there without betraying their deficiencies.

90 *Dutchmen*. Popularly thought of as great consumers of butter.

like the ace of spades or the point of a partizan, that every rib of 'em is like the tooth of a saw; and will so grate 'em with their hips and shoulders as, take 'em altogether, they were as good lie with a hurdle.

QUARLOUS

Out upon her, how she drips! She's able to give a man the sweating sickness with looking on her.

URSLA

Marry look off, with a patch o' your face and a dozen i' your breech, though they be o' scarlet, sir. I ha' seen as fine outsides as either o' yours bring lousy linings to the broker's, ere now, twice a week.

QUARLOUS

Do you think there may be a fine new cucking-stool i' the Fair to be purchased? One large enough, I mean. I know there is a pond of capacity for her.

URSLA

For your mother, you rascal! Out, you rogue, you hedge-bird, you pimp, you pannier-man's bastard you!

QUARLOUS

Ha, ha, ha!

URSLA

Do you sneer, you dog's-head, you trendle-tail? You look as you were begotten atop of a cart in harvest-time, when the whelp was hot and eager. Go snuff after your brother's bitch, Mistress Commodity. That's the livery you wear. 'Twill be out at the elbows shortly. It's time you went to't for the tother remnant.

96 *partizan* long-handled spear
101 *sweating sickness* epidemic fever prevalent in the 15th and 16th centuries
102–3 *patch . . . breech* symptoms of venereal disease
104 *broker's* ed. (Brokers F)
106 *cucking-stool* chair used for punishing scolds, who were fastened in it and then ducked in a pond
109–10 *hedge-bird* foot-pad, vagrant (one born under a hedge)
110 *pannier-man's* hawker's
112 *trendle-tail* cur, mongrel with a curly tail
115 *Commodity* (i) gain (ii) article for sale (whore)

---

104 *bring lousy linings to the broker's.* Either (i) bring lice-infested underclothes to the pawnbroker's, or (ii) bring the diseased contents of your breeches, i.e., sexual organs, to the bawd's. (Cf. *OED*, Lining, *vbl. sb.*[1], 1. b. and 3.)

KNOCKEM

Peace, Urs, peace, Urs!—They'll kill the poor whale and make oil of her.—Pray thee go in.

URSLA

I'll see 'em poxed first, and piled, and double piled.

WINWIFE

Let's away; her language grows greasier than her pigs.

URSLA

Does't so, snotty-nose? Good Lord! are you snivelling? You were engendered on a she-beggar in a barn when the bald thrasher, your sire, was scarce warm.

WINWIFE

Pray thee let's go.

QUARLOUS

No, faith; I'll stay the end of her now. I know she cannot last long; I find by her similes she wanes apace.

URSLA

Does she so? I'll set you gone. Gi' me my pig-pan hither a little. I'll scald you hence, an you will not go. [*Exit*]

KNOCKEM

Gentlemen, these are very strange vapours! And very idle vapours, I assure you!

QUARLOUS

You are a very serious ass, we assure you.

KNOCKEM

Hum'h! Ass? And serious? Nay, then pardon me my vapour. I have a foolish vapour, gentlemen: any man that does vapour me the ass, Master Quarlous—

QUARLOUS

What then, Master Jordan?

KNOCKEM

I do vapour him the lie.

QUARLOUS

Faith, and to any man that vapours me the lie, I do vapour that. [*Strikes him*]

KNOCKEM

Nay then, vapours upon vapours.

EDGWORTH }
NIGHTINGALE }

'Ware the pan, the pan, the pan! She comes with the pan, gentlemen.

120 *piled* (i) bald (from the pox) (ii) afflicted with piles (iii) threadbare, reduced to beggary

128 *set you gone* set you going

URSLA *comes in with the scalding-pan. They fight. She falls with it.*

God bless the woman!

URSLA

Oh! [*Exeunt* QUARLOUS, WINWIFE]

TRASH

What's the matter?

OVERDO

Goodly woman!

MOONCALF

Mistress!

URSLA

Curse of hell that ever I saw these fiends! Oh! I ha' scalded my leg, my leg, my leg, my leg! I ha' lost a limb in the service! Run for some cream and salad oil, quickly. [*To* MOONCALF] Are you under-peering, you baboon? Rip off my hose, an you be men, men, men.

MOONCALF

Run you for some cream, good mother Joan. I'll look to your basket. [*Exit* TRASH]

LEATHERHEAD

Best sit up i' your chair, Ursla. Help, gentlemen. [*They lift her up*]

KNOCKEM

Be of good cheer, Urs. Thou hast hindered me the currying of a couple of stallions here, that abused the good race-bawd o' Smithfield. 'Twas time for 'em to go.

NIGHTINGALE

I'faith, when the pan came. They had made you run else.— This had been a fine time for purchase, if you had ventured.

EDGWORTH

Not a whit, these fellows were too fine to carry money.

KNOCKEM

Nightingale, get some help to carry her leg out o' the air; take off her shoes. Body o' me, she has the malanders, the scratches, the crown-scab, and the quitter-bone i' the tother leg.

145 s.p. TRASH Ed. (ERA. F)
156 *currying* beating, dressing-down
157 *race-bawd* breeder of bawds, mother-bawd
160 *purchase* theft
161 *fine* smart, clever

163–4 *malanders . . . quitter-bone.* These are all diseases of the leg and hoof in horses.

URSLA

Oh, the pox! Why do you put me in mind o' my leg thus, to make it prick and shoot? Would you ha' me i' the Hospital afore my time?

KNOCKEM

Patience, Urs. Take a good heart; 'tis but a blister as big as a windgall. I'll take it away with the white of an egg, a little honey, and hog's-grease. Ha' thy pasterns well rolled, and thou shalt pace again by tomorrow. I'll tend thy booth and look to thy affairs the while. Thou shalt sit i' thy chair, and give directions, and shine Ursa major.

[*Exeunt* KNOCKEM *and* MOONCALF *with* URSLA *in her chair*]

Act II, Scene vi

[*Enter*] COKES, WASP, MISTRESS OVERDO, GRACE

OVERDO

These are the fruits of bottle-ale and tobacco! the foam of the one and the fumes of the other! Stay, young man, and despise not the wisdom of these few hairs that are grown grey in care of thee.

EDGWORTH

Nightingale, stay a little. Indeed I'll hear some o' this!

COKES

Come, Numps, come, where are you? Welcome into the Fair, Mistress Grace.

EDGWORTH

[*To* NIGHTINGALE] 'Slight, he will call company, you shall see, and put us into doings presently.

OVERDO

Thirst not after that frothy liquor, ale; for who knows, when he openeth the stopple, what may be in the bottle? Hath not a snail, a spider, yea, a neuft been found there? Thirst not after it, youth; thirst not after it.

COKES

This is a brave fellow, Numps, let's hear him.

170 *windgall* soft tumour on a horse's leg
171 *rolled* bandaged
174 *Ursa major* the constellation of the Great Bear
8 *'Slight* by God's light
14 *brave* fine, capital

170–1 *white . . . hog's-grease.* Remedies used by farriers to deal with diseases in horses.

WASP

'Sblood, how brave is he? In a guarded coat? You were best truck with him; e'en strip, and truck presently; it will become you. Why will you hear him? Because he is an ass, and may be akin to the Cokeses?

COKES

O, good Numps!

OVERDO

Neither do thou lust after that tawny weed, tobacco.

COKES

Brave words!

OVERDO

Whose complexion is like the Indian's that vents it!

COKES

Are they not brave words, sister?

OVERDO

And who can tell if, before the gathering and making up thereof, the alligarta hath not pissed thereon?

WASP

'Heart, let 'em be brave words, as brave as they will! An they were all the brave words in a country, how then? Will you away yet? Ha' you enough on him? Mistress Grace, come you away, I pray you, be not you accessary. If you do lose your licence, or somewhat else, sir, with listening to his fables, say Numps is a witch, with all my heart, do, say so.

COKES

Avoid, i' your satin doublet, Numps.

OVERDO

The creeping venom of which subtle serpent, as some late writers affirm, neither the cutting of the perilous plant, nor the drying of it, nor the lighting or burning, can any way persway or assuage.

15 *brave* well dressed
16 *truck* make an exchange (of clothes)
17 *him*? Ed. (him, F)
22 *vents* sells (*OED*, Vent, v.^{3}, 1.)
25 *alligarta* alligator
31 *witch* wizard
32 *Avoid* go away, keep off (cf. 'Avoid, Satan')
36 *persway* diminish

33–4 *some late writers*. The most famous of those who wrote to attack the use of tobacco was James I, whose *Counterblaste to Tobacco* had come out in 1604.

COKES

Good, i'faith! is't not, sister?

OVERDO

Hence it is that the lungs of the tobacconist are rotted, the liver spotted, the brain smoked like the backside of the pig-woman's booth here, and the whole body within, black as her pan you saw e'en now without.

COKES

A fine similitude that, sir! Did you see the pan?

EDGWORTH

Yes, sir.

OVERDO

Nay, the hole in the nose here of some tobacco-takers, or the third nostril, if I may so call it, which makes that they can vent the tobacco out like the ace of clubs, or rather the flower-de-lys, is caused from the tobacco, the mere tobacco! when the poor innocent pox, having nothing to do there, is miserably and most unconscionably slandered.

COKES

Who would ha' missed this, sister?

MISTRESS OVERDO

Not anybody but Numps.

COKES

He does not understand.

EDGWORTH

[*Aside*] Nor you feel. *He picketh his purse*

COKES

What would you have, sister, of a fellow that knows nothing but a basket-hilt and an old fox in't? The best music i' the Fair will not move a log.

EDGWORTH

[*Slipping the purse to* NIGHTINGALE] In to Ursla, Nightingale, and carry her comfort. See it told. This fellow was sent to us by fortune for our first fairing.

[*Exit* NIGHTINGALE]

38 *tobacconist* smoker
46 *vent* blow, exhale
55 *basket-hilt* hilt with a basket-like protection for the hand
fox sword
58 *told* counted

44–5 *hole in the nose . . . third nostril.* An effect of syphilis; but Overdo prefers to attribute it to smoking.

OVERDO

But what speak I of the diseases of the body, children of the Fair?

COKES

That's to us, sister. Brave i'faith!

OVERDO

Hark, O you sons and daughters of Smithfield! and hear what malady it doth the mind: it causeth swearing, it causeth swaggering, it causeth snuffling and snarling, and now and then a hurt.

MISTRESS OVERDO

He hath something of Master Overdo, methinks, brother.

COKES

So methought, sister, very much of my brother Overdo. And, 'tis when he speaks.

OVERDO

Look into any angle o' the town—the Straits, or the Bermudas—where the quarrelling lesson is read, and how do they entertain the time but with bottle-ale and tobacco? The lecturer is o' one side, and his pupils o' the other; but the seconds are still bottle-ale and tobacco, for which the lecturer reads and the novices pay. Thirty pound a week in bottle-ale! forty in tobacco! and ten more in ale again! Then, for a suit to drink in, so much, and, that being slavered, so much for another suit, and then a third suit, and a fourth suit! and still the bottle-ale slavereth, and the tobacco stinketh!

WASP

Heart of a madman! are you rooted here? Will you never

65 *snuffling* sniffing with contempt
70 *angle* corner
72 *entertain* occupy, while away
74 *seconds* stand-bys, main supports
78 *slavered* soiled with saliva and sweat
81 *Will* Ed. (well F)

70–1 *the Straits, or the Bermudas.* A disreputable district of narrow lanes and alleys near Charing Cross, frequented by criminals.

71 *the quarrelling lesson.* The vogue for fencing and duelling with sword and dagger, which developed in the 1590s, led to the establishment of fencing academies and to the publication of such works of instruction as Vincentio Saviola's *Practise of the Rapier and Dagger* (1594–95), which dealt, among other things, with the right way to go about making a challenge. See *As You Like It*, V.iv, 45–97, where Touchstone makes splendid fun of it all.

away? What can any man find out in this bawling fellow, to grow here for? He is a full handful higher sin' he heard him. Will you fix here? And set up a booth, sir?

OVERDO

I will conclude briefly—

WASP

Hold your peace, you roaring rascal, I'll run my head i' your chaps else. [*To* COKES] You were best build a booth, and entertain him; make your will, an you say the word, and him your heir! Heart, I never knew one taken with a mouth of a peck afore. By this light, I'll carry you away o' my back, an you will not come. *He gets him up on pickpack*

COKES

Stay, Numps, stay, set me down. I ha' lost my purse, Numps. O my purse! One o' my fine purses is gone.

MISTRESS OVERDO

Is't indeed, brother?

COKES

Ay, as I am an honest man; would I were an arrant rogue, else! A plague of all roguy damned cutpurses for me!

WASP

Bless 'em with all my heart, with all my heart, do you see! Now, as I am no infidel, that I know of, I am glad on't. Ay, I am; here's my witness! do you see, sir? I did not tell you of his fables, I? No, no, I am a dull malt-horse, I, I know nothing. Are you not justly served, i' your conscience, now? Speak i' your conscience. Much good do you with all my heart, and his good heart that has it, with all my heart again.

EDGWORTH

[*Aside*] This fellow is very charitable; would he had a purse too! But I must not be too bold all at a time.

COKES

Nay, Numps, it is not my best purse.

WASP

Not your best! Death! Why should it be your worst? Why should it be any, indeed, at all? Answer me to that. Gi' me a reason from you why it should be any.

83 *him.* Ed. (him, F)
87 *chaps* mouth, chops
88 *entertain* support, maintain
90 *a peck* the capacity of a peck
91 s.d. *pickpack* pick-a-back
98–9 *Ay, I* Ed. (I I F)
100 *malt-horse* heavy horse used to pull brewers' drays

COKES

Nor my gold, Numps; I ha' that yet. Look here else, sister.

[*Shews* MISTRESS OVERDO *his other purse*]

WASP

Why so, there's all the feeling he has!

MISTRESS OVERDO

I pray you have a better care of that, brother.

COKES

Nay, so I will, I warrant you. Let him catch this that catch can. I would fain see him get this, look you, here.

WASP

So, so, so, so, so, so, so, so! Very good.

COKES

I would ha' him come again now, and but offer at it. Sister, will you take notice of a good jest? I will put it just where th'other was, and if we ha' good luck, you shall see a delicate fine trap to catch the cutpurse nibbling.

EDGWORTH

[*Aside*] Faith, and he'll try ere you be out o' the Fair.

COKES

Come, Mistress Grace, prithee be not melancholy for my mischance; sorrow wi' not keep it, sweetheart.

GRACE

I do not think on't, sir.

COKES

'Twas but a little scurvy white money, hang it; it may hang the cutpurse one day. I ha' gold left to gi' thee a fairing yet, as hard as the world goes. Nothing angers me but that nobody here looked like a cutpurse, unless 'twere Numps.

WASP

How? I? I look like a cutpurse? Death! your sister's a cutpurse! and your mother and father, and all your kin, were cutpurses! And here is a rogue is the bawd o' the cutpurses, whom I will beat to begin with.

They speak all together; and WASP *beats the* JUSTICE

OVERDO

Hold thy hand, child of wrath and heir of anger. Make

117 *offer at* make an attempt on
125 *white money* silver

123 *wi' not keep it.* Will not bring the purse back—a version of the proverb 'Sorrow will pay no debt' (Tilley, S660).

it not Childermas day in thy fury, or the feast of the French Bartholmew, parent of the Massacre.

COKES

Numps, Numps!

MISTRESS OVERDO

Good Master Humphrey!

WASP

You are the Patrico, are you? the patriarch of the cutpurses? You share, sir, they say; let them share this with you. Are you i' your hot fit of preaching again? I'll cool you.

OVERDO

Murther, murther, murther!

[*Exeunt*]

Act III, Scene i

[*Enter*] WHIT, HAGGIS, BRISTLE, LEATHERHEAD, TRASH

WHIT

Nay, 'tish all gone now! Dish 'tish phen tou vilt not be phitin call, Master Offisher! Phat ish a man te better to lishen out noishes for tee an tou art in anoder 'orld—being very shuffishient noishes and gallantsh too? One o' their brabblesh would have fed ush all dish fortnight; but tou art so bushy about beggersh still, tou hast no leishure to intend shentlemen, an't be.

HAGGIS

Why, I told you, Davy Bristle.

BRISTLE

Come, come, you told me a pudding, Toby Haggis; a matter of nothing; I am sure it came to nothing! You said, 'Let's go

134 *Childermas day* Feast of the Holy Innocents, 28 December
138 *Patrico* hedge-priest of the gypsies and vagabonds
5 *brabblesh* brabbles, brawls
7 *intend* pay any attention to
9 *a pudding* a lot of 'tripe', with a pun on 'Haggis'

---

135 *French Bartholmew.* A reference to the great massacre of Protestants in France on 24 August 1572.

1 *'tish.* 'Tis. The curious and outlandish spellings Jonson resorts to for Whit's speeches are intended to represent an Irish brogue, which Elizabethan Englishmen, like their modern counterparts, evidently found extremely funny. Jonson, understandably, is not consistent in his attempts to reproduce it phonetically. Every now and again he forgets about it and allows Whit to lapse into standard English forms.

to Ursla's', indeed; but then you met the man with the monsters, and I could not get you from him. An old fool, not leave seeing yet?

HAGGIS

Why, who would ha' thought anybody would ha' quarrelled so early? Or that the ale o' the Fair would ha' been up so soon?

WHIT

Phy, phat o'clock toest tou tink it ish, man?

HAGGIS

I cannot tell.

WHIT

Tou art a vishe vatchman, i' te mean teeme.

HAGGIS

Why, should the watch go by the clock, or the clock by the watch, I pray?

BRISTLE

One should go by another, if they did well.

WHIT

Tou art right now! Phen didst tou ever know or hear of a shuffishient vatchman but he did tell the clock, phat bushiness soever he had?

BRISTLE

Nay, that's most true, a sufficient watchman knows what o'clock it is.

WHIT

Shleeping or vaking, ash well as te clock himshelf, or te Jack dat shtrikes him!

BRISTLE

Let's enquire of Master Leatherhead, or Joan Trash here. Master Leatherhead, do you hear, Master Leatherhead?

WHIT

If it be a Ledderhead, 'tish a very tick Ledderhead, tat sho mush noish vill not piersh him.

LEATHERHEAD

I have a little business now, good friends, do not trouble me.

WHIT

Phat? Because o' ty wrought neet-cap and ty phelvet sherkin, man? Phy, I have sheen tee in ty ledder sherkin ere now, Mashter o' de hobby-horses, as bushy and as stately as tou sheem'st to be.

29 *Jack* mechanical figure which strikes the bell on a public clock
36 *Phy*, ed. (phy? F)

TRASH

Why, what an you have, Captain Whit? He has his choice of jerkins, you may see by that, and his caps too, I assure you, when he pleases to be either sick or employed.

LEATHERHEAD

God a mercy, Joan, answer for me.

WHIT

Away, be not sheen i' my company; here be shentlemen, and men of vorship. [*Exeunt* HAGGIS, BRISTLE]

Act III, Scene ii

[*Enter to them*] QUARLOUS, WINWIFE

QUARLOUS

We had wonderful ill luck to miss this prologue o' the purse, but the best is we shall have five acts of him ere night. He'll be spectacle enough! I'll answer for't.

WHIT

O Creesh! Duke Quarlous, how dosht tou? Tou dosht not know me, I fear? I am te vishesht man, but Justish Overdo, in all Bartholmew Fair now. Gi' me twelvepence from tee, I vill help tee to a vife vorth forty marks for't, an't be.

QUARLOUS

Away, rogue; pimp, away!

WHIT

And she shall shew tee as fine cut-'ork for't in her shmock, too, as tou cansht vish i'faith. Vilt tou have her, vorshipful Vinvife? I vill help tee to her here, be an't be, in te pig-quarter, gi' me ty twel'pence from tee.

WINWIFE

Why, there's twel'pence; pray thee wilt thou be gone?

WHIT

Tou art a vorthy man, and a vorshipful man still.

QUARLOUS

Get you gone, rascal.

WHIT

I do mean it, man. Prinsh Quarlous, if tou hasht need on me,

4 *Creesh* Christ
5 *vishesht* wisest
8 *pimp*, Ed. (Pimpe F)
9 *cut-'ork* 'cut work', lace
13 *gone*? Ed. (gone. F)
14 *still* ever

tou shalt find me here at Ursla's. I vill see phat ale and punk ish i' te pigshty for tee; bless ty good vorship! [*Exit*]

QUARLOUS

Look who comes here! John Littlewit!

WINWIFE

And his wife, and my widow, her mother: the whole family.

[*Enter*] BUSY, LITTLEWIT, PURECRAFT, WIN

QUARLOUS

'Slight, you must gi' 'em all fairings now!

WINWIFE

Not I, I'll not see 'em.

QUARLOUS

They are going a feasting. What schoolmaster's that is with 'em?

WINWIFE

That's my rival, I believe, the baker!

BUSY

So, walk on in the middle way, fore-right; turn neither to the right hand nor to the left. Let not your eyes be drawn aside with vanity, nor your ear with noises.

QUARLOUS

O, I know him by that start!

LEATHERHEAD

What do you lack? What do you buy, pretty Mistress? a fine hobby-horse, to make your son a tilter? a drum, to make him a soldier? a fiddle, to make him a reveller? What is't you lack? Little dogs for your daughters? or babies, male or female?

BUSY

Look not toward them, hearken not. The place is Smithfield, or the field of smiths, the grove of hobby-horses and trinkets. The wares are the wares of devils; and the whole Fair is the shop of Satan! They are hooks and baits, very baits, that are hung out on every side to catch you, and to hold you, as it were, by the gills, and by the nostrils, as the fisher doth; therefore, you must not look, nor turn toward

26 *fore-right* straight ahead
31 *tilter* (i) jouster (ii) lecher, rake

35–6 *Smithfield, or the field of smiths.* The correct etymology is, in fact, as the earliest recorded spelling 'Smethefelda' (*c.* 1145) shows, 'Smoothfield'.

them—the heathen man could stop his ears with wax against the harlot o' the sea; do you the like, with your fingers, against the bells of the Beast.

WINWIFE

What flashes comes from him!

QUARLOUS

O, he has those of his oven! A notable hot baker 'twas, when he plied the peel. He is leading his flock into the Fair now.

WINWIFE

Rather driving 'em to the pens; for he will let 'em look upon nothing.

[*Enter*] KNOCKEM, WHIT

KNOCKEM

Gentlewomen, the weather's hot! Whither walk you? Have a care o' your fine velvet caps, the Fair is dusty.

LITTLEWIT *is gazing at the sign; which is the Pig's Head with a large writing under it*

Take a sweet delicate booth, with boughs, here i' the way, and cool yourselves i' the shade, you and your friends. The best pig and bottle-ale i' the Fair, sir. Old Ursla is cook, there you may read: the pig's head speaks it. Poor soul, she has had a stringhalt, the maryhinchco; but she's prettily amended.

WHIT

A delicate show-pig, little mistress, with shweet sauce, and crackling like de bay-leaf i' de fire, la! Tou shalt ha' de clean side o' de table-clot and dy glass vashed with phatersh of Dame Annessh Cleare.

45 *flashes* showy phrases
47 *peel* baker's shovel for putting loaves in the oven and pulling them out
52 *delicate* charming, delightful
56 *stringhalt, the maryhinchco* diseases affecting a horse's legs
58 *show-pig* sow-pig (as pronounced by Whit)

42–3 *the heathen man . . . sea.* Busy is somewhat muddled. Ulysses, 'the heathen man', had the ears of his crew stopped with wax to prevent them from hearing the song of the Sirens, and had himself lashed to the mast of his boat, so that he could hear the song but was unable to respond to its invitation. (Homer, *The Odyssey*, xii.)

45 *comes.* The third person plural in -s is very common in Elizabethan English (see Abbott, 333).

60–1 *phatersh of Dame Annessh Cleare.* Waters from a spring in Hoxton called Dame Annis (Agnes) the clear.

LITTLEWIT

This's fine, verily. 'Here be the best pigs, and she does roast 'em as well as ever she did', the pig's head says.

KNOCKEM

Excellent, excellent, mistress, with fire o' juniper and rosemary branches! The oracle of the pig's head, that, sir.

PURECRAFT

Son, were you not warned of the vanity of the eye? Have you forgot the wholesome admonition so soon?

LITTLEWIT

Good mother, how shall we find a pig if we do not look about for't? Will it run off o' the spit into our mouths, think you, as in Lubberland, and cry, 'We, we'?

BUSY

No, but your mother, religiously wise, conceiveth it may offer itself by other means to the sense, as by way of steam, which I think it doth, here in this place. Huh, huh!

BUSY *scents after it like a hound*

Yes, it doth. And it were a sin of obstinacy, great obstinacy, high and horrible obstinacy, to decline or resist the good titillation of the famelic sense, which is the smell. Therefore be bold (huh, huh, huh), follow the scent. Enter the tents of the unclean, for once, and satisfy your wife's frailty. Let your frail wife be satisfied; your zealous mother, and my suffering self, will also be satisfied.

LITTLEWIT

Come, Win, as good winny here as go farther and see nothing.

BUSY

We scape so much of the other vanities by our early entering.

PURECRAFT

It is an edifying consideration.

WIN

This is scurvy, that we must come into the Fair and not look on't.

LITTLEWIT

Win, have patience, Win, I'll tell you more anon.

76 *famelic* exciting hunger
81 *winny* stay

70 *Lubberland.* An imaginary country of plenty and idleness, also known as the Land of Cockaigne and, in German, as 'Schlaraffenland'.

KNOCKEM

Mooncalf, entertain within there; the best pig i' the booth, a pork-like pig. These are Banbury-bloods, o' the sincere stud, come a pig-hunting. Whit, wait, Whit, look to your charge. [*Exit* WHIT]

BUSY

A pig prepare presently, let a pig be prepared to us.
[*Exeunt* BUSY, LITTLEWIT, WIN, PURECRAFT]

[*Enter*] MOONCALF, URSLA

MOONCALF

'Slight, who be these?

URSLA

Is this the good service, Jordan, you'd do me?

KNOCKEM

Why, Urs? Why, Urs? Thou'lt ha' vapours i' thy leg again presently; pray thee go in; 't may turn to the scratches else.

URSLA

Hang your vapours, they are stale, and stink like you. Are these the guests o' the game you promised to fill my pit withal today?

KNOCKEM

Ay, what ail they, Urs?

URSLA

Ail they? They are all sippers, sippers o' the City. They look as they would not drink off two penn'orth of bottle-ale amongst 'em.

MOONCALF

A body may read that i' their small printed ruffs.

KNOCKEM

Away, thou art a fool, Urs, and thy Mooncalf too, i' your ignorant vapours now! Hence! Good guests, I say, right hypocrites, good gluttons. In, and set a couple o' pigs o' the board, and half a dozen of the biggest bottles afore 'em, and call Whit. I do not love to hear innocents abused: fine ambling hypocrites! and a stone-puritan with a sorrel head

90-1 *sincere stud* true breed
101 *what ail they* what's wrong with them
111 *stone-puritan* lascivious male puritan (by analogy with *stone-horse* = *stallion*)
sorrel chestnut coloured (of horses)

105 *small printed ruffs*. Puritans wore small ruffs, very carefully set; 'in print' was a synonym for 'precise'.

and beard—good-mouthed gluttons, two to a pig. Away!
[*Exit* MOONCALF]

URSLA

Are you sure they are such?

KNOCKEM

O' the right breed; thou shalt try 'em by the teeth, Urs. Where's this Whit?

[*Enter* WHIT]

WHIT

Behold, man, and see, what a worthy man am ee!
With the fury of my sword, and the shaking of my beard,
I will make ten thousand men afeard.

KNOCKEM

Well said, brave Whit! In, and fear the ale out o' the bottles into the bellies of the brethren and the sisters; drink to the cause, and pure vapours. [*Exeunt* KNOCKEM, WHIT, URSLA]

QUARLOUS

My roarer is turned tapster, methinks. Now were a fine time for thee, Winwife, to lay aboard thy widow; thou'lt never be master of a better season or place. She that will venture herself into the Fair, and a pig-box, will admit any assault, be assured of that.

WINWIFE

I love not enterprises of that suddenness, though.

QUARLOUS

I'll warrant thee, then, no wife out o' the widows' hundred. If I had but as much title to her as to have breathed once on that strait stomacher of hers, I would now assure myself to carry her yet, ere she went out of Smithfield. Or she should carry me, which were the fitter sight, I confess. But you are a

119 *fear* frighten

120 *brethren and the sisters;* Ed. (brethren, and the sisters F)

123 *lay aboard* make advances to (nautical term for the manoeuvre of bringing one ship alongside another in order to board it)

130 *stomacher* ornamental covering for the chest worn by women under the lacing of the bodice

131 *carry* win

116–18 *Behold . . . afeard.* Whit's lines smack of the traditional St George play, described by Thomas Hardy in *The Return of the Native*, Bk. II, Ch. v.

128 *the widow's hundred.* Since a hundred was a sub-division of the English shire, the meaning would seem to be 'the widows' section of the community', but some topical allusion has probably been lost.

modest undertaker, by circumstances and degrees. Come, 'tis disease in thee, not judgement. I should offer at all together.—Look, here's the poor fool again that was stung by the wasp erewhile.

Act III, Scene iii

[*Enter*] OVERDO

OVERDO

I will make no more orations shall draw on these tragical conclusions. And I begin now to think that, by a spice of collateral justice, Adam Overdo deserved this beating. For I, the said Adam, was one cause, a by-cause, why the purse was lost—and my wife's brother's purse too—which they know not of yet. But I shall make very good mirth with it at supper—that will be the sport—and put my little friend Master Humphrey Wasp's choler quite out of countenance, when, sitting at the upper end o' my table, as I use, and drinking to my brother Cokes and Mistress Alice Overdo, as I will, my wife, for their good affection to old Bradley, I deliver to 'em it was I that was cudgelled, and shew 'em the marks. To see what bad events may peep out o' the tail of good purposes! The care I had of that civil young man I took fancy to this morning—and have not left it yet—drew me to that exhortation; which drew the company, indeed; which drew the cutpurse; which drew the money; which drew my brother Cokes his loss; which drew on Wasp's anger; which drew on my beating: a pretty gradation! And they shall ha' it i' their dish, i'faith, at night for fruit. I love to be merry at my table. I had thought once, at one special blow he ga' me, to have revealed myself. But then—I thank thee, fortitude—I remembered that a wise man, and who is ever so great a part o' the Commonwealth in himself, for no

133 *undertaker* venturer, one who undertakes an enterprise
circumstances roundabout methods
134–5 *offer at all together* make an all-out attack, risk everything
1 *shall draw on* which will produce
3 *collateral* concomitant
4 *by-cause* secondary or incidental cause
22 *myself.* Ed. (my selfe? F)

23–4 *and who . . . himself.* Overdo, thinking of himself and petty officers like him as statesmen, appears to have in mind Cicero's contention (*De Re Publica*, I.iv and v) that the statesman is at least the equal of the philosopher (the wise man); 'and who' = 'and anyone who'.

particular disaster ought to abandon a public good design. The husbandman ought not, for one unthankful year, to forsake the plough; the shepherd ought not, for one scabbed sheep, to throw by his tar-box; the pilot ought not, for one leak i' the poop, to quit the helm; nor the alderman ought not, for one custard more at a meal, to give up his cloak; the constable ought not to break his staff and forswear the watch, for one roaring night; nor the piper o' the parish—*ut parvis componere magna solebam*—to put up his pipes, for one rainy Sunday. These are certain knocking conclusions; out of which I am resolved, come what come can—come beating, come imprisonment, come infamy, come banishment, nay, come the rack, come the hurdle, welcome all—I will not discover who I am till my due time. And yet still all shall be, as I said ever, in Justice' name, and the King's, and for the Commonwealth.

WINWIFE

What does he talk to himself, and act so seriously? Poor fool! [*Exit* OVERDO]

QUARLOUS

No matter what. Here's fresher argument, intend that.

Act III, Scene iv

[*Enter to them*] COKES, MISTRESS OVERDO, GRACE, WASP

COKES

Come, Mistress Grace, come sister, here's more fine sights yet, i'faith. God's lid, where's Numps?

28 *tar-box* box used by shepherds to hold tar employed as a cure for skin diseases in sheep
30 *one custard more* i.e., an extra guest
31 *cloak* i.e., office (of which the cloak was the mark)
32 *roaring* tempestuous
piper o' the parish piper employed by the parish to play at church-ales and similar functions
34 *knocking* clinching, decisive
37 *hurdle* a kind of sledge on which traitors were dragged through the streets to their execution
41 *What* for what reason, why
42 *fresher argument* more matter for a May morning
intend pay attention to

---

33 *ut parvis . . . solebam.* Virgil, *Eclogues*, i. 23, with *sic* instead of *ut*: 'thus it was my habit to compare great things to small ones'.

LEATHERHEAD

What do you lack, gentlemen? What is't you buy? Fine rattles? Drums? Babies? Little dogs? And birds for ladies? What do you lack?

COKES

Good honest Numps, keep afore, I am so afraid thou'lt lose somewhat. My heart was at my mouth when I missed thee.

WASP

You were best buy a whip i' your hand to drive me.

COKES

Nay, do not mistake, Numps, thou art so apt to mistake; I would but watch the goods. Look you now, the treble fiddle was e'en almost like to be lost

WASP

Pray you take heed you lose not yourself. Your best way were e'en get up and ride for more surety. Buy a token's worth of great pins to fasten yourself to my shoulder.

LEATHERHEAD

What do you lack, gentlemen? Fine purses, pouches, pin-cases, pipes? What is't you lack? A pair o' smiths to wake you i' the morning? Or a fine whistling bird?

COKES

Numps, here be finer things than any we ha' bought, by odds! And more delicate horses, a great deal! Good Numps, stay, and come hither.

WASP

Will you scourse with him? You are in Smithfield; you may fit yourself with a fine easy-going street-nag for your saddle again Michaelmas term, do. Has he ne'er a little odd cart for you to make a caroche on i' the country, with four pied hobby-horses? Why the measles should you stand here with your train, cheaping of dogs, birds, and babies? You ha' no children to bestow 'em on, ha' you?

COKES

No, but again I ha' children, Numps, that's all one.

21 *scourse* barter, bargain
23 *again* against, in preparation for
24 *caroche* smart carriage
26 *cheaping of* bargaining for, asking the price of
28 *again* in anticipation of the time when

16 *A pair o' smiths*. Presumably a clock of some kind with a pair of 'Jacks' in the shape of smiths.

WASP

Do, do, do, do! How many shall you have, think you? An I were as you, I'd buy for all my tenants, too. They are a kind o' civil savages that will part with their children for rattles, pipes, and knives. You were best buy a hatchet or two, and truck with 'em.

COKES

Good Numps, hold that little tongue o' thine, and save it a labour. I am resolute Bat, thou know'st.

WASP

A resolute fool you are, I know, and a very sufficient coxcomb. With all my heart—nay, you have it, sir, an you be angry—turd i' your teeth, twice, if I said it not once afore; and much good do you.

WINWIFE

Was there ever such a self-affliction? And so impertinent?

QUARLOUS

Alas! his care will go near to crack him; let's in and comfort him.

WASP

Would I had been set i' the ground, all but the head on me, and had my brains bowled at, or threshed out, when first I underwent this plague of a charge!

QUARLOUS

How now, Numps! Almost tired i' your protectorship? Overparted? Overparted?

WASP

Why, I cannot tell, sir; it may be I am. Does't grieve you?

QUARLOUS

No, I swear does't not, Numps, to satisfy you.

WASP

Numps? 'Sblood, you are fine and familiar! How long ha' we been acquainted, I pray you?

31 *civil savages* savages of a civilized country
41 *crack him* drive him crazy

43–4 *Would I . . . bowled at.* Cf. *The Merry Wives of Windsor*, III.iv, 85–6, where Anne Page responds to the suggestion that she marry Dr Caius by saying:

> Alas, I had rather be set quick i' th' earth,
> And bowl'd to death with turnips.

47 *Overparted.* Given a bigger part than you can play. Cf. *Love's Labour's Lost*, V.ii, 577–8, where Costard remarks that Sir Nathaniel was 'a little o'erparted' in taking on the role of Alexander the Great.

QUARLOUS

I think it may be remembered, Numps. That? 'Twas since morning, sure.

WASP

Why, I hope I know't well enough, sir; I did not ask to be told.

QUARLOUS

No? Why then?

WASP

It's no matter why. You see with your eyes now, what I said to you today? You'll believe me another time?

QUARLOUS

Are you removing the Fair, Numps?

WASP

A pretty question! and a very civil one! Yes faith, I ha' my lading you see, or shall have anon; you may know whose beast I am by my burden. If the pannier-man's jack were ever better known by his loins of mutton, I'll be flayed and feed dogs for him, when his time comes.

WINWIFE

How melancholy Mistress Grace is yonder! Pray thee let's go enter ourselves in grace with her.

COKES

Those six horses, friend, I'll have—

WASP

How!

COKES

And the three Jew's trumps; and half a dozen o' birds, and that drum—I have one drum already—and your smiths—I like that device o' your smiths very pretty well—and four halberts—and, le' me see, that fine painted great lady, and her three women for state, I'll have.

64 *for* in place of
66 *grace* favour
69 *trumps* harps
73 *state* ceremonial shew

---

62 *jack*. Jackass, male ass. Though *OED* cites no instance of 'jackass' prior to 1727, 'jack' was used in the sixteenth century to denote the male of some animals and birds. That a jackass is meant here is evident from the reference to 'beast' and 'burden' (l. 62) and still more from Wasp's promise to 'be flayed and feed dogs for [in place of] him, when his time comes', since this is precisely what happened to dead horses and donkeys; they were flayed and used as dog food.

WASP

No, the shop; buy the whole shop, it will be best; the shop, the shop!

LEATHERHEAD

If his worship please.

WASP

Yes, and keep it during the Fair, bobchin.

COKES

Peace, Numps. Friend, do not meddle with him, an you be wise and would shew your head above board; he will sting thorough your wrought night-cap, believe me. A set of these violins I would buy too, for a delicate young noise I have i' the country, that are every one a size less than another, just like your fiddles. I would fain have a fine young masque at my marriage, now I think on't. But I do want such a number o' things. And Numps will not help me now, and I dare not speak to him.

TRASH

Will your worship buy any gingerbread, very good bread, comfortable bread?

COKES

Gingerbread! Yes, let's see. *He runs to her shop*

WASP

There's the tother springe!

LEATHERHEAD

Is this well, Goody Joan? To interrupt my market? In the midst? And call away my customers? Can you answer this at the Pie-powders?

TRASH

Why, if his mastership have a mind to buy, I hope my ware lies as open as another's! I may shew my ware as well as you yours.

COKES

Hold your peace; I'll content you both: I'll buy up his shop, and thy basket.

79 *above board* in company
80 *thorough* through
81 *delicate* fine *noise* band of musicians
83 *masque* group of masquers
90 *springe* snare used to catch birds

---

77 *bobchin*. Defined by *OED* as 'one who bobs his chin', an action denoting folly, especially in the form of idle chatter.

WASP

Will you i'faith?

LEATHERHEAD

Why should you put him from it, friend?

WASP

Cry you mercy! You'd be sold too, would you? What's the price on you? Jerkin and all, as you stand? Ha' you any qualities?

TRASH

Yes, goodman angry-man, you shall find he has qualities, if you cheapen him.

WASP

God's so, so you ha' the selling of him! What are they? Will they be bought for love or money?

TRASH

No indeed, sir.

WASP

For what then? Victuals?

TRASH

He scorns victuals, sir, he has bread and butter at home, thanks be to God! And yet he will do more for a good meal, if the toy take him i' the belly. Marry, then they must not set him at lower end. If they do, he'll go away, though he fast. But put him atop o' the table, where his place is, and he'll do you forty fine things. He has not been sent for and sought out for nothing at your great city-suppers, to put down Coriat and Cokeley, and been laughed at for his labour. He'll play you all the puppets i' the town over, and the players, every company, and his own company too; he spares nobody!

103 *qualities* accomplishments
106 *God's so* form of *cazzo* (Italian for penis) used as an oath
so, so you ed. (so, you F)
113 *lower end* (of the table) where inferior guests sat

---

116 *Coriat*. Thomas Coryate (1577?–1617) was a great traveller and, according to Jonson, a great bore. His best-known work, *Coryats Crudities* (1611), is an account of his 'trauells in France, Sauoy, Italy . . . the Grisons . . . Switzerland, some parts of high Germany, and the Netherlands'. When it was published, Jonson contributed some mock-commendatory verses to it, together with 'The Character' of the author. (H & S, viii. 373–8.)

117 *Cokeley*. A jester of the time, who seems to have improvised at entertainments. Jonson also refers to him in *The Devil is an Ass* (I.i, 93) and in his poem 'To Mime' (*Epigrams*, cxxix. 16).

COKES

I'faith?

TRASH

He was the first, sir, that ever baited the fellow i' the bear's skin, an't like your worship. No dog ever came near him since. And for fine motions!

COKES

Is he good at those too? Can he set out a masque, trow?

TRASH

O Lord, master! sought to, far and near, for his inventions; and he engrosses all, he makes all the puppets i' the Fair.

COKES

Dost thou, in troth, old velvet jerkin? Give me thy hand.

TRASH

Nay, sir, you shall see him in his velvet jerkin, and a scarf too, at night, when you hear him interpret Master Littlewit's motion.

COKES

Speak no more, but shut up shop presently, friend. I'll buy both it and thee too, to carry down with me, and her hamper beside. Thy shop shall furnish out the masque, and hers the banquet. I cannot go less, to set out anything with credit. What's the price, at a word, o' thy whole shop, case and all, as it stands?

LEATHERHEAD

Sir, it stands me in six and twenty shillings sevenpence half-penny, besides three shillings for my ground.

COKES

Well, thirty shillings will do all, then! And what comes yours to?

123 *motions* puppet-shews
124 *set out* produce (in the theatrical sense), exhibit (*OED*, Set, *v.*, 149., h.) *trow* do you think
125 *sought* applied, resorted
126 *engrosses* monopolizes
129 *at night* this evening *interpret* ventriloquize
134 *banquet* dessert
I cannot go less it's the least I can do
137 *stands me in* costs me, is worth to me

121–2 *baited . . . bear's skin.* According to Samuel Rowlands, in his *The Knave of Harts* (1612), an actor at the Fortune Theatre, playing the part of a bear, was 'wel-nye' killed by 'Some Butchers (playing Dogs)'.

TRASH

Four shillings and elevenpence, sir, ground and all, an't like your worship.

COKES

Yes, it does like my worship very well, poor woman, that's five shillings more. What a masque shall I furnish out for forty shillings—twenty pound Scotch! And a banquet of gingerbread! There's a stately thing! Numps! Sister! And my wedding gloves too! That I never thought on afore. All my wedding gloves gingerbread! O me! what a device will there be, to make 'em eat their fingers' ends! And delicate brooches for the bridemen and all! And then I'll ha' this poesy put to 'em: 'For the best grace', meaning Mistress Grace, my wedding poesy.

GRACE

I am beholden to you, sir, and to your Bartholmew-wit.

WASP

You do not mean this, do you? Is this your first purchase?

COKES

Yes faith, and I do not think, Numps, but thou'lt say, it was the wisest act that ever I did in my wardship.

WASP

Like enough! I shall say anything, I!

Act III, Scene v

[*Enter to them*] OVERDO, EDGWORTH, NIGHTINGALE

OVERDO

[*Aside*] I cannot beget a project, with all my political brain, yet; my project is how to fetch off this proper young man from his debauched company. I have followed him all the Fair over, and still I find him with this songster; and I begin

150 *bridemen* male attendants on the bridegroom
151 *poesy* posy, motto in metrical form
153 *Bartholmew-wit* foolish attempt to be witty, cheap witticism
1 *political* shrewd
2 *fetch off* rescue, save
proper excellent

145 *twenty pound Scotch.* When the Crowns of England and Scotland were united on the accession of James I to the throne of England, the Scots pound was valued at one-twelfth of a pound sterling, i.e., 1*s.* 8*d.*

147 *wedding gloves.* It was customary to present gloves to the guests at a wedding.

shrewdly to suspect their familiarity; and the young man of a terrible taint, poetry! With which idle disease if he be infected, there's no hope of him in a state-course. *Actum est* of him for a commonwealth's-man if he go to't in rhyme once.

EDGWORTH

[*To* NIGHTINGALE] Yonder he is buying o' gingerbread. Set in quickly, before he part with too much on his money.

NIGHTINGALE [*Sings*]

My masters and friends, and good people, draw near, etc.

COKES

Ballads! Hark, hark! Pray thee, fellow, stay a little. Good Numps, look to the goods. *He runs to the ballad-man*
What ballads hast thou? Let me see, let me see myself.

WASP

Why so! He's flown to another lime-bush. There he will flutter as long more, till he ha' ne'er a feather left. Is there a vexation like this, gentlemen? Will you believe me now? Hereafter shall I have credit with you?

QUARLOUS

Yes faith, shalt thou, Numps, and thou art worthy on't, for thou sweatest for't. I never saw a young puny errant and his squire better matched.

WINWIFE

Faith, the sister comes after 'em well, too.

7 *state-course* career of public service (?)
Actum est of it's all up with
8 *commonwealth's man* good citizen
go to't indulge
10–11 *Set in* begin, go to work
16 *lime-bush* snare (literally, a bush smeared with birdlime)
17 *more* moreover, again
18–19 *now? Hereafter* Ed. (now, hereafter? F)

---

21 *puny* ed. (Pimpe F) ninny, raw novice, French *béjaune*. Cf. Nashe in his *Christs Teares Over Jerusalem* (1593): 'I see others of them [whores] sharing halfe with the Baudes their Hostesses, & laughing at the Punies they haue lurched [cheated]' (Nashe, ii. 150. 34–36). It is hard to see how Cokes, or Wasp who matches him, or Mistress Overdo who resembles ('comes after') him, or Overdo who completes the foursome ('mess'), can properly be described as a 'pimp' in any recorded sense of that word. All four are, however, very emphatically 'punies'; and 'Punye', in Jonson's handwriting, might easily have been misread as 'Pimpe', especially if a tiny splutter of ink had fallen above the first stroke of the 'u'.

GRACE
Nay, if you saw the Justice her husband, my guardian, you were fitted for the mess. He is such a wise one his way—

WINWIFE
I wonder we see him not here.

GRACE
O! he is too serious for this place, and yet better sport than the other three, I assure you, gentlemen, where'er he is, though't be o' the bench.

COKES
How dost thou call it? *A Caveat against Cutpurses*! A good jest, i'faith. I would fain see that demon, your cutpurse you talk of, that delicate-handed devil. They say he walks hereabout; I would see him walk now. Look you, sister, here, here, let him come, sister, and welcome.

He shews his purse boastingly

Ballad-man, does any cutpurses haunt hereabout? Pray thee raise me one or two; begin and shew me one.

NIGHTINGALE
Sir, this is a spell against 'em, spick and span new; and 'tis made as 'twere in mine own person, and I sing it in mine own defence. But 'twill cost a penny alone, if you buy it.

COKES
No matter for the price. Thou dost not know me, I see; I am an odd Bartholmew.

MISTRESS OVERDO
Has't a fine picture, brother?

COKES
O sister, do you remember the ballads over the nursery chimney at home o' my own pasting up? There be brave pictures! Other manner of pictures than these, friend.

WASP
Yet these will serve to pick the pictures out o' your pockets, you shall see.

COKES
So I heard 'em say. Pray thee mind him not, fellow; he'll have an oar in everything.

NIGHTINGALE
It was intended, sir, as if a purse should chance to be cut in

25 *mess* group of four persons who ate together (*OED*, Mess *sb*. II.4); cf. *Love's Labour's Lost*, IV.iii, 203: 'you three fools lack'd me fool to make up the mess'

27–8 *than the* Ed. (then then the F)

46 *pictures* coins (stamped with the king's head)

my presence, now, I may be blameless though; as by the sequel will more plainly appear.

COKES

We shall find that i' the matter. Pray thee begin.

NIGHTINGALE

To the tune of *Paggington's Pound*, sir.

COKES [*Sings*]

Fa, la la la, la la la, fa la la la. Nay, I'll put thee in tune, and all! Mine own country dance! Pray thee begin.

NIGHTINGALE

It is a gentle admonition, you must know, sir, both to the purse-cutter and the purse-bearer.

COKES

Not a word more out o' the tune, an thou lov'st me. [*Sings*] *Fa, la la la, la la la, fa la la la.* Come, when?

NIGHTINGALE [*Sings*]

My masters and friends, and good people, draw near,
And look to your purses, for that I do say;

COKES

Ha, ha, this chimes! Good counsel at first dash.

NIGHTINGALE

And though little money in them you do bear,
It cost more to get than to lose in a day.

(COKES

Good!)

You oft have been told,
Both the young and the old;
And bidden beware of the cutpurse so bold;
Then if you take heed not, free me from the curse,
Who both give you warning, for and the cutpurse.

(COKES

Well said! He were to blame that would not, i'faith.)

Youth, youth, thou hadst better been starved by thy nurse,
Than live to be hangèd for cutting a purse.

51 *though* nevertheless
59 *out o'* extraneous to, not part of
62 *for that* because of what
63 *chimes* rings true, goes well
at first dash from the start
70 *for and* and moreover

---

54 *Paggington's Pound.* Also known as *Packington's Pound*, this old country-dance tune still survives.

COKES

Good i'faith, how say you, Numps? Is there any harm i' this?

NIGHTINGALE

It hath been upbraided to men of my trade,
That oftentimes we are the cause of this crime.

(COKES

The more coxcombs they that did it, I wusse.)

Alack and for pity, why should it be said?
As if they regarded or places, or time.
Examples have been
Of some that were seen,
In Westminster Hall, yea the pleaders between;
Then why should the judges be free from this curse,
More than my poor self, for cutting the purse?

(COKES

God a mercy for that! Why should they be more free indeed?)

Youth, youth, thou hadst better been starved by thy nurse,
Than live to be hangèd for cutting a purse.

COKES

That again, good ballad-man, that again!

He sings the burden with him

O rare! I would fain rub mine elbow now, but I dare not pull out my hand. On, I pray thee. He that made this ballad shall be poet to my masque.

NIGHTINGALE

At Worcester 'tis known well, and even i' the jail,
A knight of good worship did there shew his face,
Against the foul sinners, in zeal for to rail,
And lost (ipso facto) *his purse in the place.*

90 *rub mine elbow* (as a sign of glee)

76–7 *It hath . . . crime.* The accusation had been made by Robert Greene in his *The Third and Last Part of Cony-Catching* (1592), where one of the stories is very similar to the action of this scene. See *Three Elizabethan Pamphlets*, ed. G. R. Hibbard (London, 1951), pp. 49–51; or *The Elizabethan Underworld*, ed. A. V. Judges (London, 1930) pp. 189–190.

83 *In Westminster Hall.* The courts of Common Pleas, of the King's Bench, and of Chancery all sat in the great hall of the Palace of Westminster. H & S note that Thomas Dekker, in his *Iests to make you Merie* (1607), 'has a story of a foreman of the jury, taking pity on a young man who had picked a purse, got him acquitted; the man "in recompence presently vpon his discharge, paying his fees, came to the place where this Juror was, and pickt his pocket" ' (H & S, x. 199).

(COKES
Is it possible?)

Nay, once from the seat
Of judgement so great,
A judge there did lose a fair pouch of velvet.

(COKES
I'faith?)

O Lord for thy mercy, how wicked or worse
Are those that so venture their necks for a purse!
Youth, youth, etc.

COKES [*Sings the burden with him again*]
Youth, youth, etc.
Pray thee stay a little, friend. Yet o' thy conscience, Numps, speak; is there any harm i' this?

WASP
To tell you true, 'tis too good for you, 'less you had grace to follow it.

OVERDO
[*Aside*] It doth discover enormity, I'll mark it more; I ha' not liked a paltry piece of poetry so well a good while.

COKES
Youth, youth, etc.
Where's this youth now? A man must call upon him, for his own good, and yet he will not appear. Look here, here's for him; handy-dandy, which hand will he have?
He shews his purse

106 *stay* pause, break off
friend. Yet Ed. (friend, yet F)
108 *'less* unless
115 *handy-dandy* take your choice (from a children's game of guessing in which hand an object is hidden)

98–100 *Nay . . . velvet.* The allusion is to a story preserved by Cresacre More in his *The Life and Death of Sir Thomas Moore* (1631), pp. 115–17. It tells how More grew tired of hearing one of the Justices at Newgate upbraid victims of purse-cutting for not keeping their purses more warily and thus encouraging cutpurses in their activities. Accordingly, he got in touch with a cutpurse who was about to be tried, and promised to stand his friend 'if he would cut that Iustice's purse, whilst he sate . . . on the Benche'. The cutpurse agreed. Coming before the Bench, he asked to speak privately with the Justice, and, while whispering to him, cut his purse. This he handed to More, who then restored it to its owner, telling him not to be so censorious in future. The incident is dramatized, with some alteration, in *Sir Thomas More*, the play in which Shakespeare probably had a hand. See *Sir Thomas More*, I.ii, in *The Shakespeare Apocrypha*, ed. C. F. Tucker Brooke (Oxford, 1918), pp. 387–90.

On, I pray thee, with the rest. I do hear of him, but I cannot see him, this Master Youth, the cutpurse.

NIGHTINGALE

At plays and at sermons, and at the sessions,
'Tis daily their practice such booty to make:
Yea, under the gallows, at executions,
They stick not the stare-abouts' purses to take—
Nay, one without grace,
At a far better place,
At court, and in Christmas, before the King's face.

(COKES

That was a fine fellow! I would have him, now.)

Alack then for pity, must I bear the curse,
That only belongs to the cunning cutpurse?

COKES

But where's their cunning now, when they should use it? They are all chained now, I warrant you.
Youth, youth, thou hadst better, etc.
The rat-catcher's charm! Are all fools and asses to this? A pox on 'em, that they will not come! that a man should have such a desire to a thing and want it.

QUARLOUS

'Fore God, I'd give half the Fair, an 'twere mine, for a cutpurse for him, to save his longing.

COKES

Look you, sister, here, here, where is't now? which pocket is't in, for a wager? *He shews his purse again*

123 *a far better* Ed. (a better F)
133 *to* for
want be unable to get

122–4 *Nay . . . face.* The cutpurse in question, John Selman, picked a purse during a celebration of the sacrament in the King's Chapel at the Palace of Whitehall on Christmas Day 1611. He was hanged for it on 7 January 1612.

131 *The rat-catcher's charm!* Cf. *As You Like It*, III.ii, 163–5, where Rosalind says, referring to Orlando's verses: 'I was never so berhym'd since Pythagoras' time that I was an Irish rat, which I can hardly remember'. The Irish peasantry held the superstitious belief that their bards could kill rats or drive them away by the use of magical verses. *charm! Are . . . this?* ed. (charme, are . . . this! F). The Folio punctuation does not make sense. Cokes, frustrated by the failure of the cutpurses to appear, puts their reluctance down to the effect of the ballad, which has, he says, scared them off and made fools and asses of them; 'this' is in apposition to 'charm'.

WASP

I beseech you leave your wagers, and let him end his matter, an't may be.

COKES

O, are you edified, Numps?

OVERDO

[*Aside*] Indeed he does interrupt him too much. There Numps spoke to purpose.

COKES

Sister, I am an ass, I cannot keep my purse?

[*He shews his purse*] *again*

On, on, I pray thee, friend.

[*While* COKES *listens to the song*] EDGWORTH *gets up to him, and tickles him in the ear with a straw twice, to draw his hand out of his pocket*

NIGHTINGALE

But O, you vile nation of cutpurses all,
Relent and repent, and amend and be sound,
And know that you ought not, by honest men's fall,
Advance your own fortunes, to die above ground;

(WINWIFE

Will you see sport? Look, there's a fellow gathers up to him, mark.)

And though you go gay,
In silks as you may,
It is not the highway to heaven, as they say.

(QUARLOUS

Good, i'faith! O, he has lighted on the wrong pocket.)

Repent then, repent you, for better, for worse;
And kiss not the gallows for cutting a purse.

(WINWIFE

He has it! 'Fore God, he is a brave fellow; pity he should be detected.)

Youth, youth, thou hadst better been starved by thy nurse,
Than live to be hangèd for cutting a purse.

ALL

An excellent ballad! an excellent ballad!

EDGWORTH

Friend, let me ha' the first, let me ha' the first, I pray you.

[*He slips the purse to* NIGHTINGALE]

138 *matter* business, performance
143 *purse*? ed. (purse: F)
146 *Relent* abandon your wicked ways
148 *above ground* on the scaffold

COKES

Pardon me, sir. First come, first served; and I'll buy the whole bundle too.

WINWIFE

That conveyance was better than all, did you see't? He has given the purse to the ballad-singer.

QUARLOUS

Has he?

EDGWORTH

Sir, I cry you mercy; I'll not hinder the poor man's profit; pray you, mistake me not.

COKES

Sir, I take you for an honest gentleman, if that be mistaking. I met you today afore. Ha! humh! O God! my purse is gone, my purse, my purse, etc.

WASP

Come, do not make a stir, and cry yourself an ass thorough the Fair afore your time.

COKES

Why, hast thou it, Numps? Good Numps, how came you by it? I mar'l!

WASP

I pray you seek some other gamester to play the fool with. You may lose it time enough, for all your Fair-wit.

COKES

By this good hand, glove and all, I ha' lost it already, if thou hast it not; feel else. And Mistress Grace's handkercher, too, out o' the tother pocket.

WASP

Why, 'tis well; very well, exceeding pretty and well.

EDGWORTH

Are you sure you ha' lost it, sir?

COKES

O God! yes; as I am an honest man, I had it but e'en now, at 'Youth, youth'.

NIGHTINGALE

I hope you suspect not me, sir.

EDGWORTH

Thee? that were a jest indeed! Dost thou think the gentleman

170 *gentleman, . . . mistaking*. Ed. (Gentleman; . . . mistaking, F)
173 *thorough* throughout, from end to end of
176 *mar'l* marvel
177 *gamester* playmate

is foolish? Where hadst thou hands, I pray thee? Away, ass, away.

[*Exit* NIGHTINGALE]

OVERDO

[*Aside and beginning to go*] I shall be beaten again if I be spied.

EDGWORTH

Sir, I suspect an odd fellow, yonder, is stealing away.

MISTRESS OVERDO

Brother, it is the preaching fellow! You shall suspect him. He was at your tother purse, you know!—Nay, stay, sir, and view the work you ha' done; an you be beneficed at the gallows, and preach there, thank your own handiwork.

COKES

Sir, you shall take no pride in your preferment: you shall be silenced quickly.

OVERDO

What do you mean, sweet buds of gentility?

COKES

To ha' my pennyworths out on you, bud! No less than two purses a day serve you? I thought you a simple fellow when my man Numps beat you i' the morning, and pitied you—

MISTRESS OVERDO

So did I, I'll be sworn, brother. But now I see he is a lewd and pernicious enormity, as Master Overdo calls him.

OVERDO

[*Aside*] Mine own words turned upon me, like swords.

COKES

Cannot a man's purse be at quiet for you i' the master's pocket, but you must entice it forth and debauch it?

WASP

Sir, sir, keep your 'debauch' and your fine Bartholmew-terms to yourself, and make as much on 'em as you please. But gi' me this from you i' the mean time. I beseech you see if I can look to this. [*Tries to take the box*]

COKES

Why, Numps?

193 *shall* ought to, have every reason to
200 *pennyworths* revenge
207 *debauch it* induce it to desert

195–6 *an you . . . there.* If you, who are so given to preaching, suffer a hanging as your church living—a reference to the speeches of repentance which were a common feature of executions at the time.

WASP

Why? Because you are an ass, sir. There's a reason the shortest way, an you will needs ha' it. Now you ha' got the trick of losing, you'd lose your breech an 'twere loose. I know you, sir. Come, deliver.

WASP *takes the licence from him*

You'll go and crack the vermin you breed now, will you? 'Tis very fine! Will you ha' the truth on't? They are such retchless flies as you are, that blow cutpurses abroad in every corner; your foolish having of money makes 'em. An there were no wiser than I, sir, the trade should lie open for you, sir, it should i'faith, sir. I would teach your wit to come to your head, sir, as well as your land to come into your hand, I assure you, sir.

WINWIFE

Alack, good Numps.

WASP

Nay, gentlemen, never pity me, I am not worth it. Lord send me at home once, to Harrow o' the Hill again; if I travel any more, call me Coriat, with all my heart.

[*Exeunt* WASP, COKES, MISTRESS OVERDO, *with* OVERDO]

QUARLOUS

Stay, sir, I must have a word with you in private. Do you hear?

EDGWORTH

With me, sir? What's your pleasure, good sir?

QUARLOUS

Do not deny it. You are a cutpurse, sir; this gentleman here, and I, saw you; nor do we mean to detect you, though we can sufficiently inform ourselves toward the danger of concealing you; but you must do us a piece of service.

EDGWORTH

Good gentlemen, do not undo me; I am a civil young man, and but a beginner, indeed.

216 s.d. WASP *takes the licence from him* (at l. 211 in F)
219 *retchless* heedless
blow beget (as a fly deposits its eggs and breeds maggots)
220–1 *An there . . . I* if I might have my way without interference
221 *the trade . . . you* you would be apprenticed to some trade
233 *nor do we* and yet we do not
detect expose, inform on
234 *toward* about
236 *civil* orderly, respectable

QUARLOUS

Sir, your beginning shall bring on your ending, for us. We are no catchpoles nor constables. That you are to undertake is this: you saw the old fellow with the black box here?

EDGWORTH

The little old governor, sir?

QUARLOUS

That same. I see you have flown him to a mark already. I would ha' you get away that box from him, and bring it us.

EDGWORTH

Would you ha' the box and all, sir? Or only that that is in't? I'll get you that, and leave him the box to play with still—which will be the harder o' the two—because I would gain your worships' good opinion of me.

WINWIFE

He says well, 'tis the greater mastery, and 'twill make the more sport when 'tis missed.

EDGWORTH

Ay, and 'twill be the longer a-missing, to draw on the sport.

QUARLOUS

But look you do it now, sirrah, and keep your word, or—

EDGWORTH

Sir, if ever I break my word with a gentleman, may I never read word at my need. Where shall I find you?

QUARLOUS

Somewhere i' the Fair, hereabouts. Dispatch it quickly. [*Exit* EDGWORTH]

I would fain see the careful fool deluded! Of all beasts, I love the serious ass: he that takes pains to be one, and plays the fool with the greatest diligence that can be.

GRACE

Then you would not choose, sir, but love my guardian, Justice Overdo, who is answerable to that description in every hair of him.

QUARLOUS

So I have heard. But how came you, Mistress Wellborn, to be his ward, or have relation to him, at first?

238 *for us* for all we care
239 *That* that which, what
241 *governor* tutor
242 *flown him to a mark* identified him (cf. II. iv, 41)
248 *mastery* feat, exercise of skill
253 *word* the neck-verse (cf. I, iv, 6–7)
256 *ass: he* Ed. (Asse. He F)

GRACE

Faith, through a common calamity: he bought me, sir. And now he will marry me to his wife's brother, this wise gentleman that you see, or else I must pay value o' my land.

QUARLOUS

'Slid, is there no device of disparagement, or so? Talk with some crafty fellow, some picklock o' the Law. Would I had studied a year longer i' the Inns of Court, an't had been but i' your case!

WINWIFE

[*Aside*] Ay, Master Quarlous, are you proffering?

GRACE

You'd bring but little aid, sir.

WINWIFE

[*Aside*] I'll look to you i'faith, gamester.—An unfortunate foolish tribe you are fallen into, lady; I wonder you can endure 'em.

GRACE

Sir, they that cannot work their fetters off must wear 'em.

WINWIFE

You see what care they have on you, to leave you thus.

GRACE

Faith, the same they have of themselves, sir. I cannot greatly complain, if this were all the plea I had against 'em.

WINWIFE

'Tis true! But will you please to withdraw with us a little, and make them think they have lost you? I hope our manners ha' been such hitherto, and our language, as will give you no cause to doubt yourself in our company.

270 *proffering* making an offer, making advances
272 *look to* keep an eye on, beware of
282 *doubt* have fears for

---

263 *he bought me.* Grace is the victim of one of the major abuses of the age. The Court of Wards, established under Henry VIII, administered the estates of all wards of the crown, i.e., minors and lunatics inheriting from tenants of the King. The Court had the power to sell the guardianship, including control of the ward's marriage, to anyone it pleased for ready cash. See Joel Hurstfield, *The Queen's Wards* (1958), *passim.*

265 *or else . . . land.* If the ward refused to accept the spouse chosen by the guardian, the guardian was entitled to recover the value of the marriage from the ward.

266 *disparagement.* Disparagement was involved, and the match could not go forward, if the guardian sought to wed his ward to one of inferior rank.

GRACE

Sir, I will give myself no cause; I am so secure of mine own manners as I suspect not yours.

QUARLOUS

Look where John Littlewit comes.

WINWIFE

Away, I'll not be seen by him.

QUARLOUS

No, you were not best, he'd tell his mother, the widow.

WINWIFE

Heart, what do you mean?

QUARLOUS

Cry you mercy, is the wind there? Must not the widow be named?

[*Exeunt* GRACE, WINWIFE, QUARLOUS]

Act III, Scene vi

[*Enter to them*] LITTLEWIT, WIN

LITTLEWIT

Do you hear, Win, Win?

WIN

What say you, John?

LITTLEWIT

While they are paying the reckoning, Win, I'll tell you a thing, Win: we shall never see any sights i' the Fair, Win, except you long still, Win. Good Win, sweet Win, long to see some hobby-horses, and some drums, and rattles, and dogs, and fine devices, Win. The bull with the five legs, Win, and the great hog. Now you ha' begun with pig, you may long for anything, Win, and so for my motion, Win.

WIN

But we sha' not eat o' the bull and the hog, John. How shall I long then?

LITTLEWIT

O yes, Win! You may long to see as well as to taste, Win. How did the pothecary's wife, Win, that longed to see the

283 *secure of* confident in
284 *manners* moral code of behaviour
287 *were not best* had best not
289 *is the wind there* is that the case (proverbial, Tilley, W421)

anatomy, Win? Or the lady, Win, that desired to spit i' the great lawyer's mouth after an eloquent pleading? I assure you they longed, Win. Good Win, go in, and long.

[*Exeunt* LITTLEWIT, WIN]

TRASH

I think we are rid of our new customer, Brother Leatherhead, we shall hear no more of him.

They plot to be gone

LEATHERHEAD

All the better. Let's pack up all, and be gone, before he find us.

TRASH

Stay a little, yonder comes a company; it may be we may take some more money.

[*Enter*] KNOCKEM, BUSY

KNOCKEM

Sir, I will take your counsel, and cut my hair, and leave vapours. I see that tobacco, and bottle-ale, and pig, and Whit, and very Ursla herself, is all vanity.

BUSY

Only pig was not comprehended in my admonition, the rest were. For long hair, it is an ensign of pride, a banner, and the world is full of those banners, very full of banners. And bottle-ale is a drink of Satan's, a diet-drink of Satan's, devised to puff us up, and make us swell in this latter age of vanity, as the smoke of tobacco to keep us in mist and error. But the fleshly woman, which you call Ursla, is above all to be avoided, having the marks upon her of the three enemies of man: the World, as being in the Fair; the Devil, as being in the fire; and the Flesh, as being herself.

[*Enter*] PURECRAFT

PURECRAFT

Brother Zeal-of-the-land, what shall we do? My daughter, Win-the-fight, is fallen into her fit of longing again.

BUSY

For more pig? There is no more, is there?

14 *anatomy* skeleton
14–15 *to spit . . . mouth* (as a form of reward and encouragement—proverbial, Tilley, M1255 and M1259)
27 *For* as for
29 *diet-drink* medicine
35 *and the* Ed. (and and the F)

PURECRAFT

To see some sights, i' the Fair.

BUSY

Sister, let her fly the impurity of the place swiftly, lest she partake of the pitch thereof. Thou art the seat of the Beast, O Smithfield, and I will leave thee. Idolatry peepeth out on every side of thee.

KNOCKEM

An excellent right hypocrite! Now his belly is full, he falls a-railing and kicking, the jade. A very good vapour! I'll in, and joy Ursla with telling how her pig works; two and a half he ate to his share. And he has drunk a pailful. He eats with his eyes, as well as his teeth. [*Exit*]

LEATHERHEAD

What do you lack, gentlemen? What is't you buy? Rattles, drums, babies—

BUSY

Peace, with thy apocryphal wares, thou profane publican— thy bells, thy dragons, and thy Toby's dogs. Thy hobby-horse is an idol, a very idol, a fierce and rank idol; and thou the Nebuchadnezzar, the proud Nebuchadnezzar of the Fair, that sett'st it up, for children to fall down to and worship.

LEATHERHEAD

Cry you mercy, sir, will you buy a fiddle to fill up your noise?

[*Enter* LITTLEWIT, WIN]

LITTLEWIT

Look, Win; do look o' God's name, and save your longing. Here be fine sights.

PURECRAFT

Ay, child, so you hate 'em, as our brother Zeal does, you may look on 'em.

LEATHERHEAD

Or what do you say to a drum, sir?

51 *apocryphal* sham, spurious (the Puritans rejected the Apocrypha completely)
publican heathen, excommunicated person
54 *Nebuchadnezzar* King of Babylon who set up a golden idol (Daniel, iii)
58 *noise?* Ed. (noise. F)
63 *drum,* Ed. (Drumme. F)

52 *thy bells . . . Toby's dogs.* See *Tobit,* v. 16 and *Bel and the Dragon,* in the Apocrypha.

BUSY
It is the broken belly of the Beast, and thy bellows there are his lungs, and these pipes are his throat, those feathers are of his tail, and thy rattles the gnashing of his teeth.

TRASH
And what's my gingerbread, I pray you?

BUSY
The provender that pricks him up. Hence with thy basket of popery, thy nest of images, and whole legend of ginger-work.

LEATHERHEAD
Sir, if you be not quiet the quicklier, I'll ha' you clapped fairly by the heels, for disturbing the Fair.

BUSY
The sin of the Fair provokes me, I cannot be silent.

PURECRAFT
Good brother Zeal!

LEATHERHEAD
Sir, I'll make you silent, believe it.

LITTLEWIT
I'd give a shilling you could, i' faith, friend.

LEATHERHEAD
Sir, give me your shilling; I'll give you my shop if I do not, and I'll leave it in pawn with you, i' the mean time.

LITTLEWIT
A match i' faith; but do it quickly then.

[*Exit* LEATHERHEAD]

BUSY *He speaks to the widow*
Hinder me not, woman. I was moved in spirit, to be here, this day, in this Fair, this wicked and foul Fair—and fitter may it be called a foul than a Fair—to protest against the abuses of it, the foul abuses of it, in regard of the afflicted saints, that are troubled, very much troubled, exceedingly troubled, with the opening of the merchandise of Babylon again, and the peeping of popery upon the stalls here, here in

68 *pricks him up* makes him high-spirited (proverbial, Tilley, P615)
75 *shilling you could*, Ed. (shilling, you could F) shilling if you could
81 *be called* Ed. (be a called F)
83 *saints* Puritans

69 *images . . . legend of ginger-work*. The Puritans were, of course, strongly opposed to the use of images in churches—some of Trash's wares are, presumably, in the shape of St Bartholomew—and they regarded *The Golden Legend*, the great mediaeval collection of saints' lives, as a pack of lies.

the high places. See you not Goldylocks, the purple strumpet, there? in her yellow gown, and green sleeves? the profane pipes, the tinkling timbrels? A shop of relics!

LITTLEWIT

Pray you forbear, I am put in trust with 'em.

BUSY

And this idolatrous grove of images, this flasket of idols! which I will pull down— *Overthrows the gingerbread*

TRASH

O my ware, my ware, God bless it.

BUSY

—in my zeal, and glory to be thus exercised.

LEATHERHEAD *enters with officers*

LEATHERHEAD

Here he is. Pray you lay hold on his zeal; we cannot sell a whistle, for him, in tune. Stop his noise first!

BUSY

Thou canst not; 'tis a sanctified noise. I will make a loud and most strong noise, till I have daunted the profane enemy. And for this cause—

LEATHERHEAD

Sir, here's no man afraid of you, or your cause. You shall swear it, i' the stocks, sir.

BUSY

I will thrust myself into the stocks, upon the pikes of the land.

LEATHERHEAD

Carry him away.

PURECRAFT

What do you mean, wicked men?

BUSY

Let them alone; I fear them not.

[*Exeunt officers with* BUSY, *followed by* PURECRAFT]

LITTLEWIT

Was not this shilling well ventured, Win, for our liberty? Now we may go play, and see over the Fair, where we list, ourselves. My mother is gone after him, and let her e'en go, and loose us.

90 *flasket* long shallow basket
95 *for* because of
100 *swear it* do your swearing
101 *thrust myself . . . upon the pikes* rush to destruction (like a martyr)

WIN

Yes, John, but I know not what to do.

LITTLEWIT

For what, Win?

WIN

For a thing I am ashamed to tell you, i'faith, and 'tis too far to go home.

LITTLEWIT

I pray thee be not ashamed, Win. Come, i'faith thou shall not be ashamed. Is it anything about the hobby-horse-man? An't be, speak freely.

WIN

Hang him, base bobchin, I scorn him. No, I have very great what-sha-callum, John.

LITTLEWIT

O! Is that all, Win? We'll go back to Captain Jordan, to the pig-woman's, Win. He'll help us, or she with a dripping pan, or an old kettle, or something. The poor greasy soul loves you, Win. And after we'll visit the Fair all over, Win, and see my puppet play, Win. You know it's a fine matter, Win.

[*Exeunt* LITTLEWIT, WIN]

LEATHERHEAD

Let's away. I counselled you to pack up afore, Joan.

TRASH

A pox of his Bedlam purity! He has spoiled half my ware. But the best is: we lose nothing if we miss our first merchant.

LEATHERHEAD

It shall be hard for him to find, or know us, when we are translated, Joan.

[*Exeunt*]

Act IV, Scene i

[*Enter*] TROUBLE-ALL, BRISTLE, HAGGIS, COKES, OVERDO

TROUBLE-ALL

My masters, I do make no doubt but you are officers.

BRISTLE

What then, sir?

118 *what-sha-callum* need to make water
127 *miss* avoid meeting, keep clear of
merchant customer
128–9 *are translated* (i) have moved elsewhere (ii) have disguised ourselves

TROUBLE-ALL

And the King's loving and obedient subjects.

BRISTLE

Obedient, friend? Take heed what you speak, I advise you: Oliver Bristle advises you. His loving subjects, we grant you; but not his obedient, at this time, by your leave; we know ourselves a little better than so; we are to command, sir, and such as you are to be obedient. Here's one of his obedient subjects, going to the stocks, and we'll make you such another, if you talk.

TROUBLE-ALL

You are all wise enough i' your places, I know.

BRISTLE

If you know it, sir, why do you bring it in question?

TROUBLE-ALL

I question nothing, pardon me. I do only hope you have warrant for what you do, and so, quit you, and so, multiply you. *He goes away again*

HAGGIS

What's he?—Bring him up to the stocks there. Why bring you him not up?

[TROUBLE-ALL] *comes again*

TROUBLE-ALL

If you have Justice Overdo's warrant, 'tis well; you are safe; that is the warrant of warrants. I'll not give this button for any man's warrant else.

BRISTLE

Like enough, sir. But let me tell you, an you play away your buttons thus, you will want 'em ere night; for any store I see about you, you might keep 'em, and save pins, I wusse.

[TROUBLE-ALL] *goes away*

OVERDO

[*Aside*] What should he be, that doth so esteem and advance my warrant? He seems a sober and discreet person! It is a

7 *than so* than that
14–15 *quit you . . . you* God reward you and increase your family
22–3 *night; . . . you,* ed. (night, . . . you: F)
22 *store* plenty, abundant supply
24 *should* might, can
advance extol (OED, Advance *v.*, 12)

---

5 *Oliver Bristle.* At III.i, 8, Haggis called him 'Davy Bristle', but Jonson appears to have forgotten this.

comfort to a good conscience to be followed with a good fame in his sufferings. The world will have a pretty taste by this, how I can bear adversity; and it will beget a kind of reverence toward me, hereafter, even from mine enemies, when they shall see I carry my calamity nobly, and that it doth neither break me nor bend me.

HAGGIS

Come, sir, here's a place for you to preach in. Will you put in your leg?

They put him in the stocks

OVERDO

That I will, cheerfully.

BRISTLE

O' my conscience, a seminary! He kisses the stocks.

COKES

Well, my masters, I'll leave him with you. Now I see him bestowed, I'll go look for my goods, and Numps.

HAGGIS

You may, sir, I warrant you. Where's the tother bawler? Fetch him too. You shall find 'em both fast enough.

[*Exit* COKES]

OVERDO

[*Aside*] In the midst of this tumult, I will yet be the author of mine own rest, and, not minding their fury, sit in the stocks in that calm as shall be able to trouble a triumph.

[TROUBLE-ALL] *comes again*

TROUBLE-ALL

Do you assure me upon your words? May I undertake for you, if I be asked the question, that you have this warrant?

HAGGIS

What's this fellow, for God's sake?

TROUBLE-ALL

Do but shew me 'Adam Overdo', and I am satisfied.

Goes out

BRISTLE

He is a fellow that is distracted, they say—one Trouble-all.

35 *seminary* recusant (cf. II. i, 33)
41 *rest* (i) tranquillity of mind (ii) arrest
42 *trouble* mar

---

33 *leg*. The stocks used here secure the victim by one leg only, not two, as was more normal. See also the s.d. at IV.vi, 73.

He was an officer in the court of Pie-powders here last year, and put out on his place by Justice Overdo.

OVERDO

Ha!

BRISTLE

Upon which he took an idle conceit, and's run mad upon't. So that, ever since, he will do nothing but by Justice Overdo's warrant: he will not eat a crust, nor drink a little, nor make him in his apparel ready. His wife, sir-reverence, cannot get him make his water, or shift his shirt, without his warrant.

OVERDO

[*Aside*] If this be true, this is my greatest disaster! How am I bound to satisfy this poor man, that is, of so good a nature to me, out of his wits, where there is no room left for dissembling!

[TROUBLE-ALL] *comes in*

TROUBLE-ALL

If you cannot shew me 'Adam Overdo', I am in doubt of you. I am afraid you cannot answer it. *Goes again*

HAGGIS

Before me, neighbour Bristle, and now I think on't better, Justice Overdo is a very parantory person.

BRISTLE

O! are you advised of that? And a severe justicer, by your leave.

OVERDO

[*Aside*] Do I hear ill o' that side, too?

BRISTLE

He will sit as upright o' the bench, an you mark him, as a candle i' the socket, and give light to the whole court in every business.

49 *on* of
51 *took an idle conceit* became the victim of a groundless delusion
53–4 *make him in his apparel ready* get dressed
55 *shift* change
58 *is,* Ed. (is F)
of as a consequence of
62 *answer it* give a satisfactory answer
63 *Before me* upon my word
64 *parantory* peremptory
65 *are you advised* have you taken note

HAGGIS

But he will burn blue, and swell like a boil, God bless us, an he be angry.

BRISTLE

Ay, and he will be angry too, when 'has list, that's more; and when he is angry, be it right or wrong, he has the law on's side ever. I mark that too.

OVERDO

[*Aside*] I will be more tender hereafter. I see compassion may become a Justice, though it be a weakness, I confess, and nearer a vice than a virtue.

HAGGIS

Well, take him out o' the stocks again. We'll go a sure way to work; we'll ha' the ace of hearts of our side, if we can.

They take the Justice out

[*Enter*] POCHER, BUSY, PURECRAFT

POCHER

Come, bring him away to his fellow there. Master Busy, we shall rule your legs, I hope, though we cannot rule your tongue.

BUSY

No, minister of darkness, no, thou canst not rule my tongue; my tongue it is mine own, and with it I will both knock and mock down your Bartholmew-abhominations, till you be made a hissing to the neighbour parishes round about.

HAGGIS

Let him alone, we have devised better upon't.

PURECRAFT

And shall he not into the stocks then?

BRISTLE

No, mistress, we'll have 'em both to Justice Overdo, and let him do over 'em as is fitting. Then I, and my gossip Haggis, and my beadle Pocher are discharged.

73 *'has list* ed. (his list F) feels so inclined
80 *of* on
87 *hissing* object of scorn and opprobrium (cf. Jeremiah, xix. 8)
92 *discharged* freed of responsibility

86 *Bartholmew-abhominations*. This spelling of 'abomination', very common in the sixteenth century, arose from the mistaken view that the word was derived from 'ab homine', meaning 'inhuman'. Jonson, who knew better, puts this form of the word in Busy's mouth as a further indication of the preacher's ignorance.

PURECRAFT

O, I thank you, blessed, honest men!

BRISTLE

Nay, never thank us, but thank this madman that comes here, he put it in our heads.

[TROUBLE-ALL] *comes again*

PURECRAFT

Is he mad? Now heaven increase his madness, and bless it, and thank it! Sir, your poor handmaid thanks you.

TROUBLE-ALL

Have you a warrant? An you have a warrant, shew it.

PURECRAFT

Yes, I have a warrant out of the Word, to give thanks for removing any scorn intended to the brethren.

TROUBLE-ALL

It is Justice Overdo's warrant that I look for; if you have not that, keep your word, I'll keep mine. Quit ye, and multiply ye.

[*Exeunt all but* TROUBLE-ALL]

Act IV, Scene ii

[*Enter to him*] EDGWORTH, NIGHTINGALE

EDGWORTH

Come away, Nightingale, I pray thee.

TROUBLE-ALL

Whither go you? Where's your warrant?

EDGWORTH

Warrant for what, sir?

TROUBLE-ALL

For what you go about; you know how fit it is. An you have no warrant, bless you, I'll pray for you, that's all I can do.

Goes out

EDGWORTH

What means he?

NIGHTINGALE

A madman that haunts the Fair; do you not know him? It's marvel he has not more followers after his ragged heels.

97 *it*! Ed. (it, F)
99 *the Word* the Bible

EDGWORTH

Beshrew him, he startled me; I thought he had known of our plot. Guilt's a terrible thing! Ha' you prepared the costard-monger?

NIGHTINGALE

Yes, and agreed for his basket of pears. He is at the corner here, ready. And your prize, he comes down, sailing, that way, all alone, without his protector. He is rid of him, it seems.

EDGWORTH

Ay, I know. I should ha' followed his protectorship for a feat I am to do upon him; but this offered itself so i' the way, I could not let it scape. Here he comes. Whistle. Be this sport called 'Dorring the Dottrel'.

[*Enter*] COKES

NIGHTINGALE *Whistles*

Wh, wh, wh, wh, etc.

[*Enter*] COSTARD-MONGER

COKES

By this light, I cannot find my gingerbread-wife, nor my hobby-horse-man, in all the Fair, now, to ha' my money again. And I do not know the way out on't, to go home for more. Do you hear, friend, you that whistle, what tune is that you whistle?

NIGHTINGALE

A new tune I am practising, sir.

COKES

Dost thou know where I dwell, I pray thee? Nay, on with thy tune; I ha' no such haste for an answer. I'll practise with thee.

9 *Beshrew* curse, a plague on
12 *agreed* settled on a price
13 *prize* prey (Cokes is seen as a ship to be captured)
17–18 *i' the way* invitingly, opportunely
23 *again* back

---

19 *Dorring the Dottrel.* Hoaxing the simpleton. 'To dor' was 'to make a fool of', and the dottrel is a kind of plover proverbial for its foolishness (Tilley, D364) in allowing itself to be easily caught. The fatuous Norfolk squire in Jonson's next play, *The Devil is an Ass*, is called Fitz-Dottrell.

COSTARD-MONGER

Buy any pears, very fine pears, pears fine.

NIGHTINGALE *sets his foot afore him, and he falls with his basket*

COKES

God's so! A muss, a muss, a muss, a muss!

COSTARD-MONGER

Good gentleman, my ware, my ware! I am a poor man. Good sir, my ware.

NIGHTINGALE

Let me hold your sword, sir, it troubles you.

COKES

Do, and my cloak, an thou wilt, and my hat, too.

COKES *falls a-scrambling whilst they run away with his things*

EDGWORTH

A delicate great boy! Methinks he out-scrambles 'em all. I cannot persuade myself but he goes to grammar-school yet, and plays the truant today.

NIGHTINGALE

Would he had another purse to cut, Zekiel!

EDGWORTH

Purse! A man might cut out his kidneys, I think, and he never feel 'em, he is so earnest at the sport.

NIGHTINGALE

His soul is half-way out on's body at the game.

EDGWORTH

Away, Nightingale, that way!

[*Exit* NIGHTINGALE *with sword, cloak, and hat*]

COKES

I think I am furnished for Cather'ne pears, for one under-meal. Gi' me my cloak.

COSTARD-MONGER

Good gentleman, give me my ware.

COKES

Where's the fellow I ga' my cloak to? My cloak? and my hat? Ha! God's lid, is he gone? Thieves, thieves! Help me to cry, gentlemen. *He runs out*

EDGWORTH

Away, costermonger, come to us to Ursla's.

[*Exit* COSTARD-MONGER]

31 *muss* scramble
35 s.d. COKES *falls . . . things* (at l. 34 in F)
44–5 *undermeal* afternoon meal, snack

Talk of him to have a soul? 'Heart, if he have any more than a thing given him instead of salt, only to keep him from stinking, I'll be hanged afore my time, presently. Where should it be, trow? In his blood? He has not so much to'ard it in his whole body as will maintain a good flea. And if he take this course, he will not ha' so much land left as to rear a calf within this twelvemonth. Was there ever green plover so pulled? That his little overseer had been here now, and been but tall enough, to see him steal pears in exchange for his beaver-hat and his cloak thus! I must go find him out next, for his black box, and his patent, it seems he has, of his place; which I think the gentleman would have a reversion of, that spoke to me for it so earnestly. [*Exit*]

He [COKES] *comes again*

COKES

Would I might lose my doublet, and hose too, as I am an honest man, and never stir, if I think there be anything but thieving and coz'ning i' this whole Fair. Bartholmew Fair, quoth he! An ever any Bartholmew had that luck in't that I have had, I'll be martyred for him, and in Smithfield too. I ha' paid for my pears. A rot on 'em, I'll keep 'em no longer.

Throws away his pears

You were choke-pears to me. I had been better ha' gone to mum-chance for you, I wusse. Methinks the Fair should not have used me thus, an 'twere but for my name's sake. I

58 *pulled* plucked clean
61 *patent, it seems* ed. (Patent (it seemes) F)
70 *choke-pears* (i) coarse unpalatable pears (ii) a harsh reproof
71 *mum-chance* dicing game popular among costermongers
for instead of

51–3 *Talk . . . stinking*. An allusion to the notion that just as salt preserves meat so the soul prevents man from going rotten, which he does, of course, when the soul leaves the body. H & S aptly quote Herrick's epigram:

> The body's salt, the soule is; which when gon,
> The flesh soone sucks in putrifaction. (*Works*, ed. L. C. Martin, Oxford, 1956, p. 332.)

61–3 *patent . . . reversion of*. Edgworth thinks the box contains a document confirming Wasp in his position as Cokes's tutor, and that Quarlous wants the document in order to make sure of taking over Wasp's position.

68 *martyred . . . Smithfield too*. A reference to the Smithfield Martyrs, the Protestants who were burned there during the reign of Mary Tudor.

would not ha' used a dog o' the name so. O, Numps will triumph now!

TROUBLE-ALL *comes again*

Friend, do you know who I am? Or where I lie? I do not myself, I'll be sworn. Do but carry me home, and I'll please thee, I ha' money enough there. I ha' lost myself, and my cloak and my hat, and my fine sword, and my sister, and Numps, and Mistress Grace, a gentlewoman that I should ha' married, and a cut-work handkercher she ga' me, and two purses, today. And my bargain o' hobby-horses and gingerbread, which grieves me worst of all.

TROUBLE-ALL
By whose warrant, sir, have you done all this?

COKES
Warrant? Thou art a wise fellow indeed—as if a man need a warrant to lose anything with.

TROUBLE-ALL
Yes, Justice Overdo's warrant a man may get and lose with, I'll stand to't.

COKES
Justice Overdo? Dost thou know him? I lie there, he is my brother-in-law, he married my sister. Pray thee shew me the way; dost thou know the house?

TROUBLE-ALL
Sir, shew me your warrant. I know nothing without a warrant, pardon me.

COKES
Why, I warrant thee. Come along, thou shalt see I have wrought pillows there, and cambric sheets, and sweet bags too. Pray thee guide me to the house.

TROUBLE-ALL
Sir, I'll tell you. Go you thither yourself first alone; tell your worshipful brother your mind; and but bring me three lines of his hand, or his clerk's, with 'Adam Overdo'

75 *lie* lodge
76 *carry* escort, take
please satisfy, reward
80 *cut-work* embroidered
93 *thee. Come along,* ed. (thee, come along: F)
94 *wrought* embroidered
sweet bags bags containing fragrant herbs to perfume the linen

underneath. Here I'll stay you, I'll obey you, and I'll guide you presently.

COKES

[*Aside*] 'Slid, this is an ass, I ha' found him. Pox upon me, what do I talking to such a dull fool?—Farewell. You are a very coxcomb, do you hear?

TROUBLE-ALL

I think I am. If Justice Overdo sign to it, I am, and so we are all. He'll quit us all, multiply us all.

[*Exeunt*]

Act IV, Scene iii

[*Enter*] GRACE. *They* (QUARLOUS, WINWIFE) *enter with their swords drawn*

GRACE

Gentlemen, this is no way that you take. You do but breed one another trouble and offence, and give me no contentment at all. I am no she that affects to be quarrelled for, or have my name or fortune made the question of men's swords.

QUARLOUS

'Slood, we love you.

GRACE

If you both love me, as you pretend, your own reason will tell you but one can enjoy me; and to that point there leads a directer line than by my infamy, which must follow if you fight. 'Tis true—I have professed it to you ingenuously—that, rather than to be yoked with this bridegroom is appointed me, I would take up any husband, almost, upon any trust; though Subtlety would say to me—I know—he is a fool, and has an estate, and I might govern him, and enjoy a friend beside. But these are not my aims. I must have a

99 *stay* wait for
101 *found him* discovered his true character, sized him up
3 *affects* likes
6 *pretend* claim
10 *is* who is
11 *take up* accept
almost, ed. (almost F)
11–12 *upon any trust* without further investigation of his credentials
12 *he* Cokes
14 *friend* lover

husband I must love, or I cannot live with him. I shall ill make one of these politic wives!

WINWIFE

Why, if you can like either of us, lady, say which is he, and the other shall swear instantly to desist.

QUARLOUS

Content, I accord to that willingly.

GRACE

Sure you think me a woman of an extreme levity, gentlemen, or a strange fancy, that, meeting you by chance in such a place as this, both at one instant, and not yet of two hours' acquaintance, neither of you deserving afore the other of me, I should so forsake my modesty, though I might affect one more particularly, as to say, 'This is he', and name him.

QUARLOUS

Why, wherefore should you not? What should hinder you?

GRACE

If you would not give it to my modesty, allow it yet to my wit; give me so much of woman, and cunning, as not to betray myself impertinently. How can I judge of you, so far as to a choice, without knowing you more? You are both equal and alike to me, yet; and so indifferently affected by me, as each of you might be the man, if the other were away; for you are reasonable creatures; you have understanding and discourse; and if fate send me an understanding husband, I have no fear at all but mine own manners shall make him a good one.

QUARLOUS

Would I were put forth to making for you, then.

GRACE

It may be you are; you know not what's toward you. Will you consent to a motion of mine, gentlemen?

16 *politic* scheming
28 *wit* intelligence
cunning knowledge of the world
29 *impertinently* unbecomingly
31 *indifferently affected* impartially regarded
33 *away; for* ed. (away. For F)
34 *discourse* the ability to reason
37 *put forth to making* apprenticed to be trained
38 *toward* in store for
39 *motion* proposal, suggestion

WINWIFE

Whatever it be, we'll presume reasonableness, coming from you.

QUARLOUS

And fitness, too.

GRACE

I saw one of you buy a pair of tables, e'en now.

WINWIFE

Yes, here they be, and maiden ones too, unwritten in.

GRACE

The fitter for what they may be employed in. You shall write, either of you, here a word or a name, what you like best, but of two or three syllables at most. And the next person that comes this way—because Destiny has a high hand in business of this nature—I'll demand which of the two words he or she doth approve; and, according to that sentence, fix my resolution, and affection, without change.

QUARLOUS

Agreed, my word is conceived already.

WINWIFE

And mine shall not be long creating after.

GRACE

But you shall promise, gentlemen, not to be curious to know which of you it is, is taken; but give me leave to conceal that till you have brought me, either home, or where I may safely tender myself.

WINWIFE

Why, that's but equal.

QUARLOUS

We are pleased.

GRACE

Because I will bind both your endeavours to work together, friendly and jointly, each to the other's fortune, and have

43 *tables* writing tablets
46 *either* each
46–7 *what you like best* whichever you prefer
55 *is, is taken* Ed. (is, taken F)
57 *tender myself* offer myself for acceptance
58 *but equal* fair enough

48–9 *because Destiny . . . nature.* Alluding to one or more proverbs: 'Marriage is destiny' (Tilley, M682); 'Marriage and magistrate be destinies of heaven' (Tilley, M680); and the familiar 'Wedding and hanging go by destiny' (Tilley, W232).

myself fitted with some means to make him that is forsaken a part of amends.

QUARLOUS

These conditions are very courteous. Well, my word is out of the *Arcadia*, then: 'Argalus'.

WINWIFE

And mine out of the play: 'Palemon'.

TROUBLE-ALL *comes again*

TROUBLE-ALL

Have you any warrant for this, gentlemen?

QUARLOUS }
WINWIFE }

Ha?

TROUBLE-ALL

There must be a warrant had, believe it.

WINWIFE

For what?

TROUBLE-ALL

For whatsoever it is, anything indeed, no matter what.

QUARLOUS

'Slight, here's a fine ragged prophet, dropped down i' the nick!

TROUBLE-ALL

Heaven quit you, gentlemen.

QUARLOUS

Nay, stay a little. Good lady, put him to the question.

GRACE

You are content, then?

WINWIFE }
QUARLOUS }

Yes, yes.

GRACE

Sir, here are two names written—

62 *forsaken* rejected, refused
63 *a part of* some
72–3 *i' the nick* at exactly the right moment

---

65 *Argalus*. A character in Sir Philip Sidney's *Arcadia*, whose love for Parthenia forms one of the episodes in that work.

66 *Palemon*. Either Palamon in *The Two Noble Kinsmen* by Shakespeare and Fletcher, first performed in 1613, or Palaemon in Samuel Daniel's *The Queen's Arcadia*, played at Christ Church, Oxford, on 30 August 1605, during the course of a royal visit to the University.

TROUBLE-ALL

Is Justice Overdo one?

GRACE

How, sir? I pray you read 'em to yourself—it is for a wager between these gentlemen—and, with a stroke or any difference, mark which you approve best.

TROUBLE-ALL

They may be both worshipful names for aught I know, mistress, but Adam Overdo had been worth three of 'em, I assure you, in this place; that's in plain English.

GRACE

This man amazes me! I pray you, like one of 'em, sir.

TROUBLE-ALL

I do like him there, that has the best warrant. Mistress, to save your longing, and multiply him, it may be this.

[*He marks the book*]

But I am aye still for Justice Overdo, that's my conscience. And quit you. [*Exit*]

WINWIFE

Is't done, lady?

GRACE

Ay, and strangely as ever I saw! What fellow is this, trow?

QUARLOUS

No matter what, a fortune-teller we ha' made him. Which is't, which is't?

GRACE

Nay, did you not promise, not to enquire?

[*Enter*] EDGWORTH

QUARLOUS

'Slid, I forgot that, pray you pardon me. Look, here's our Mercury come; the licence arrives i' the finest time, too! 'Tis but scraping out Cokes his name, and 'tis done.

79 *Justice* Ed. (*Iudice* F)
80 *to yourself* silently
81–2 *difference* distinguishing mark
87 *warrant.* Ed. (warrant, F)
88 *and multiply him* Ed. (and (multiply him) F)
89 *aye* Ed. (I F)
conscience conviction
94 *is't?* Ed. (is't. F)

---

97 *Mercury.* As well as being the messenger of the gods, Mercury was also the god of thieves.

WINWIFE

How now, lime-twig? Hast thou touched?

EDGWORTH

Not yet, sir; except you would go with me, and see't, it's not worth speaking on. The act is nothing, without a witness. Yonder he is, your man with the box, fallen into the finest company, and so transported with vapours. They ha' got in a northern clothier, and one Puppy, a western man, that's come to wrestle before my Lord Mayor anon, and Captain Whit, and one Val Cutting, that helps Captain Jordan to roar, a circling boy; with whom your Numps is so taken that you may strip him of his clothes, if you will. I'll undertake to geld him for you; if you had but a surgeon ready, to sear him. And Mistress Justice, there, is the goodest woman! She does so law 'em all over, in terms of justice, and the style of authority, with her hood upright, that—that I beseech you come away, gentlemen, and see't.

QUARLOUS

'Slight, I would not lose it for the Fair. What'll you do, Ned?

99 *lime-twig* thief, one whose fingers are 'limed' so that things stick to them
touched? Ed. (touch'd. F) carried out the theft

100 *sir;* Ed. (Sir, F)
except unless

103 *vapours. They* Ed. (vapours, they F)

110 *goodest* most important

112 *upright, that—that* ed. (vpright—that F)

113 *come away* come along

---

104 *a western man.* Cornwall was famous for its wrestlers.

105 *before my Lord Mayor.* Wrestling in the presence of the Lord Mayor was a regular feature of Bartholomew Fair on the afternoon of the opening day.

107 *a circling boy.* Since no other example of this term is known, it is difficult to say precisely what it means. Cutting is evidently a 'roarer'; he makes use of a circle for quarrelling purposes (see IV.iv, 115–22); and he 'gives the lie in circle', i.e., circuitously, indirectly (*OED*, Circle, *sb.*, †24., quoting from *The Alchemist*, III.iv, 38–9). The last of these activities is probably the reason for the term.

111 *law* ed. (loue F) argue with, lay down the law to. It is difficult to see how one can 'love . . . in terms of justice, and the style of authority'. Nor is it what Mistress Overdo does at IV.iv, 125–8. Nashe, in *Nashes Lenten Stuffe* (1599), launches a vigorous attack on lawyers' jargon, and then continues: 'I stand lawing heere' (Nashe, iii. 216. 16). Mistress Overdo also 'stands lawing'. If Jonson wrote 'lawe', as this editor believes he did, a compositor might easily read it as 'loue'.

WINWIFE

Why, stay here about for you; Mistress Wellborn must not be seen.

QUARLOUS

Do so, and find out a priest i' the mean time; I'll bring the licence.—Lead, which way is't?

EDGWORTH

Here, sir, you are o' the backside o' the booth already, you may hear the noise.

[*Exeunt*]

Act IV, Scene iv

[*Enter*] KNOCKEM, NORTHERN, PUPPY, CUTTING, WHIT, WASP, MISTRESS OVERDO

KNOCKEM

Whit, bid Val Cutting continue the vapours for a lift, Whit, for a lift.

NORTHERN

I'll ne mare, I'll ne mare, the eale's too meeghty.

KNOCKEM

How now, my Galloway Nag, the staggers? Ha! Whit, gi' him a slit i' the forehead. Cheer up, man; a needle and thread to stitch his ears. I'd cure him now, an I had it, with a little butter, and garlic, long-pepper, and grains. Where's my horn? I'll gi' him a mash, presently, shall take away this dizziness.

PUPPY

Why, where are you, zurs? Do you vlinch, and leave us i' the zuds, now?

1 *for a lift* in preparation for a theft
4 *the staggers* disease of horses, marked by a staggering gait
7 *long-pepper* very strong kind of pepper
grains refuse of malt
8 *horn* drenching-horn
10 *vlinch* flinch (as pronounced in the West Country), weaken in your drinking
10–11 *i' the zuds* (literally, in the suds) i.e., in trouble

---

3 *ne mare . . . too meeghty.* No more, the ale's too mighty. Jonson's attempt to represent the northern dialect.

4 *Galloway Nag.* Breed of small horses from the south-west of Scotland, noted for their hardiness and powers of endurance.

4–7 *gi' him . . . grains.* The cure recommended in Jonson's day for a horse suffering from the staggers.

NORTHERN
I'll ne mare, I is e'en as vull as a paiper's bag, by my troth, I.

PUPPY
Do my northern cloth zhrink i' the wetting, ha?

KNOCKEM
Why, well said, old flea-bitten, thou'lt never tire, I see.
They fall to their vapours again

CUTTING
No, sir, but he may tire, if it please him.

WHIT
Who told dee sho? that he vuld never teer, man?

CUTTING
No matter who told him so, so long as he knows.

KNOCKEM
Nay, I know nothing, sir, pardon me there.

[*Enter*] EDGWORTH, QUARLOUS

EDGWORTH
They are at it still, sir, this they call vapours.

WHIT
He shall not pardon dee, captain, dou shalt not be pardoned. Pre'de shweetheart, do not pardon him.

CUTTING
'Slight, I'll pardon him, an I list, whosoever says nay to't.

QUARLOUS
Where's Numps? I miss him.

WASP
Why, I say nay to't.

QUARLOUS
O there he is!

KNOCKEM
To what do you say nay, sir?
Here they continue their game of vapours, which is nonsense: every man to oppose the last man that spoke, whether it concerned him, or no

12 *paiper's* piper's
26 s.d. *Here they . . . no* (at l. 23 in F)

13 *Do my . . . wetting.* The complaint that Northern cloth shrank easily was a common one.
14 *flea-bitten . . . tire.* 'A flea-bitten horse never tires' was a proverb (Tilley, H640). 'Flea-bitten' refers to the horse's colour—dappled.

WASP

To anything, whatsoever it is, so long as I do not like it.

WHIT

Pardon me, little man, dou musht like it a little.

CUTTING

No, he must not like it at all, sir; there you are i' the wrong.

WHIT

I tink I be; he musht not like it, indeed.

CUTTING

Nay, then he both must and will like it, sir, for all you.

KNOCKEM

If he have reason, he may like it, sir.

WHIT

By no meansh, captain, upon reason, he may like nothing upon reason.

WASP

I have no reason, nor I will hear of no reason, nor I will look for no reason, and he is an ass that either knows any, or looks for't from me.

CUTTING

Yes, in some sense you may have reason, sir.

WASP

Ay, in some sense, I care not if I grant you.

WHIT

Pardon me, thou ougsht to grant him nothing, in no shensh, if dou do love dyshelf, angry man.

WASP

Why then, I do grant him nothing; and I have no sense.

CUTTING

'Tis true, thou hast no sense indeed.

WASP

'Slid, but I have sense, now I think on't better, and I will grant him anything, do you see?

KNOCKEM

He is i' the right, and does utter a sufficient vapour.

CUTTING

Nay, it is no sufficient vapour, neither, I deny that.

KNOCKEM

Then it is a sweet vapour.

CUTTING

It may be a sweet vapour.

WASP

Nay, it is no sweet vapour, neither, sir; it stinks, and I'll stand to't.

WHIT

Yes, I tink it doesh shtink, captain. All vapour doesh shtink.

WASP

Nay, then it does not stink, sir, and it shall not stink.

CUTTING

By your leave, it may, sir.

WASP

Ay, by my leave, it may stink; I know that.

WHIT

Pardon me, thou knowesht nothing; it cannot by thy leave, angry man.

WASP

How can it not?

KNOCKEM

Nay, never question him, for he is i' the right.

WHIT

Yesh, I am i' de right, I confesh it; so ish de little man too.

WASP

I'll have nothing confessed that concerns me. I am not i' the right, nor never was i' the right, nor never will be i' the right, while I am in my right mind.

CUTTING

Mind? Why, here's no man minds you, sir, nor anything else.

They drink again

PUPPY

Vriend, will you mind this that we do?

QUARLOUS

Call you this vapours? This is such belching of quarrel as I never heard. Will you mind your business, sir?

EDGWORTH

You shall see, sir.

NORTHERN

I'll ne mair, my waimb warks too mickle with this auready.

EDGWORTH

Will you take that, Master Wasp, that nobody should mind you?

WASP

Why? What ha' you to do? Is't any matter to you?

67 *mind your business* get on with your job (of stealing the licence)

69 *waimb warks too mickle* stomach is too upset

72 *What ha' you to do* what business of yours is it

EDGWORTH

No, but methinks you should not be unminded, though.

WASP

Nor I wu' not be, now I think on't; do you hear, new acquaintance, does no man mind me, say you?

CUTTING

Yes, sir, every man here minds you, but how?

WASP

Nay, I care as little how as you do; that was not my question.

WHIT

No, noting was ty question; tou art a learned man, and I am a valiant man, i'faith la; tou shalt speak for me, and I vill fight for tee.

KNOCKEM

Fight for him, Whit? A gross vapour; he can fight for himself.

WASP

It may be I can, but it may be I wu' not, how then?

CUTTING

Why, then you may choose.

WASP

Why, and I'll choose whether I'll choose or no.

KNOCKEM

I think you may, and 'tis true; and I allow it for a resolute vapour.

WASP

Nay, then I do think you do not think, and it is no resolute vapour.

CUTTING

Yes, in some sort he may allow you.

KNOCKEM

In no sort, sir, pardon me, I can allow him nothing. You mistake the vapour.

WASP

He mistakes nothing, sir, in no sort.

WHIT

Yes, I pre dee now, let him mistake.

73 *unminded* left unnoticed

90, 93 *sort* (i) sense (ii) company

WASP

A turd i' your teeth! Never pre dee me, for I will have nothing mistaken.

KNOCKEM

Turd, ha, turd? A noisome vapour! Strike, Whit.

They fall by the ears

[EDGWORTH *steals the licence from the box, and exit*]

MISTRESS OVERDO

Why gentlemen, why gentlemen, I charge you upon my authority, conserve the peace. In the King's name, and my husband's, put up your weapons; I shall be driven to commit you myself, else.

QUARLOUS

Ha, ha, ha!

WASP

Why do you laugh, sir?

QUARLOUS

Sir, you'll allow me my Christian liberty. I may laugh, I hope.

CUTTING

In some sort you may, and in some sort you may not, sir.

KNOCKEM

Nay, in some sort, sir, he may neither laugh, nor hope, in this company.

WASP

Yes, then he may both laugh and hope in any sort, an't please him.

QUARLOUS

Faith, and I will then, for it doth please me exceedingly.

WASP

No exceeding neither, sir.

KNOCKEM

No, that vapour is too lofty.

QUARLOUS

Gentlemen, I do not play well at your game of vapours, I am not very good at it, but—

97 s.d. *They fall by the ears* they fight
100–1 *commit you* send you to prison
111 *exceeding* excess, going too far

CUTTING
Do you hear, sir? I would speak with you in circle!
He draws a circle on the ground

QUARLOUS
In circle, sir? What would you with me in circle?

CUTTING
Can you lend me a piece, a Jacobus, in circle?

QUARLOUS
'Slid, your circle will prove more costly than your vapours, then. Sir, no, I lend you none.

CUTTING
Your beard's not well turned up, sir.

QUARLOUS
How, rascal? Are you playing with my beard? I'll break circle with you.
They draw all, and fight

PUPPY }
NORTHERN }
Gentlemen, gentlemen!

KNOCKEM
Gather up, Whit, gather up, Whit. Good vapours!
[*Exeunt* KNOCKEM *and* WHIT *with the cloaks*]

MISTRESS OVERDO
What mean you? Are you rebels, gentlemen? Shall I send out a sergeant-at-arms, or a writ o' rebellion, against you? I'll commit you, upon my womanhood, for a riot, upon my justice-hood, if you persist.
[*Exeunt* QUARLOUS, CUTTING]

WASP
Upon your justice-hood? Marry, shit o' your hood! You'll commit? Spoke like a true Justice of Peace's wife, indeed, and a fine female lawyer! Turd i' your teeth for a fee, now.

MISTRESS OVERDO
Why, Numps, in Master Overdo's name, I charge you.

WASP
Good Mistress Underdo, hold your tongue.

117 *Jacobus* gold coin, 'sovereign', issued by James I
130 *commit* (i) send to prison (ii) fornicate

115–22 *Do you . . . with you.* The drawing of the circle is an indirect challenge, which Quarlous fails to understand. Cutting then asks for the loan of a Jacobus, knowing that it will be refused and thus provide the pretext for the final insult, his playing with Quarlous's beard which precipitates the fight.

MISTRESS OVERDO

Alas! poor Numps.

WASP

Alas! And why alas from you, I beseech you? Or why poor Numps, Goody Rich? Am I come to be pitied by your tuftaffeta now? Why, mistress, I knew Adam, the clerk, your husband, when he was Adam Scrivener, and writ for two-pence a sheet, as high as he bears his head now, or you your hood, dame.

The watch comes in [*accompanied by* WHIT]

What are you, sir?

BRISTLE

We be men, and no infidels. What is the matter here, and the noises? Can you tell?

WASP

Heart, what ha' you to do? Cannot a man quarrel in quietness, but he must be put out on't by you? What are you?

BRISTLE

Why, we be His Majesty's Watch, sir.

WASP

Watch? 'Sblood, you are a sweet watch, indeed. A body would think, an you watched well o' nights, you should be contented to sleep at this time o' day. Get you to your fleas, and your flock-beds, you rogues, your kennels, and lie down close.

BRISTLE

Down? Yes, we will down, I warrant you.—Down with him in His Majesty's name, down, down with him, and carry him away, to the pigeon-holes.

[WASP *is arrested*]

MISTRESS OVERDO

I thank you, honest friends, in the behalf o' the Crown, and

136 *Goody* Goodwife
137 *tuftaffeta* a kind of taffeta with a pile or nap arranged in tufts (*OED*)
145 *put out on't* debarred from doing it
148 *watched* (i) stayed awake (ii) did your duties as watchmen
154 *pigeon-holes* stocks

---

138 *Adam Scrivener*. There may be an allusion here to Chaucer's little poem 'Chaucers Wordes unto Adam, his own Scriveyn', reproving Adam for his carelessness in copying.

140 s.d. *accompanied by* WHIT ed. (not in F). Whit's entry here, like his exit at 124, is demanded by his collusion with the Watch established in III.i.

the peace, and in Master Overdo's name, for suppressing enormities.

WHIT

Stay, Bristle, here ish a noder brashe o' drunkards, but very quiet, special drunkards, will pay dee five shillings very well. Take 'em to dee, in de graish o' God: one of 'em does change cloth for ale in the Fair here, te toder ish a strong man, a mighty man, my Lord Mayor's man, and a wrestler. He has wreshled so long with the bottle, here, that the man with the beard hash almosht streek up hish heelsh.

BRISTLE

'Slid, the Clerk o' the Market has been to cry him all the Fair over, here, for my Lord's service.

WHIT

Tere he ish, pre de taik him hensh, and make ty best on him.

[*Exit watch with* WASP, NORTHERN, PUPPY]

How now, woman o' shilk, vat ailsh ty shweet faish? Art tou melancholy?

MISTRESS OVERDO

A little distempered with these enormities. Shall I entreat a courtesy of you, Captain?

WHIT

Entreat a hundred, velvet voman, I vill do it, shpeak out.

MISTRESS OVERDO

I cannot with modesty speak it out, but—

[*She whispers to him*]

WHIT

I vill do it, and more, and more, for dee. What Ursla, an't be bitch, an't be bawd, an't be!

[*Enter*] URSLA

URSLA

How now, rascal? What roar you for, old pimp?

158 *brashe* Ed. (brash F) brace
164 *streek up hish heelsh* struck up his heels, i.e., overthrown him
165 *cry* summon
166 *Lord's* Lord Mayor's
170 *distempered with* upset by
176 *for, old pimp?* Ed. (for? old Pimpe. F)

163–4 *the man with the beard.* A kind of drinking-jug, pot-bellied but with a narrow neck decorated with a bearded face.

165 *Clerk o' the Market.* An officer appointed by the City to collect market dues and inspect the market.

WHIT

Here, put up de cloaks, Ursh, de purchase. Pre dee now, shweet Ursh, help dis good brave voman to a jordan, an't be.

URSLA

'Slid, call your Captain Jordan to her, can you not?

WHIT

Nay, pre dee leave dy consheits, and bring the velvet woman to de—

URSLA

I bring her? Hang her! Heart, must I find a common pot for every punk i' your purlieus?

WHIT

O good voordsh, Ursh; it ish a guest o' velvet, i' fait la!

URSLA

Let her sell her hood, and buy a sponge, with a pox to her. My vessel? Employed, sir. I have but one, and 'tis the bottom of an old bottle. An honest proctor and his wife are at it within. If she'll stay her time, so.

WHIT

As soon ash tou cansht, shweet Ursh. Of a valiant man I tink I am the patientsh man i' the world, or in all Smithfield.

[*Enter* KNOCKEM]

KNOCKEM

How now, Whit? Close vapours? stealing your leaps? covering in corners, ha?

WHIT

No fait, Captain, dough tou beesht a vishe man, dy vit is a mile hence now. I vas procuring a shmall courtesy for a woman of fashion here.

MISTRESS OVERDO

Yes, Captain, though I am Justice of Peace's wife, I do love men of war, and the sons of the sword, when they come before my husband.

KNOCKEM

Say'st thou so, filly? Thou shalt have a leap presently, I'll horse thee myself else.

177 *purchase.* Ed. (purchase, F) booty

183 *your purlieus* the brothel areas

185–6 *her. My vessel? Employed, sir.* ed. (her, my vessell, employed Sir. F)

192 *covering* (technical term for a stallion mating with a mare) copulating

URSLA
Come, will you bring her in now? And let her take her turn?

WHIT
Gramercy, good Ursh, I tank dee.

MISTRESS OVERDO
Master Overdo shall thank her. [*Exit*]

Act IV, Scene v

[*Enter to them*] LITTLEWIT, WIN

LITTLEWIT
Good Gammer Urs, Win and I are exceedingly beholden to you, and to Captain Jordan, and Captain Whit. Win, I'll be bold to leave you i' this good company, Win, for half an hour or so, Win, while I go and see how my matter goes forward, and if the puppets be perfect. And then I'll come and fetch you, Win.

WIN
Will you leave me alone with two men, John?

LITTLEWIT
Ay, they are honest gentlemen, Win, Captain Jordan and Captain Whit, they'll use you very civilly, Win. God b'w'you, Win. [*Exit*]

URSLA
What's her husband gone?

KNOCKEM
On his false gallop, Urs, away.

URSLA
An you be right Bartholmew-birds, now shew yourselves so. We are undone for want of fowl i' the Fair here. Here will be Zekiel Edgworth, and three or four gallants with him at night, and I ha' neither plover nor quail for 'em. Persuade this between you two, to become a bird o' the game, while I work the velvet woman within, as you call her.

KNOCKEM
I conceive thee, Urs! Go thy ways. [*Exit* URSLA]
Dost thou hear, Whit? Is't not pity my delicate dark chest-

201 *take* Ed. (talke F)
5 *be perfect* know their parts, are word-perfect
12 *false gallop* Ed. (false, gallop F) canter, with a quibble on 'false' = 'unwise'
14 *fowl* 'birds', wenches
16 *neither plover nor quail* no wenches at all
19 *ways.* Ed. (waies, F)

nut here—with the fine lean head, large forehead, round eyes, even mouth, sharp ears, long neck, thin crest, close withers, plain back, deep sides, short fillets, and full flanks; with a round belly, a plump buttock, large thighs, knit knees, straight legs, short pasterns, smooth hoofs, and short heels—should lead a dull honest woman's life, that might live the life of a lady?

WHIT

Yes, by my fait and trot, it is, Captain. De honesht woman's life is a scurvy dull life, indeed, la!

WIN

How, sir? Is an honest woman's life a scurvy life?

WHIT

Yes, fait, shweetheart, believe him, de leef of a bondwoman! But if dou vilt harken to me, I vill make tee a free-woman, and a lady; dou shalt live like a lady, as te captain saish.

KNOCKEM

Ay, and be honest too, sometimes; have her wires, and her tires, her green gowns, and velvet petticoats.

WHIT

Ay, and ride to Ware and Romford i' dy coash, shee de players, be in love vit 'em; sup vit gallantsh, be drunk, and cost de noting.

KNOCKEM

Brave vapours!

WHIT

And lie by twenty on 'em, if dou pleash, shweetheart.

WIN

What, and be honest still? That were fine sport.

WHIT

'Tish common, shweetheart, tou may'st do it, by my hand.

23 *plain* flat
26 *honest* (i) respectable (ii) chaste
27 *lady* (i) woman of rank (ii) 'lady of pleasure'
34 *wires* frames of wire used to stiffen ruffs and to support the hair
35 *tires* head-dresses and dresses in general
41 *still? That* Ed. (still, that F)
42 *it,* Ed. (it F)

---

35 *green gowns*. Knockem is quibbling; 'to give a wench a green gown' was to seduce her by rolling her over in the grass. Hence green gowns came to be associated with prostitutes.

36 *Ware and Romford*. Ware, famous for its 'great bed' (eleven feet square), and Romford were notorious as places of assignation within easy reach of London.

It shall be justified to ty husband's faish, now: tou shalt be as honesht as the skin between his hornsh, la!

KNOCKEM

Yes, and wear a dressing, top and topgallant, to compare with e'er a husband on 'em all, for a fore-top. It is the vapour of spirit, in the wife, to cuckold, nowadays, as it is the vapour of fashion, in the husband, not to suspect. Your prying cat-eyed citizen is an abominable vapour.

WIN

Lord, what a fool have I been!

WHIT

Mend then, and do everyting like a lady hereafter; never know ty husband from another man.

KNOCKEM

Nor any one man from another, but i' the dark.

WHIT

Ay, and then it ish no dishgrash to know any man.

[*Enter* URSLA]

URSLA

Help, help here!

KNOCKEM

How now? What vapour's there?

URSLA

O, you are a sweet ranger, and look well to your walks! Yonder is your punk of Turnbull, Ramping Alice, has fallen upon the poor gentlewoman within, and pulled her hood over her ears, and her hair through it.

ALICE *enters, beating the Justice's wife*

MISTRESS OVERDO

Help, help, i' the King's name!

51 *Mend* reform yourself

---

44 *as honesht . . . hornsh.* 'As honest as the skin between his brows' was, and still is, proverbial (Tilley, S506), but Whit substitutes the horns of the cuckold for 'brows'.

45–6 *dressing . . . fore-top.* The elaborate head-dresses and 'hair-dos' of the time are described in nautical terms, comparing the effect to that of a ship under full sail, by Shakespeare in *The Merry Wives of Windsor*, III.iii, 46–9, and by Nashe in his *Christs Teares Over Jerusalem*, where he writes: 'Theyr heads, with theyr top and top gallant Lawne baby-caps, and Snow-resembled siluer curlings, they make a playne Puppet stage of' (Nashe, ii. 137. 31–3). Got up in this fashion, Knockem says, Win's head will be a fit match for her husband's horns (foretop).

ALICE

A mischief on you! They are such as you are that undo us and take our trade from us, with your tuftaffeta haunches.

KNOCKEM

How now, Alice!

ALICE

The poor common whores can ha' no traffic for the privy rich ones. Your caps and hoods of velvet call away our customers, and lick the fat from us.

URSLA

Peace, you foul ramping jade, you—

ALICE

Od's foot, you bawd in grease, are you talking?

KNOCKEM

Why, Alice, I say.

ALICE

Thou sow of Smithfield, thou.

URSLA

Thou tripe of Turnbull.

KNOCKEM

Catamountain vapours, ha!

URSLA

You know where you were tawed lately, both lashed and slashed you were in Bridewell.

ALICE

Ay, by the same token, you rid that week, and broke out the bottom o' the cart, night-tub.

62 *undo* ruin
63 *tuftaffeta haunches* artificial haunches made of silk and designed to improve the figure
65 *for* because of
privy clandestine
66 *velvet* Ed. (veluet, F)
69 *in grease* fat, in prime condition for killing
73 *Catamountain* wildcat, ferocious
74 *tawed* flogged
75 *slashed* cut with the scourge
76 *rid* rode in the cart for whores
77 *night-tub* tub for excrement or night-soil

---

67 *lick the fat from us.* 'To lick the fat from one's lips' was proverbial (Tilley F80) for depriving one of one's best customers.

75 *Bridewell.* The London prison, where sexual offenders in particular were confined and punished.

KNOCKEM

Why, lion face, ha! Do you know who I am? Shall I tear ruff, slit waistcoat, make rags of petticoat, ha? Go to, vanish, for fear of vapours. Whit, a kick, Whit, in the parting vapour.

[*They kick* ALICE *out*]

Come, brave woman, take a good heart, thou shalt be a lady too.

WHIT

Yes fait, dey shall all both be ladies, and write Madam. I vill do't myself for dem. *Do* is the vord, and *D* is the middle letter of *Madam*, *DD*, put 'em together and make deeds, without which all words are alike, la!

KNOCKEM

'Tis true. Ursla, take 'em in, open thy wardrobe, and fit 'em to their calling. Green gowns, crimson petticoats, green women! My Lord Mayor's green women! guests o' the game, true bred. I'll provide you a coach, to take the air in.

WIN

But do you think you can get one?

KNOCKEM

O, they are as common as wheelbarrows where there are great dunghills. Every pettifogger's wife has 'em; for first he buys a coach, that he may marry, and then he marries that he may be made cuckold in't. For if their wives ride not to their cuckolding, they do 'em no credit. 'Hide and be hidden, ride and be ridden', says the vapour of experience.

[*Exeunt* URSLA, WIN, MISTRESS OVERDO]

Act IV, Scene vi

[*Enter to them*] TROUBLE-ALL

TROUBLE-ALL

By what warrant does it say so?

79 *petticoat, ha*? ed. (petticoat? ha! F)
83 *write* sign themselves, style themselves
93 *pettifogger* lawyer of inferior status
97 *ridden* mounted sexually by a man

---

79 *waistcoat*. When worn without a gown over it, the waistcoat was the mark of a prostitute, who was sometimes called a 'waistcoateer'.

88–9 *green women . . . green women*. (i) loose women, whores (ii) female equivalents of the 'green men', i.e., men dressed in green to represent wild men of the woods or woodwoses, as they were called, who were a common feature of the Lord Mayor's Show.

KNOCKEM
Ha! mad child o' the Pie-powders, art thou there? Fill us a fresh can, Urs, we may drink together.

TROUBLE-ALL
I may not drink without a warrant, Captain.

KNOCKEM
'Slood, thou'll not stale without a warrant, shortly. Whit, give me pen, ink and paper. I'll draw him a warrant presently.

TROUBLE-ALL
It must be Justice Overdo's!

KNOCKEM
I know, man. Fetch the drink, Whit.

WHIT
I pre dee now, be very brief, Captain; for de new ladies stay for dee.

KNOCKEM
O, as brief as can be; here 'tis already. 'Adam Overdo'.

TROUBLE-ALL
Why, now I'll pledge you, Captain.

KNOCKEM
Drink it off. I'll come to thee, anon, again.

[*Exeunt*]

[*Enter*] QUARLOUS, EDGWORTH

QUARLOUS *To the cutpurse*
Well, sir. You are now discharged; beware of being spied, hereafter.

EDGWORTH
Sir, will it please you, enter in here at Ursla's, and take part of a silken gown, a velvet petticoat, or a wrought smock. I am promised such, and I can spare any gentleman a moiety.

QUARLOUS
Keep it for your companions in beastliness, I am none of 'em, sir. If I had not already forgiven you a greater trespass, or thought you yet worth my beating, I would instruct your manners to whom you made your offers. But go your ways, talk not to me, the hangman is only fit to discourse with you;

3 *we* which we
5 *stale* urinate
16 *will it* if it will
take part partake
18 *moiety* share, portion
21–2 *I would . . . offers* I would teach you proper behaviour towards the man to whom you make your offers

the hand of beadle is too merciful a punishment for your trade of life. [*Exit* EDGWORTH]
I am sorry I employed this fellow, for he thinks me such: *Facinus quos inquinat, aequat.* But it was for sport. And would I make it serious, the getting of this licence is nothing to me, without other circumstances concur. I do think how impertinently I labour, if the word be not mine that the ragged fellow marked; and what advantage I have given Ned Winwife in this time now of working her, though it be mine. He'll go near to form to her what a debauched rascal I am, and fright her out of all good conceit of me. I should do so by him, I am sure, if I had the opportunity. But my hope is in her temper yet; and it must needs be next to despair, that is grounded on any part of a woman's discretion. I would give, by my troth, now, all I could spare, to my clothes and my sword, to meet my tattered soothsayer again, who was my judge i' the question, to know certainly whose word he has damned or saved. For, till then, I live but under a reprieve. I must seek him. Who be these?

Enter WASP *with the officers*

WASP
Sir, you are a Welsh cuckold, and a prating runt, and no constable.

BRISTLE
You say very well. Come, put in his leg in the middle roundel, and let him hole there.

WASP
You stink of leeks, metheglin, and cheese, you rogue.

26 *such* such a one as he is
27–8 *would I make it serious* if I wanted to take it seriously
30 *impertinently* pointlessly
32 *working* influencing
33 *form* state explicitly
34 *conceit* opinion
36 *temper* character
38 *to* down to but not including
43 *runt* ignoramus
45 *roundel* round hole (of the stocks)
47 *metheglin* Welsh mead
cheese, you Ed. (cheese. You F)

---

27 *Facinus quos inquinat, aequat.* 'Crime puts those it corrupts on the same footing' (Lucan, *Pharsalia*, v. 290).

BRISTLE
Why, what is that to you, if you sit sweetly in the stocks in the mean time? If you have a mind to stink too, your breeches sit close enough to your bum. Sit you merry, sir.

QUARLOUS
How now, Numps?

WASP
It is no matter how; pray you look off.

QUARLOUS
Nay, I'll not offend you, Numps. I thought you had sat there to be seen.

WASP
And to be sold, did you not? Pray you mind your business, an you have any.

QUARLOUS
Cry you mercy, Numps. Does your leg lie high enough?

[Enter] HAGGIS, OVERDO, BUSY

BRISTLE
How now, neighbour Haggis, what says Justice Overdo's worship to the other offenders?

HAGGIS
Why, he says just nothing. What should he say? Or where should he say? He is not to be found, man. He ha' not been seen i' the Fair, here, all this livelong day, never since seven o'clock i' the morning. His clerks know not what to think on't. There is no court of Pie-powders yet. Here they be returned.

BRISTLE
What shall be done with 'em, then, in your discretion?

HAGGIS
I think we were best put 'em in the stocks, in discretion—there they will be safe in discretion—for the valour of an hour, or such a thing, till his worship come.

BRISTLE
It is but a hole matter if we do, neighbour Haggis. Come, sir, here is company for you. Heave up the stocks.

66 *discretion* opinion
68 *valour* length (literally, value or quantity)

67–8 *in discretion . . . in discretion.* (i) as an act of prudence (ii) in separation. The proverb 'Discretion is the better part of valour' (Tilley, D354) seems to be in Haggis's muddled mind, since he goes on to speak of 'valour' (= space, length).

WASP

[*Aside*] I shall put a trick upon your Welsh diligence, perhaps.

As they open the stocks, WASP *puts his shoe on his hand, and slips it in for his leg*

BRISTLE

Put in your leg, sir.

QUARLOUS

What, Rabbi Busy! Is he come?

They bring BUSY *and put him in*

BUSY

I do obey thee; the lion may roar, but he cannot bite. I am glad to be thus separated from the heathen of the land, and put apart in the stocks, for the holy cause.

WASP

What are you, sir?

BUSY

One that rejoiceth in his affliction, and sitteth here to prophesy the destruction of Fairs and May-games, Wakes, and Whitsun-ales, and doth sigh and groan for the reformation of these abuses.

[*They put* OVERDO *in the stocks*]

WASP

And do you sigh and groan too, or rejoice in your affliction?

OVERDO

I do not feel it, I do not think of it, it is a thing without me. Adam, thou art above these batteries, these contumelies. *In te manca ruit fortuna*, as thy friend Horace says; thou art one, *Quem neque pauperies, neque mors, neque vincula terrent.* And therefore, as another friend of thine says—I think it be thy friend Persius—*Non te quaesiveris extra.*

86 *batteries* series of heavy blows

---

82 *Whitsun-ales.* Parish festivals held at Whitsuntide and given over to feasting, sports, and merrymaking, Whitsun ales were opposed by the Puritans.

85 *it is a thing without me.* Overdo expresses the Stoic doctrine that no external factors can have any effect on the man who is conscious of his own virtue.

87 *In te manca ruit fortuna.* Fortune maims herself when she attacks you (Horace, *Satires*, II.vii. 88).

88 *Quem . . . terrent.* Whom neither poverty, nor death, nor shackles can affright (ibid., 84).

90 *Non . . . extra.* Look to no one outside yourself (Persius, *Satires*, i. 7).

QUARLOUS

What's here? A stoic i' the stocks? The fool is turned philosopher.

BUSY

Friend, I will leave to communicate my spirit with you, if I hear any more of those superstitious relics, those lists of Latin, the very rags of Rome, and patches of Popery.

WASP

Nay, an you begin to quarrel, gentlemen, I'll leave you. I ha' paid for quarrelling too lately. Look you, a device, but shifting in a hand for a foot. God b'w'you. *He gets out*

BUSY

Wilt thou then leave thy brethren in tribulation?

WASP

For this once, sir. [*Exit*]

BUSY

Thou art a halting neutral—stay him there, stop him—that will not endure the heat of persecution.

BRISTLE

How now, what's the matter?

BUSY

He is fled, he is fled, and dares not sit it out.

BRISTLE

What, has he made an escape? Which way? Follow, neighbour Haggis. [*Exit* HAGGIS]

[*Enter*] PURECRAFT

PURECRAFT

O me! In the stocks! Have the wicked prevailed?

BUSY

Peace, religious sister, it is my calling, comfort yourself, an extraordinary calling, and done for my better standing, my surer standing, hereafter.

The madman enters

TROUBLE-ALL

By whose warrant, by whose warrant, this?

93 *leave* cease
94 *lists* strips, selvages, shreds
97–8 *but shifting in a hand for a foot* merely slipping in a hand in place of a foot

---

91 *A stoic . . . stocks.* The association of Stoics with stocks (= senseless things) was a fairly common witticism (cf. *The Taming of the Shrew*, I.i, 31).

QUARLOUS

O, here's my man dropped in, I looked for.

OVERDO

Ha!

PURECRAFT

O good sir, they have set the faithful here to be wondered at; and provided holes for the holy of the land.

TROUBLE-ALL

Had they warrant for it? Shewed they Justice Overdo's hand? If they had no warrant, they shall answer it.

[*Enter* HAGGIS]

BRISTLE

Sure you did not lock the stocks sufficiently, neighbour Toby!

HAGGIS

No? See if you can lock 'em better.

BRISTLE

They are very sufficiently locked, and truly, yet something is in the matter.

TROUBLE-ALL

True, your warrant is the matter that is in question; by what warrant?

BRISTLE

Madman, hold your peace; I will put you in his room else, in the very same hole, do you see?

QUARLOUS

How? Is he a madman?

TROUBLE-ALL

Shew me Justice Overdo's warrant, I obey you.

HAGGIS

You are a mad fool, hold your tongue.

TROUBLE-ALL

In Justice Overdo's name, I drink to you, and here's my warrant. *Shews his can*

[*Exeunt* HAGGIS, BRISTLE]

OVERDO

[*Aside*] Alas, poor wretch! How it earns my heart for him!

QUARLOUS

[*Aside*] If he be mad, it is in vain to question him. I'll try,

112 *man* Ed. (man! F)
I whom I
127 *warrant*, Ed. (warrant. F)
131 *earns* grieves

though.—Friend, there was a gentlewoman shewed you two names, some hour since, Argalus and Palemon, to mark in a book. Which of 'em was it you marked?

TROUBLE-ALL

I mark no name but Adam Overdo; that is the name of names; he only is the sufficient magistrate; and that name I reverence. Shew it me.

QUARLOUS

[*Aside*] This fellow's mad indeed. I am further off now than afore.

OVERDO

[*Aside*] I shall not breathe in peace till I have made him some amends.

QUARLOUS

[*Aside*] Well, I will make another use of him, is come in my head: I have a nest of beards in my trunk, one something like his. [*Exit*]

The watchmen come back again

BRISTLE

This mad fool has made me that I know not whether I have locked the stocks or no; I think I locked 'em.

TROUBLE-ALL

Take Adam Overdo in your mind, and fear nothing.

BRISTLE

'Slid, madness itself, hold thy peace, and take that.

TROUBLE-ALL

Strikest thou without a warrant? Take thou that.

The madman fights with 'em, and they leave open the stocks

BUSY

We are delivered by miracle. Fellow in fetters, let us not refuse the means; this madness was of the spirit. The malice of the enemy hath mocked itself.

[*Exeunt* BUSY, OVERDO]

PURECRAFT

Mad do they call him! The world is mad in error, but he is mad in truth. I love him o' the sudden—the cunning man said all true—and shall love him more and more. How well it becomes a man to be mad in truth! O, that I might be his

133 *though.—Friend,* Ed. (though, friend: F)
144 *nest* set, collection
trunk trunk-hose, baggy padded breeches reaching to the knee
146 *I have* Ed. (I I haue F)
150 s.d. *The madman . . . stocks* (at l.149 in F)

yoke-fellow, and be mad with him! What a many should we draw to madness in truth with us! [*Exit*]

The watch, missing them, are affrighted

BRISTLE

How now? All scaped? Where's the woman? It is witchcraft! Her velvet hat is a witch, o' my conscience, or my key, t'one! The madman was a devil, and I am an ass; so bless me, my place, and mine office!

[*Exeunt*]

Act V, Scene i

[*Enter*] LEATHERHEAD, FILCHER, SHARKWELL

LEATHERHEAD

Well, Luck and Saint Bartholmew! Out with the sign of our invention, in the name of Wit, and do you beat the drum the while. All the foul i' the Fair, I mean all the dirt in Smithfield—that's one of Master Littlewit's carwhitchets now—will be thrown at our banner today, if the matter does not please the people. O the motions that I, Lantern Leatherhead, have given light to, i' my time, since my Master Pod died! *Jerusalem* was a stately thing, and so was *Nineveh*, and *The City of Norwich*, and *Sodom and Gomorrah*, with the rising o' the prentices, and pulling down the bawdy-houses there, upon Shrove Tuesday; but *The Gunpowder Plot*, there was a

161 *t'one* the one or the other

1–2 *sign of our invention* painted cloth depicting the subject of the puppet-shew

4 *carwhitchets* puns

6 *motions* puppet-shews

10 *prentices*, Ed. (prentises; F)

---

s.d. LEATHERHEAD Ed. (LANTHORNE. F). From this point onwards to the end of the play Leatherhead is almost consistently LANTHORNE or LANTERNE in stage directions and LAN. in speech prefixes. Transformed from hobby-horse-seller into puppet-master and suitably disguised for the new role, he has taken on another identity which prevents Cokes from recognizing him. See his whispered request to Littlewit at V.iii, 48.

7 *my Master Pod.* F has the marginal note 'Pod *was a Master of motions before him.*' Jonson also refers to Pod in *Every Man Out of His Humour* (IV.v, 62) and in two of his *Epigrams*, xcvii and cxxix.

8–9 *Jerusalem . . . Gomorrah.* The destruction of Jerusalem by the Romans, the fall of Nineveh in which Jonah and the whale figured prominently, the building of Norwich, and the destruction of Sodom and Gomorrah were common themes for puppet-shews.

9–11 *rising . . . Shrove Tuesday.* The apprentices of London made a regular habit of wrecking brothels and playhouses on Shrove Tuesday.

get-penny! I have presented that to an eighteen-, or twenty-pence audience, nine times in an afternoon. Your home-born projects prove ever the best, they are so easy, and familiar. They put too much learning i' their things nowadays; and that, I fear, will be the spoil o' this. Littlewit? I say, Micklewit! if not too mickle! Look to your gathering there, Goodman Filcher.

FILCHER

I warrant you, sir.

LEATHERHEAD

An there come any gentlefolks, take twopence apiece, Sharkwell.

SHARKWELL

I warrant you, sir; threepence an we can.

[*Exeunt*]

Act V, Scene ii

The Justice comes in like a porter

OVERDO

This later disguise, I have borrowed of a porter, shall carry me out to all my great and good ends; which, however interrupted, were never destroyed in me. Neither is the hour of my severity yet come, to reveal myself, wherein, cloud-like, I will break out in rain and hail, lightning and thunder, upon the head of enormity. Two main works I have to prosecute first: one is to invent some satisfaction for the poor kind wretch who is out of his wits for my sake; and yonder I see him coming. I will walk aside, and project for it.

[*Enter*] WINWIFE, GRACE

WINWIFE

I wonder where Tom Quarlous is, that he returns not; it may be he is struck in here to seek us.

12 *get-penny* draw, profitable operation
14 *projects* designs
familiar readily understood
16 *spoil* spoiling, ruination
17 *mickle* great
gathering collecting of entrance money (technical theatrical term)
1–2 *carry me out to* enable me to achieve
7 *prosecute first:* ed. (prosecute: first, F)
invent find, devise
9 *project* think of some plan
11 *is struck* has turned

GRACE

See, here's our madman again.

[*Enter*] QUARLOUS, PURECRAFT. QUARLOUS, *in the habit of the madman, is mistaken by* MISTRESS PURECRAFT

QUARLOUS

[*Aside*] I have made myself as like him as his gown and cap will give me leave.

PURECRAFT

Sir, I love you, and would be glad to be mad with you in truth.

WINWIFE

[*Aside*] How? My widow in love with a madman?

PURECRAFT

Verily, I can be as mad in spirit as you.

QUARLOUS

By whose warrant? Leave your canting. [*To* GRACE] Gentlewoman, have I found you?—Save ye, quit ye, and multiply ye.—Where's your book? 'Twas a sufficient name I marked, let me see't, be not afraid to shew't me.

He desires to see the book of MISTRESS GRACE

GRACE

What would you with it, sir?

QUARLOUS

Mark it again, and again, at your service.

GRACE

Here it is, sir; this was it you marked.

QUARLOUS

Palemon! Fare you well, fare you well.

WINWIFE

How, Palemon!

GRACE

Yes, faith, he has discovered it to you now, and therefore 'twere vain to disguise it longer; I am yours, sir, by the benefit of your fortune.

WINWIFE

And you have him, Mistress, believe it, that shall never give you cause to repent her benefit, but make you rather to think that in this choice she had both her eyes.

19 *canting* Puritan jargon
30 *benefit* favour, kindness

33 *she had both her eyes.* Winwife is referring to the proverb 'Fortune is blind (= blindfolded)' (Tilley, F604).

GRACE

I desire to put it to no danger of protestation.

[*Exeunt* GRACE, WINWIFE]

QUARLOUS

Palemon the word, and Winwife the man!

PURECRAFT

Good sir, vouchsafe a yoke-fellow in your madness; shun not one of the sanctified sisters, that would draw with you, in truth.

QUARLOUS

Away! You are a herd of hypocritical proud ignorants, rather wild than mad; fitter for woods, and the society of beasts, than houses, and the congregation of men. You are the second part of the society of canters, outlaws to order and discipline, and the only privileged church-robbers of Christendom. Let me alone. Palemon the word, and Winwife the man!

PURECRAFT

[*Aside*] I must uncover myself unto him, or I shall never enjoy him, for all the cunning men's promises.—Good sir, hear me, I am worth six thousand pound; my love to you is become my rack; I'll tell you all, and the truth, since you hate the hypocrisy of the parti-coloured brotherhood. These seven years, I have been a wilful holy widow only to draw feasts and gifts from my entangled suitors. I am also, by office, an assisting sister of the deacons, and a devourer, instead of a distributor, of the alms. I am a special maker of marriages for our decayed brethren with our rich widows, for a third part of their wealth, when they are married, for the relief of the poor elect; as also our poor handsome young virgins' with our

35, 45 *man!* Ed. (man? F)
48 *you is* Ed. (you, is F)
49 *truth,* Ed. (truth: F)
50 *parti-coloured* of several colours, i.e., inconsistent
57 *virgins'* ed. (Virgins, F), i.e., virgins' marriages

---

34 *put . . . protestation.* An allusion to the proverb 'Too much protesting makes the truth suspected' (Tilley, P614); cf. *Hamlet,* III.ii, 225: 'The lady doth protest too much, methinks'.

42 *second . . . canters.* The first part of the society of canters would be those who spoke thieves' cant, i.e., the rogues and vagabonds of the time. Thomas Harman, in his *A Caveat or Warning for Common Cursitors* (1566), provides some specimens of this cant. The pamphlet is edited by A. V. Judges in his *The Elizabethan Underworld*, London, 1930.

wealthy bachelors or widowers, to make them steal from their husbands, when I have confirmed them in the faith, and got all put into their custodies. And if I ha' not my bargain, they may sooner turn a scolding drab into a silent minister than make me leave pronouncing reprobation and damnation unto them. Our elder, Zeal-of-the-land, would have had me; but I know him to be the capital knave of the land, making himself rich by being made feoffee in trust to deceased brethren, and cozening their heirs by swearing the absolute gift of their inheritance. And thus, having eased my conscience, and uttered my heart with the tongue of my love —enjoy all my deceits together, I beseech you. I should not have revealed this to you, but that in time I think you are mad; and I hope you'll think me so too, sir.

QUARLOUS

Stand aside, I'll answer you presently.

He considers with himself of it

Why should not I marry this six thousand pound, now I think on't? And a good trade too, that she has beside, ha? The tother wench, Winwife is sure of; there's no expectation for me there! Here I may make myself some saver yet, if she continue mad; there's the question. It is money that I want; why should I not marry the money, when 'tis offered me? I have a licence and all; it is but razing out one name and putting in another. There's no playing with a man's fortune! I am resolved! I were truly mad, an I would not!—Well, come your ways, follow me; an you will be mad, I'll shew you a warrant! *He takes her along with him*

PURECRAFT

Most zealously, it is that I zealously desire.

The Justice calls him

OVERDO

Sir, let me speak with you.

61 *into* Ed. (in to F)
65 *feoffee in trust* trustee invested with a freehold estate in land (*OED*)
69 *together*, *I* Ed. (together. I F)
70 *in time* not too late
71 *sir*. Ed. (Sir? F)
72 s.d. *considers* Ed. (*consider* F)
75 *Winwife* Ed. (*Winwife*, F)
76 *saver* compensation for loss (gambler's term)

---

61 *silent minister*. One of the Puritan clergy who had been put out of their livings as a result of the Hampton Court conference of 1604. Cf. I.ii, 60–1 and note.

QUARLOUS

By whose warrant?

OVERDO

The warrant that you tender and respect so: Justice Overdo's! I am the man, friend Trouble-all, though thus disguised, as the careful magistrate ought, for the good of the republic in the Fair, and the weeding out of enormity. Do you want a house, or meat, or drink, or clothes? Speak; whatsoever it is, it shall be supplied you. What want you?

QUARLOUS

Nothing but your warrant.

OVERDO

My warrant? For what?

QUARLOUS

To be gone, sir.

OVERDO

Nay, I pray thee stay. I am serious, and have not many words nor much time to exchange with thee; think what may do thee good.

QUARLOUS

Your hand and seal will do me a great deal of good; nothing else in the whole Fair, that I know.

OVERDO

If it were to any end, thou should'st have it willingly.

QUARLOUS

Why, it will satisfy me—that's end enough—to look on. An you will not gi' it me, let me go.

OVERDO

Alas! thou shalt ha' it presently. I'll but step into the scrivener's hereby, and bring it. Do not go away.

The JUSTICE *goes out*

QUARLOUS

Why, this madman's shape will prove a very fortunate one, I think! Can a ragged robe produce these effects? If this be the wise Justice, and he bring me his hand, I shall go near to make some use on't.

The JUSTICE *returns*

87 *tender* have regard for

88–9 *as the careful magistrate ought* as befits the watchful magistrate

89 *republic* state, commonwealth

91 *Speak; whatsoever* ed. (speake whatsoeuer F)

102 *me—that's end enough—to* ed. (me, that's end enough, to F)
on at

109 s.d. *The* JUSTICE *returns* Ed. (*and returns.* F)

He is come already!

OVERDO

Look thee! here is my hand and seal, 'Adam Overdo'. If there be anything to be written above in the paper, that thou want'st now, or at any time hereafter, think on't. It is my deed, I deliver it so. Can your friend write?

QUARLOUS

Her hand for a witness, and all is well.

OVERDO

With all my heart. *He urgeth* MISTRESS PURECRAFT

QUARLOUS

[*Aside*] Why should not I ha' the conscience to make this a bond of a thousand pound now? Or what I would else?

OVERDO

Look you, there it is; and I deliver it as my deed again.

QUARLOUS

Let us now proceed in madness.

He takes her in with him

OVERDO

Well, my conscience is much eased; I ha' done my part. Though it doth him no good, yet Adam hath offered satisfaction! The sting is removed from hence. Poor man, he is much altered with his affliction, it has brought him low! Now for my other work: reducing the young man I have followed so long in love, from the brink of his bane to the centre of safety. Here, or in some such-like vain place, I shall be sure to find him. I will wait the good time.

Act V, Scene iii

[*Enter*] COKES, SHARKWELL, FILCHER

COKES

How now? What's here to do? Friend, art thou the Master of the Monuments?

117 *ha' the conscience* have the effrontery (*OED*, Conscience, 12.)
118 *pound now*? Ed. (pound? now, F)
125 *reducing* leading back
126 *bane* destruction, ruin
128 *good time* propitious moment
1 *to do* going on

1–2 *Master of the Monuments.* Exactly what Cokes has in mind is not clear. He obviously takes Sharkwell for an official in charge of effigies, perhaps seeing him, as H & S suggest, as the equivalent of the guide who took people around Westminster Abbey.

SHARKWELL
'Tis a motion, an't please your worship.

OVERDO
[*Aside*] My fantastical brother-in-law, Master Bartholmew Cokes!

COKES
A motion, what's that? *He reads the bill*
'The ancient modern history of *Hero and Leander*, otherwise called *The Touchstone of True Love*, with as true a trial of friendship between Damon and Pythias, two faithful friends o' the Bankside'? Pretty i'faith! What's the meaning on't? Is't an interlude? or what is't?

FILCHER
Yes, sir. Please you come near, we'll take your money within.
The boys o' the Fair follow him [COKES]

COKES
Back with these children; they do so follow me up and down.

[*Enter*] LITTLEWIT

LITTLEWIT
By your leave, friend.

FILCHER
You must pay, sir, an you go in.

LITTLEWIT
Who, I? I perceive thou know'st not me. Call the master o' the motion.

SHARKWELL
What, do you not know the author, fellow Filcher? You must take no money of him; he must come in *gratis*. Master Littlewit is a voluntary; he is the author.

4 *fantastical* fanciful, unpredictable
11 *interlude* play
20 *voluntary* volunteer, amateur, one who serves without pay

---

7–10 *The ancient . . . Bankside.* The puppet play, like the 'tedious brief scene of young Pyramus/And his love Thisby; very tragical mirth' in *A Midsummer Night's Dream*, is a burlesque of the kind of interlude (l. 11) that was popular in the early years of Elizabeth's reign, and, in particular, of Richard Edwards's *The Excellent Comedie of two the moste faithfullest Freendes, Damon and Pithias.* 'Newly Imprinted' in 1571, this work is described in the Prologue to it (l. 38) as a 'tragical comedy'. Marlowe's *Hero and Leander*, which is brutally travestied by Littlewit, had first appeared in print in 1598 and had proved enormously popular. It had also been burlesqued, in prose, by Nashe, in his *Nashes Lenten Stuffe* (1599); see Nashe, iii. 195–201.

LITTLEWIT

Peace, speak not too loud; I would not have any notice taken that I am the author, till we see how it passes.

COKES

Master Littlewit, how dost thou?

LITTLEWIT

Master Cokes! you are exceeding well met. What, in your doublet and hose, without a cloak or a hat?

COKES

I would I might never stir, as I am an honest man, and by that fire; I have lost all i' the Fair, and all my acquaintance too. Didst thou meet anybody that I know, Master Littlewit? My man Numps, or my sister Overdo, or Mistress Grace? Pray thee, Master Littlewit, lend me some money to see the interlude here. I'll pay thee again, as I am a gentleman—if thou'lt but carry me home, I have money enough there.

LITTLEWIT

O sir, you shall command it. What, will a crown serve you?

COKES

I think it will. What do we pay for coming in, fellows?

FILCHER

Twopence, sir.

COKES

Twopence? There's twelvepence, friend. Nay, I am a gallant, as simple as I look now, if you see me with my man about me, and my artillery, again.

LITTLEWIT

Your man was i' the stocks e'en now, sir.

COKES

Who, Numps?

LITTLEWIT

Yes, faith.

COKES

For what i'faith? I am glad o' that. Remember to tell me on't anon; I have enough now! What manner of matter is this,

22 *passes* goes down, is received
27 *fire* probably refers to the fire in Ursla's booth, but could be the fire of hell
31 *gentleman—if* ed. (Gentleman. If F)
34 *will. What* Ed. (well, what F)
37 *as simple as* humble though
38 *artillery* full equipment
42 *i'faith*? Ed. (i'faith, F)

Master Littlewit? What kind of actors ha' you? Are they good actors?

[*Enter*] LEATHERHEAD

LITTLEWIT

Pretty youths, sir, all children, both old and young, here's the master of 'em—

LEATHERHEAD *whispers to* LITTLEWIT

LEATHERHEAD

Call me not Leatherhead, but Lantern.

LITTLEWIT

—Master Lantern, that gives light to the business.

COKES

In good time, sir! I would fain see 'em, I would be glad to drink with the young company. Which is the tiring-house?

LEATHERHEAD

Troth sir, our tiring-house is somewhat little; we are but beginners yet, pray pardon us; you cannot go upright in't.

COKES

No? Not now my hat is off? What would you have done with me if you had had me, feather and all, as I was once today? Ha' you none of your pretty impudent boys, now, to bring stools, fill tobacco, fetch ale, and beg money, as they have at other houses? Let me see some o' your actors.

LITTLEWIT

Shew him 'em, shew him 'em. Master Lantern, this is a gentleman that is a favourer of the quality.

50 *In good time* well met
50–1 *glad to drink* Ed. (glad drinke F)
51 *tiring-house* area at the back of the stage where the actors dressed (attired) themselves
53 *go upright* walk without stooping
60 *quality* acting profession

46–7 *Pretty youths . . . 'em.* Probably an allusion to the Children of the Chapel Royal, for whom Edwards, their Master, wrote *Damon and Pithias*; though it could refer to the Boys' Companies which enjoyed a great revival in the early seventeenth century.

48 *Call me . . . Lantern.* Leatherhead does not wish to be recognized by Cokes, whom he has swindled.

56–8 *Ha' you . . . houses.* There is a splendid satirical account of the way in which the young fops who sat on the stage behaved in Thomas Dekker's *The Gull's Horn-Book* (1609); see *Thomas Dekker*, ed. E. D. Pendry, London, 1967, pp. 98–102.

OVERDO

[*Aside*] Ay, the favouring of this licentious quality is the consumption of many a young gentleman; a pernicious enormity.

He [LEATHERHEAD] *brings them out in a basket*

COKES

What, do they live in baskets?

LEATHERHEAD

They do lie in a basket, sir, they are o' the small players.

COKES

These be players minors, indeed. Do you call these players?

LEATHERHEAD

They are actors, sir, and as good as any, none dispraised, for dumb shows: indeed, I am the mouth of 'em all!

COKES

Thy mouth will hold 'em all. I think one Taylor would go near to beat all this company, with a hand bound behind him.

LITTLEWIT

Ay, and eat 'em all, too, an they were in cake-bread.

COKES

I thank you for that, Master Littlewit, a good jest! Which is your Burbage now?

LEATHERHEAD

What mean you by that, sir?

COKES

Your best actor. Your Field?

62 *consumption* financial ruin
68 *mouth* interpreter, voice
71 *in cake-bread* made of cake-bread

---

69 *one Taylor.* There may be as many as three allusions here: (i) to the notion that tailors are cowardly, enshrined in the proverb 'Nine tailors make a man' (Tilley, T23); (ii) to the actor Joseph Taylor, a member of the company that first played *Bartholmew Fair*; (iii) to John Taylor, the water-poet as he was called, who had challenged William Fennor, a pamphleteer and hack-writer, to a combat of wit at the Hope Theatre in October 1614. Fennor, having accepted the challenge, failed to show up.

71 *eat 'em all.* Tailors were popularly supposed to have enormous appetites.

73 *Burbage.* Richard Burbage, who died in 1619, was the leading player of the King's Men, Shakespeare's company, and the most celebrated actor of the time.

75 *Field.* Nathan Field (1587–1619?) was the chief actor of the Lady Elizabeth's Servants when they put on *Bartholmew Fair*. A dramatist as well as a player, Field was on very good terms with Jonson.

LITTLEWIT

Good i'faith! You are even with me, sir.

LEATHERHEAD

This is he that acts young Leander, sir. He is extremely beloved of the womenkind, they do so affect his action, the green gamesters that come here; and this is lovely Hero; this with the beard, Damon; and this, pretty Pythias. This is the ghost of King Dionysius in the habit of a scrivener, as you shall see anon, at large.

COKES

Well, they are a civil company, I like 'em for that. They offer not to fleer, nor jeer, nor break jests, as the great players do. And then there goes not so much charge to the feasting of 'em, or making 'em drunk, as to the other, by reason of their littleness. Do they use to play perfect? Are they never flustered?

LEATHERHEAD

No, sir, I thank my industry and policy for it; they are as well-governed a company, though I say it—And here is young Leander, is as proper an actor of his inches, and shakes his head like an hostler.

COKES

But do you play it according to the printed book? I have read that.

78 *affect his action* like his acting (with a quibble on 'action' = 'sexual activity')
79 *green gamesters* young loose wenches
81 *the habit of a scrivener* cf. V. iv, 297.
82 *at large* in full
83 *Well,* Ed. (Well F)
84 *fleer* gibe, laugh mockingly
great adult, full-grown
87 *perfect* word-perfect
91 *of his inches* for his size

91–2 *shakes . . . hostler.* There may be an allusion here to the actor William Ostler, a member of the King's Men.

93 *the printed book.* Marlowe's *Hero and Leander* (1598) and, with Chapman's continuation of it, 1598, 1600, 1606, 1609, 1613. The first four lines run thus:

On Hellespont, guilty of true love's blood,
In view and opposite two cities stood,
Sea-borderers, disjoin'd by Neptune's might:
The one Abydos, the other Sestos hight.

LEATHERHEAD

By no means, sir.

COKES

No? How then?

LEATHERHEAD

A better way, sir. That is too learned and poetical for our audience. What do they know what Hellespont is? 'Guilty of true love's blood'? Or what Abydos is? Or 'the other Sestos hight'?

COKES

Th'art i' the right, I do not know myself.

LEATHERHEAD

No, I have entreated Master Littlewit to take a little pains to reduce it to a more familiar strain for our people.

COKES

How, I pray thee, good Master Littlewit?

LITTLEWIT

It pleases him to make a matter of it, sir. But there is no such matter, I assure you. I have only made it a little easy, and modern for the times, sir, that's all. As, for the Hellespont, I imagine our Thames here; and then Leander I make a dyer's son, about Puddle Wharf; and Hero a wench o' the Bankside, who going over one morning to Old Fish Street, Leander spies her land at Trig Stairs, and falls in love with her. Now do I introduce Cupid having metamorphosed himself into a drawer, and he strikes Hero in love with a pint of sherry. And other pretty passages there are o' the friendship, that will delight you, sir, and please you of judgement.

COKES

I'll be sworn they shall. I am in love with the actors already, and I'll be allied to them presently.—They respect gentle-

97 *sir. That* Ed. (Sir, that F)
100 *hight* called
107 *modern* up-to-date
113 *drawer* tapster
with by means of
114 *sherry. And* Ed. (*Sherry*, and F)
117 *be allied to them* make them members of my family

109 *Puddle Wharf.* Between Blackfriars and Paul's Stairs, it was one of the water-gates of London.
110 *Old Fish Street.* As the name implies, the centre of the fish trade in Jonson's London.
111 *Trig Stairs.* Stairs leading down to the Thames next to Puddle Wharf.

men, these fellows.—Hero shall be my fairing. But which of my fairings? Le'me see—i'faith, my fiddle! and Leander my fiddle-stick. Then Damon my drum, and Pythias my pipe, and the ghost of Dionysius my hobby-horse. All fitted.

Act V, Scene iv

[Enter] to them WINWIFE, GRACE

WINWIFE

Look, yonder's your Cokes gotten in among his playfellows; I thought we could not miss him at such a spectacle.

GRACE

Let him alone, he is so busy he will never spy us.

LEATHERHEAD

Nay, good sir.

COKES *is handling the puppets*

COKES

I warrant thee, I will not hurt her, fellow; what, dost think me uncivil? I pray thee be not jealous; I am toward a wife.

LITTLEWIT

Well, good Master Lantern, make ready to begin, that I may fetch my wife; and look you be perfect, you undo me else i' my reputation.

LEATHERHEAD

I warrant you, sir. Do not you breed too great an expectation of it among your friends; that's the only hurter of these things.

LITTLEWIT

No, no, no. *[Exit]*

COKES

I'll stay here and see; pray thee let me see.

WINWIFE

How diligent and troublesome he is!

GRACE

The place becomes him, methinks.

OVERDO

[Aside] My ward, Mistress Grace, in the company of a stranger? I doubt I shall be compelled to discover myself before my time!

120 *pipe*, Ed. (*Pipe* F)
5 *what*, Ed. (what F)
6 *toward* about to marry
15 *diligent and troublesome* diligently troublesome (hendiadys)
18 *doubt* fear

[*Enter*] KNOCKEM, WHIT, EDGWORTH, WIN, MISTRESS OVERDO [*the ladies masked*]

The door-keepers speak

FILCHER

Twopence apiece, gentlemen, an excellent motion.

KNOCKEM

Shall we have fine fireworks and good vapours?

SHARKWELL

Yes, Captain, and waterworks too.

WHIT

I pree dee take a care o' dy shmall lady there, Edgworth; I will look to dish tall lady myself.

LEATHERHEAD

Welcome, gentlemen; welcome, gentlemen.

WHIT

Predee, mashter o' de' monshtersh, help a very sick lady here to a chair to shit in.

LEATHERHEAD

Presently, sir.

They bring MISTRESS OVERDO *a chair*

WHIT

Good fait now, Ursla's ale and *aqua vitae* ish to blame for't. Shit down, shweetheart, shit down and shleep a little.

EDGWORTH

[*To* WIN] Madam, you are very welcome hither.

KNOCKEM

Yes, and you shall see very good vapours.

OVERDO *By* EDGWORTH

[*Aside*] Here is my care come! I like to see him in so good company; and yet I wonder that persons of such fashion should resort hither!

EDGWORTH

This is a very private house, madam.

The cutpurse courts MISTRESS LITTLEWIT

21 *vapours*? Ed. (vapours! F)

22 *waterworks* a pageant exhibited on the water (much of the puppet-shew is supposed to take place on the Thames)

32 s.d. *By* referring to

---

36 *private house*. Edgworth quibbles on (i) house that affords us privacy (ii) private playhouse, i.e., one that was, unlike the public theatres such as the Globe or the Hope, entirely roofed in. It was also more expensive than the public theatres.

LEATHERHEAD

Will it please your ladyship sit, madam?

WIN

Yes, goodman. They do so all-to-be-madam me, I think they think me a very lady!

EDGWORTH

What else, madam?

WIN

Must I put off my mask to him?

EDGWORTH

O, by no means.

WIN

How should my husband know me, then?

KNOCKEM

Husband? an idle vapour. He must not know you, nor you him; there's the true vapour.

OVERDO

[*Aside*] Yea, I will observe more of this. [*To* WHIT] Is this a lady, friend?

WHIT

Ay, and dat is anoder lady, shweetheart. If dou hasht a mind to 'em, give me twelvepence from tee, and dou shalt have eder-oder on 'em!

OVERDO

Ay? [*Aside*] This will prove my chiefest enormity, I will follow this.

EDGWORTH

Is not this a finer life, lady, than to be clogged with a husband?

WIN

Yes, a great deal. When will they begin, trow, in the name o' the motion?

EDGWORTH

By and by, madam, they stay but for company.

KNOCKEM

Do you hear, puppet-master, these are tedious vapours; when begin you?

LEATHERHEAD

We stay but for Master Littlewit, the author, who is gone for his wife; and we begin presently.

38 *all-to-be-madam me* persist in calling me madam
50 *eder-oder* one or the other
55 *trow* do you think

WIN
That's I, that's I.

EDGWORTH
That was you, lady, but now you are no such poor thing.

KNOCKEM
Hang the author's wife, a running vapour! Here be ladies will stay for ne'er a Delia o' 'em all.

WHIT
But hear me now, here ish one o' de ladish ashleep. Stay till she but vake, man.

[*Enter*] *to them* WASP

The door-keepers again

WASP
How now, friends? What's here to do?

FILCHER
Twopence apiece, sir, the best motion in the Fair.

WASP
I believe you lie. If you do, I'll have my money again, and beat you.

WINWIFE
Numps is come!

WASP
Did you see a master of mine come in here, a tall young squire of Harrow o' the Hill, Master Bartholmew Cokes?

FILCHER
I think there be such a one within.

WASP
Look he be, you were best; but it is very likely. I wonder I found him not at all the rest. I ha' been at the Eagle, and the Black Wolf, and the Bull with the five legs and two pizzles—he was a calf at Uxbridge Fair, two years agone—and at the Dogs that dance the morris, and the Hare o' the tabor, and missed him at all these! Sure this must needs be some fine sight that holds him so, if it have him.

72 s.p. WINWIFE Ed. (WIN. F)

---

65 *a Delia.* Delia is the name of the lady to whom Samuel Daniel addressed his sonnet sequence *Delia*, first published in 1592. Probably an anagram of 'ideal', the name is here synonymous with 'self-important lady'.

77–80 *the Eagle . . . tabor.* Various attractions at the Fair. The 'Bull with five legs', first mentioned at III.vi, 7, has now acquired an extra pizzle (penis) and has been joined by some other animals, including a hare that plays on the tabor.

COKES

Come, come, are you ready now?

LEATHERHEAD

Presently, sir.

WASP

Hoyday, he's at work in his doublet and hose. Do you hear, sir? Are you employed, that you are bare-headed and so busy?

COKES

Hold your peace, Numps; you ha' been i' the stocks, I hear.

WASP

Does he know that? Nay, then the date of my authority is out; I must think no longer to reign, my government is at an end. He that will correct another must want fault in himself.

WINWIFE

Sententious Numps! I never heard so much from him before.

LEATHERHEAD

Sure Master Littlewit will not come. Please you take your place, sir, we'll begin.

COKES

I pray thee do, mine ears long to be at it, and my eyes too. O Numps, i' the stocks, Numps? Where's your sword, Numps?

WASP

I pray you intend your game, sir, let me alone.

COKES

Well then, we are quit for all. Come, sit down, Numps; I'll interpret to thee. Did you see Mistress Grace? It's no matter neither now I think on't, tell me anon.

WINWIFE

A great deal of love and care he expresses.

GRACE

Alas! Would you have him to express more than he has? That were tyranny.

COKES

Peace, ho! now, now.

LEATHERHEAD

Gentles, that no longer your expectations may wander,

89–90 *date of my authority is out* term of my authority is up

91 *want* be free from

97 *intend* pay attention to

98 *quit* even (with one another)

Behold our chief actor, amorous Leander,
With a great deal of cloth lapped about him like a scarf,
For he yet serves his father, a dyer at Puddle Wharf,
Which place we'll make bold with, to call it our Abydus,
As the Bankside is our Sestos, and let it not be denied us.
Now, as he is beating, to make the dye take the fuller,
Who chances to come by but fair Hero in a sculler;
And seeing Leander's naked leg and goodly calf,
Cast at him, from the boat, a sheep's eye and a half.
Now she is landed, and the sculler come back;
By and by you shall see what Leander doth lack.

PUPPET LEANDER
Cole, Cole, old Cole.

LEATHERHEAD *That is the sculler's name without control.*

PUPPET LEANDER
Cole, Cole, I say, Cole.

LEATHERHEAD *We do hear you.*

PUPPET LEANDER *Old Cole.*

LEATHERHEAD
Old coal? Is the dyer turned collier? How do you sell?

PUPPET LEANDER
A pox o' your manners, kiss my hole here, and smell.

LEATHERHEAD
Kiss your hole, and smell? There's manners indeed.

PUPPET LEANDER
Why, Cole, I say, Cole.

LEATHERHEAD *It's the sculler you need!*

PUPPET LEANDER
Ay, and be hanged.

LEATHERHEAD *Be hanged? Look you yonder;*
Old Cole, you must go hang with Master Leander.

---

106 *Leander*, Ed. (Leander. F)
111 *fuller* more completely
117 *Cole* often used as the name for a pander
118 *We do hear you* Ed. (roman in F)
119 *collier* (i) seller of coal (ii) term of abuse, because coal-sellers were black from their trade and were notorious cheats
How at what price

---

106 *amorous Leander*. The words are Marlowe's (*Hero and Leander*, i. 51).
114 *Cast . . . eye*. 'He casts a sheep's eye at her' was proverbial (Tilley, S323) and still is.
117 *without control*. The normal meaning of this phrase is 'freely', but here 'beyond all contradiction' would seem more to the point.

PUPPET COLE

Where is he?

PUPPET LEANDER *Here, Cole. What fairest of fairs*
Was that fare that thou landedst but now at Trig Stairs?

COKES

What was that, fellow? Pray thee tell me, I scarce understand 'em.

LEATHERHEAD

Leander does ask, sir, what fairest of fairs
Was the fare that he landed, but now, at Trig Stairs.

PUPPET COLE

It is lovely Hero.

PUPPET LEANDER *Nero?*

PUPPET COLE *No, Hero.*

LEATHERHEAD *It is lovely Hero*
Of the Bankside, he saith, to tell you truth without erring,
Is come over into Fish Street to eat some fresh herring.
Leander says no more, but as fast as he can,
Gets on all his best clothes, and will after to the Swan.

COKES

Most admirable good, is't not?

LEATHERHEAD

Stay, sculler.

PUPPET COLE *What say you?*

LEATHERHEAD *You must stay for Leander,*
And carry him to the wench.

PUPPET COLE *You rogue, I am no pander.*

COKES

He says he is no pander. 'Tis a fine language; I understand it now.

LEATHERHEAD

Are you no pander, Goodman Cole? Here's no man says you are.
You'll grow a hot Cole, it seems, pray you stay for your fare.

PUPPET COLE

Will he come away?

LEATHERHEAD *What do you say?*

PUPPET COLE *I'd ha' him come away.*

LEATHERHEAD

Would you ha' Leander come away? Why pray, sir, stay.

126 *at* Ed. (*a* F)
130 *that he* Ed. (*thhe* F)
131 *is lovely Hero* ed. (*is* Hero. F)

You are angry, Goodman Cole. I believe the fair maid
Came over w' you o' trust. Tell us, sculler, are you paid?

PUPPET COLE
Yes, Goodman Hogrubber o' Pickt-hatch.

LEATHERHEAD
How? Hogrubber o' Pickt-hatch?

PUPPET COLE
Ay, Hogrubber o' Pickt-hatch.
Take you that. The puppet strikes him over the pate

LEATHERHEAD *O, my head!*

PUPPET COLE *Harm watch, harm catch.*

COKES
'Harm watch, harm catch,' he says. Very good i'faith! The sculler had like to ha' knocked you, sirrah.

LEATHERHEAD
Yes, but that his fare called him away.

PUPPET LEANDER
Row apace, row apace, row, row, row, row, row.

LEATHERHEAD
You are knavishly loaden, sculler, take heed where you go.

PUPPET COLE
Knave i' your face, Goodman Rogue.

PUPPET LEANDER *Row, row, row, row, row, row.*

COKES
He said 'knave i' your face,' friend.

LEATHERHEAD
Ay, sir, I heard him. But there's no talking to these watermen, they will ha' the last word.

COKES
God's my life! I am not allied to the sculler yet. He shall be Dauphin my boy. But my fiddle-stick does fiddle in and out

146 *paid*? Ed. (*paid.* F)
149 *Harm watch, harm catch* if you do harm, you suffer harm (proverbial, Tilley, H167)
151 *had like to ha' knocked* seemed on the point of beating
157–8 *watermen, they will ha' the last word* a variant on the proverbial 'Women will have the last word' (Tilley, W723)
160 *my fiddle-stick* i.e., Leander (cf. V. iii, 119–20)

---

147 *Hogrubber o' Pickt-hatch.* Hogrubber seems to have been a derisive term for a swineherd, while Pickt-hatch was a very unsavoury area of London, the haunt of thieves and prostitutes. It looks as though Leatherhead is being accused of bestiality.
160 *Dauphin my boy.* Also referred to by Edgar in *King Lear* (III.iv, 99) as 'Dolphin my boy', this snatch (from some lost ballad or song?) still remains unexplained.

too much. I pray thee speak to him on't; tell him I would have him tarry in my sight more.

LEATHERHEAD

I pray you be content; you'll have enough on him, sir.
Now gentles, I take it, here is none of you so stupid,
But that you have heard of a little god of love, called Cupid;
Who out of kindness to Leander, hearing he but saw her,
This present day and hour, doth turn himself to a drawer.
And because he would have their first meeting to be merry,
He strikes Hero in love to him, with a pint of sherry.
Which he tells her from amorous Leander is sent her,
Who after him into the room of Hero doth venter.

PUPPET JONAS

A pint of sack, score a pint of sack i' the Coney.

Puppet Leander goes into MISTRESS HERO's room

COKES

Sack? You said but e'en now it should be sherry.

PUPPET JONAS

Why so it is; sherry, sherry, sherry.

COKES

'Sherry, sherry, sherry.' By my troth he makes me merry. I must have a name for Cupid too. Let me see. Thou mightest help me now, an thou wouldest, Numps, at a dead lift, but thou art dreaming o' the stocks still! Do not think on't, I have forgot it. 'Tis but a nine days' wonder, man; let it not trouble thee.

WASP

I would the stocks were about your neck, sir; condition I hung by the heels in them, till the wonder wore off from you, with all my heart.

COKES

Well said, resolute Numps!—But hark you, friend, where is

171 *venter* venture
177–8 *at a dead lift* at a pinch (proverbial, Tilley, L271)
179 *a nine days' wonder* (proverbial, Tilley, W728)
181 *condition* on condition that
184 *said*, Ed. (said F)

---

172 *the Coney*. Rooms in Elizabethan inns were named not numbered.
173 *Sack? . . . sherry*. Cokes loses no opportunity of demonstrating his ignorance. Sack was the name by which all white wines, including sherry, were called.
182 *wore* Ed. (were F). Cf. 'These few days' wonder will be quickly worn' (2 *Henry VI*, II.iv, 69).

the friendship, all this while, between my drum, Damon, and my pipe, Pythias?

LEATHERHEAD

You shall see by and by, sir.

COKES

You think my hobby-horse is forgotten too. No, I'll see 'em all enact before I go; I shall not know which to love best, else.

KNOCKEM

This gallant has interrupting vapours, troublesome vapours, Whit, puff with him.

WHIT

No, I pre dee, Captain, let him alone. He is a child i'faith, la!

LEATHERHEAD

Now gentles, to the friends, who in number are two,
And lodged in that ale-house in which fair Hero does do.
Damon, for some kindness done him the last week,
Is come fair Hero, in Fish Street, this morning to seek.
Pythias does smell the knavery of the meeting,
And now you shall see their true friendly greeting.

PUPPET PYTHIAS

You whoremasterly slave, you!

COKES

'Whoremasterly slave, you?' Very friendly and familiar, that.

PUPPET DAMON *Whoremaster i' thy face,*
Thou hast lien with her thyself, I'll prove't i' this place.

COKES

Damon says Pythias has lien with her himself, he'll prove't in this place.

LEATHERHEAD

They are whoremasters both, sir, that's a plain case.

PUPPET PYTHIAS

You lie like a rogue.

LEATHERHEAD *Do I lie like a rogue?*

PUPPET PYTHIAS

A pimp and a scab.

192 *puff with* bully, quarrel with
196 *do* work
209 *scab* scoundrel

---

188 *my hobby-horse is forgotten.* A much-quoted line from some lost song; cf. *Hamlet*, III.ii, 130.

LEATHERHEAD *A pimp and a scab?*
I say between you, you have both but one drab.

PUPPET DAMON
You lie again.

LEATHERHEAD *Do I lie again?*

PUPPET DAMON
Like a rogue again.

LEATHERHEAD *Like a rogue again?*

PUPPET PYTHIAS
And you are a pimp again.

COKES
And you are a pimp again, he says.

PUPPET DAMON *And a scab again.*

COKES
And a scab again, he says.

LEATHERHEAD
And I say again, you are both whoremasters again,
And you have both but one drab again.

They fight

PUPPET DAMON } PUPPET PYTHIAS } *Dost thou, dost thou, dost thou?*

LEATHERHEAD
What, both at once?

PUPPET PYTHIAS *Down with him, Damon.*

PUPPET DAMON
Pink his guts, Pythias.

LEATHERHEAD *What, so malicious?*
Will ye murder me, masters both, i' mine own house?

COKES
Ho! well acted my drum, well acted my pipe, well acted still!

WASP
Well acted, with all my heart!

LEATHERHEAD
Hold, hold your hands.

COKES
Ay, both your hands, for my sake! for you ha' both done well.

PUPPET DAMON
Gramercy, pure Pythias.

PUPPET PYTHIAS *Gramercy, dear Damon.*

221 *Pink* pierce, stab
226 *Hold* Ed. (*Hld* F)
227 *for* Ed. (for. F)

COKES
Gramercy to you both, my pipe, and my drum.

PUPPET PYTHIAS }
PUPPET DAMON } *Come now we'll together to breakfast to Hero.*

LEATHERHEAD
'Tis well, you can now go to breakfast to Hero,
You have given me my breakfast, with a 'hone and 'honero.

COKES
How is it, friend, ha' they hurt thee?

LEATHERHEAD
O no!
Between you and I, sir, we do but make shew.
Thus, gentles, you perceive, without any denial,
'Twixt Damon and Pythias here, friendship's true trial.
Though hourly they quarrel thus, and roar each with other,
They fight you no more than does brother with brother.
But friendly together, at the next man they meet
They let fly their anger, as here you might see't.

COKES
Well, we have seen't, and thou hast felt it, whatsoever thou sayest. What's next? What's next?

LEATHERHEAD
This while young Leander with fair Hero is drinking,
And Hero grown drunk, to any man's thinking!
Yet was it not three pints of sherry could flaw her,
Till Cupid, distinguished like Jonas the drawer,
From under his apron, where his lechery lurks,
Put love in her sack. Now mark how it works.

PUPPET HERO
O Leander, Leander, my dear, my dear Leander,
I'll for ever be thy goose, so thou'lt be my gander.

COKES
Excellently well said, fiddle! She'll ever be his goose, so he'll be her gander; was't not so?

231 *to Hero* with Hero
233 *me my* Ed. (*mmy* F)
234 *is it* ed. (is't F)
243 *sayest.* Ed. (sayest, F)
246 *flaw her,* Ed. (*flaw her.* F) make her drunk (earliest example in *OED* 1673)
247 *distinguished* dressed, disguised
249 *sack* (i) sherry (ii) loose gown

---

233 *a 'hone and 'honero.* An Irish and Scottish exclamation of grief, from the Irish and Gaelic 'ochòin', meaning 'alas'.

LEATHERHEAD

Yes, sir, but mark his answer, now.

PUPPET LEANDER

And sweetest of geese, before I go to bed,
I'll swim o'er the Thames, my goose, thee to tread.

COKES

Brave! he will swim o'er the Thames and tread his goose tonight, he says.

LEATHERHEAD

Ay, peace, sir, they'll be angry if they hear you eavesdropping, now they are setting their match.

PUPPET LEANDER

But lest the Thames should be dark, my goose, my dear friend,
Let thy window be provided of a candle's end.

PUPPET HERO

Fear not, my gander, I protest I should handle
My matters very ill, if I had not a whole candle.

PUPPET LEANDER

Well then, look to't, and kiss me to boot.

LEATHERHEAD

Now here come the friends again, Pythias and Damon,
And under their cloaks they have of bacon a gammon.

DAMON and PYTHIAS enter

PUPPET PYTHIAS

Drawer, fill some wine here.

LEATHERHEAD *How, some wine there?*
There's company already, sir, pray forbear!

PUPPET DAMON

'Tis Hero.

LEATHERHEAD *Yes, but she will not be taken,*
After sack and fresh herring, with your Dunmow-bacon.

PUPPET PYTHIAS

You lie, it's Westfabian.

LEATHERHEAD *Westphalian, you should say.*

259 *they'll* Ed. (the'll F)
260 *setting their match* fixing a time for their (amorous) encounter
263 *not,* Ed. (*not* F)

---

271 *Dunmow-bacon.* 'To fetch a flitch of bacon from Dunmow' was synonymous with marital fidelity (Tilley, F375), since the village of Dunmow, in Essex, gives a flitch of bacon to the couple who can show that they have not quarrelled since they were married. Leatherhead's point is that after her meal Hero will be feeling lecherous.

272 *Westphalian.* Westphalia, in Germany, was famous for its bacon and ham.

PUPPET DAMON

If you hold not your peace, you are a coxcomb, I would say.

LEANDER and HERO are kissing

PUPPET [PYTHIAS]

What's here? What's here? Kiss, kiss upon kiss.

LEATHERHEAD

Ay, wherefore should they not? What harm is in this?
'Tis Mistress Hero.

PUPPET DAMON *Mistress Hero's a whore.*

LEATHERHEAD

Is she a whore? Keep you quiet, or, sir knave, out of door.

PUPPET DAMON

Knave out of door?

PUPPET HERO *Yes, knave, out of door.*

PUPPET DAMON

Whore out of door.

PUPPET HERO *I say, knave, out of door.*

Here the *PUPPETS* quarrel and fall together by the ears

PUPPET DAMON

I say, whore, out of door.

PUPPET PYTHIAS *Yea, so say I too.*

PUPPET HERO

Kiss the whore o' the arse.

LEATHERHEAD *Now you ha' something to do:*
You must kiss her o' the arse, she says.

PUPPET DAMON }
PUPPET PYTHIAS } *So we will, so we will*

[They kick her]

PUPPET HERO

O my haunches, O my haunches, hold, hold!

LEATHERHEAD *Stand'st thou still?*
Leander, where art thou? Stand'st thou still like a sot,
And not offer'st to break both their heads with a pot?
See who's at thine elbow there! Puppet Jonas and Cupid.

PUPPET JONAS

Upon 'em, Leander, be not so stupid.

They fight

PUPPET LEANDER

You goat-bearded slave!

PUPPET DAMON *You whoremaster knave!*

PUPPET LEANDER

Thou art a whoremaster.

PUPPET JONAS *Whoremasters all.*

LEATHERHEAD

See, Cupid with a word has ta'en up the brawl.

KNOCKEM

These be fine vapours!

COKES

By this good day they fight bravely! Do they not, Numps?

WASP

Yes, they lacked but you to be their second, all this while.

LEATHERHEAD

This tragical encounter, falling out thus to busy us,
It raises up the ghost of their friend Dionysius,
Not like a monarch, but the master of a school,
In a scrivener's furred gown, which shews he is no fool.
For therein he hath wit enough to keep himself warm.
'O Damon,' he cries, 'and Pythias, what harm
Hath poor Dionysius done you in his grave,
That after his death you should fall out thus, and rave,
And call amorous Leander whoremaster knave?'

PUPPET DIONYSIUS

I cannot, I will not, I promise you, endure it.

Act V, Scene v

[Enter] to them BUSY

BUSY

Down with Dagon, down with Dagon! 'Tis I, will no longer endure your profanations.

LEATHERHEAD

What mean you, sir?

BUSY

I will remove Dagon there, I say, that idol, that heathenish idol, that remains, as I may say, a beam, a very beam, not a

298 *wit enough . . . warm* proverbial (Tilley, K10)
1 *will* who will, and I will

295–6 *Dionysius . . . school.* According to some accounts, Dionysius the younger, tyrant of Syracuse (367–343 B.C.) became a schoolmaster after his abdication.

1 *Dagon.* The national god of the Philistines, represented as half man and half fish, was regarded as the very type of an idol. Hence comes Busy's ridiculous equation of the puppets, whom he sees as idols, with Dagon. See I Samuel, v.

beam of the sun, nor a beam of the moon, nor a beam of a balance, neither a house-beam, nor a weaver's beam, but a beam in the eye, in the eye of the brethren; a very great beam, an exceeding great beam; such as are your stage-players, rhymers, and morris-dancers, who have walked hand in hand, in contempt of the brethren, and the cause; and been borne out by instruments of no mean countenance.

LEATHERHEAD

Sir, I present nothing but what is licensed by authority.

BUSY

Thou art all licence, even licentiousness itself, Shimei!

LEATHERHEAD

I have the Master of the Revels' hand for't, sir.

BUSY

The Master of Rebels' hand, thou hast—Satan's! Hold thy peace; thy scurrility shut up thy mouth; thy profession is damnable, and in pleading for it, thou dost plead for Baal. I have long opened my mouth wide, and gaped, I have gaped as the oyster for the tide, after thy destruction, but cannot compass it by suit, or dispute; so that I look for a bickering, ere long, and then a battle.

KNOCKEM

Good Banbury-vapours.

6–7 *beam of a balance* transverse bar from the ends of which the scales of a balance are suspended

7 *weaver's beam* cylinder in a loom

7–8 *a beam in the eye* alluding to the figure of the mote and the beam (Matthew, vii. 3–5)

12 *borne out* supported
instruments agents (of the devil)
countenance position, rank

17 *thy scurrility shut up* let thy scurrility shut up

19–20 *gaped as the oyster for the tide* proverbial (Tilley, 0114)

21 *bickering* skirmish

---

14 *Shimei*. Shimei, who cursed David, had, according to David himself, God's authority (licence) for doing it (II Samuel, xvi. 5–13).

15 *Master of the Revels*. An officer of the court who was responsible for, among other things, the licensing of plays.

18 *Baal*. The heathen god of the Midianites whose altar was cast down by Gideon (Judges, vi. 25–32). Busy sees himself as a Gideon.

COKES

Friend, you'd have an ill match on't if you bicker with him here; though he be no man o' the fist, he has friends that will go to cuffs for him. Numps, will not you take our side?

EDGWORTH

Sir, it shall not need; in my mind, he offers him a fairer course—to end it by disputation!—Hast thou nothing to say for thyself, in defence of thy quality?

LEATHERHEAD

Faith, sir, I am not well studied in these controversies between the hypocrites and us. But here's one of my motion, Puppet Dionysius, shall undertake him, and I'll venture the cause on't.

COKES

Who? My hobby-horse? Will he dispute with him?

LEATHERHEAD

Yes, sir, and make a hobby-ass of him, I hope.

COKES

That's excellent! Indeed he looks like the best scholar of 'em all. Come, sir, you must be as good as your word, now.

BUSY

I will not fear to make my spirit and gifts known! Assist me, zeal, fill me, fill me, that is, make me full.

WINWIFE

What a desperate, profane wretch is this! Is there any ignorance or impudence like his? To call his zeal to fill him against a puppet?

GRACE

I know no fitter match than a puppet to commit with an hypocrite!

25 *here;* Ed. (here, F)
26 *him.* Ed. (him, F)
27 *need;* Ed. (need, F)
29 *quality* profession
32 *undertake him* take him on
43 *commit* do battle

---

43 S.P. GRACE Ed. (QVA. F). As Waith points out, Quarlous is not on stage. Having made his exit at V.ii, 120, he does not return until the opening of V.vi. A misreading of 'GRA.' as 'QVA.' by the compositor is the likeliest explanation of the mistake.

BUSY

First, I say unto thee, idol, thou hast no calling.

PUPPET DIONYSIUS

You lie, I am called Dionysius.

LEATHERHEAD

The motion says you lie, he is called Dionysius i' the matter, and to that calling he answers.

BUSY

I mean no vocation, idol, no present lawful calling.

PUPPET DIONYSIUS

Is yours a lawful calling?

LEATHERHEAD

The motion asketh if yours be a lawful calling.

BUSY

Yes, mine is of the spirit.

PUPPET DIONYSIUS

Then idol is a lawful calling.

LEATHERHEAD

He says, then idol is a lawful calling! For you called him idol, and your calling is of the spirit.

COKES

Well disputed, hobby-horse!

BUSY

Take not part with the wicked, young gallant. He neigheth and hinnyeth, all is but hinnying sophistry. I call him idol again. Yet, I say, his calling, his profession is profane; it is profane, idol.

PUPPET DIONYSIUS

It is not profane!

LEATHERHEAD

It is not profane, he says.

BUSY

It is profane.

47 *matter* puppet-play, text
57 *wicked*, Ed. (wicked F)

---

45 *no calling.* As Busy explains at l.49, he means 'no lawful occupation'. The Puritans, and opponents of the stage in general, took the view that acting was not a genuine occupation at all; and they had the law on their side, for the player was liable to arrest as a rogue and a vagabond, unless he could show that he was in the service of the court or of some great man. It was for this reason that each acting company secured the patronage of a member of the royal family, or of a noble, and called themselves 'The Lord Chamberlain's Men', 'The Lady Elizabeth's Servants', and the like.

PUPPET DIONYSIUS

It is not profane.

BUSY

It is profane.

PUPPET DIONYSIUS

It is not profane.

LEATHERHEAD

Well said, confute him with 'not', still. You cannot bear him down with your base noise, sir.

BUSY

Nor he me with his treble creaking, though he creak like the chariot wheels of Satan. I am zealous for the cause—

LEATHERHEAD

As a dog for a bone.

BUSY

And I say it is profane, as being the page of Pride, and the waiting-woman of Vanity.

PUPPET DIONYSIUS

Yea? What say you to your tire-women, then?

LEATHERHEAD

Good.

PUPPET DIONYSIUS

Or feather-makers i' the Friars, that are o' your faction of faith? Are not they, with their perukes, and their puffs, their fans, and their huffs, as much pages of Pride, and waiters upon Vanity? What say you? What say you? What say you?

BUSY

I will not answer for them.

PUPPET DIONYSIUS

Because you cannot, because you cannot. Is a bugle-maker a lawful calling? Or the confect-maker's?—Such you have there. —Or your French fashioner? You'd have all the sin within yourselves, would you not? would you not?

69 *creaking* speaking in a strident tone
74 *tire-women* dressmakers
77 *puffs* soft protuberant mass of material on the dress
78 *huffs* paddings used to raise the shoulders of dresses
81 *bugle-maker* maker of tube-shaped glass beads
82 *confect-maker's* that of the maker of sweetmeats
83 *fashioner* tailor or dressmaker

---

76 *feather-makers i' the Friars.* The traders in feathers, who lived in the Blackfriars area, also happened to be Puritans. The contradiction between their occupation, ministering to vanity, and their religious leanings did not escape their opponents.

BUSY

No, Dagon.

PUPPET DIONYSIUS

What then, Dagonet? Is a puppet worse than these?

BUSY

Yes, and my main argument against you is that you are an abomination; for the male among you putteth on the apparel of the female, and the female of the male.

PUPPET DIONYSIUS

You lie, you lie, you lie abominably.

COKES

Good, by my troth, he has given him the lie thrice.

PUPPET DIONYSIUS

It is your old stale argument against the players, but it will not hold against the puppets, for we have neither male nor female amongst us. And that thou may'st see, if thou wilt, like a malicious purblind zeal as thou art!

The PUPPET *takes up his garment*

EDGWORTH

By my faith, there he has answered you, friend, by plain demonstration.

PUPPET DIONYSIUS

Nay, I'll prove, against e'er a Rabbin of 'em all, that my standing is as lawful as his; that I speak by inspiration, as well as he; that I have as little to do with learning as he; and do scorn her helps as much as he.

BUSY

I am confuted, the cause hath failed me.

PUPPET DIONYSIUS

Then be converted, be converted.

LEATHERHEAD

Be converted, I pray you, and let the play go on!

BUSY

Let it go on. For I am changed, and will become a beholder with you!

86 *Dagonet* King Arthur's fool
99 *standing* profession

88–9 *an abomination . . . male.* This 'old stale argument against the players', used long before 1614 and long after it, is based on Deuteronomy, xxii. 5: 'The woman shall not wear that which pertaineth unto a man, neither shall a man put on a woman's garment: for all that do so are abomination unto the Lord thy God'. The text was indeed an inviting weapon for the enemies of a theatre in which all female roles were played by boys.

COKES

That's brave i'faith. Thou hast carried it away, hobby-horse. On with the play!

The JUSTICE *discovers himself*

OVERDO

Stay. Now do I forbid, I, Adam Overdo! Sit still, I charge you.

COKES

What, my brother-i'-law!

GRACE

My wise guardian!

EDGWORTH

Justice Overdo!

OVERDO

It is time to take enormity by the forehead, and brand it; for I have discovered enough.

Act V, Scene vi

[*Enter*] *to them,* QUARLOUS (*like the madman*), PURECRAFT

QUARLOUS

Nay, come, Mistress bride. You must do as I do now. You must be mad with me, in truth. I have here Justice Overdo for it.

OVERDO

Peace, good Trouble-all; come hither, and you shall trouble none. I will take the charge of you and your friend too. (*To the cutpurse and* MISTRESS LITTLEWIT) You also, young man, shall be my care, stand there.

EDGWORTH

Now mercy upon me.

The rest are stealing away

107 *carried it away* won
5 *too.* Ed. (too, F)
6 *man,* Ed. (man F)

s.d. *Enter to them,* QUARLOUS (*like the madman*), PURECRAFT Ed. (*To them,* QVARLOVS. (*like the Man-man*) PVRECRAFT. (*a while after*) IOHN. *to them* TROVBLE-ALL. VRSLA. NIGHTIGALE. F). Since Quarlous is speaking to Dame Purecraft as he enters, it is clear that the words *a while after* are intended to apply to John Littlewit, who does not appear until l. 13.

KNOCKEM

Would we were away, Whit! These are dangerous vapours; best fall off with our birds, for fear o' the cage.

OVERDO

Stay, is not my name your terror?

WHIT

Yesh faith, man, and it ish for tat we would be gone, man.

[*Enter*] LITTLEWIT

LITTLEWIT

O gentlemen, did you not see a wife of mine? I ha' lost my little wife, as I shall be trusted, my little pretty Win. I left her at the great woman's house in trust yonder, the pig-woman's, with Captain Jordan and Captain Whit, very good men, and I cannot hear of her. Poor fool, I fear she's stepped aside. Mother, did you not see Win?

OVERDO

If this grave matron be your mother, sir, stand by her, *et digito compesce labellum*; I may perhaps spring a wife for you anon. Brother Bartholmew, I am sadly sorry to see you so lightly given, and such a disciple of enormity, with your grave governor Humphrey. But stand you both there in the middle place; I will reprehend you in your course. Mistress Grace, let me rescue you out of the hands of the stranger.

WINWIFE

Pardon me, sir, I am a kinsman of hers.

OVERDO

Are you so? Of what name, sir?

WINWIFE

Winwife, sir.

OVERDO

Master Winwife? I hope you have won no wife of her, sir. If you have, I will examine the possibility of it at fit leisure.

9 *Whit!* Ed. (*Whit*, F)
10 *fall off* withdraw
cage gaol
12 *gone*, Ed. (gone F)
17 *fool* sweet
17–18 *stepped aside* gone astray
20 *spring* put up (as a partridge is 'put up' from cover)
24 *course* turn

19–20 *et digito compesce labellum*. Adapted from Juvenal (*Satires*, i. 160): 'and check any movement of your lips with your finger', i.e., 'don't give yourself away'.

Now to my enormities! Look upon me, O London! and see me, O Smithfield! the example of Justice, and Mirror of Magistrates; the true top of formality, and scourge of enormity. Hearken unto my labours and but observe my discoveries; and compare Hercules with me, if thou dar'st, of old; or Columbus, Magellan, or our countryman Drake of later times. Stand forth you weeds of enormity and spread. (*To* BUSY) First, Rabbi Busy, thou superlunatical hypocrite. (*To* LANTERN) Next, thou other extremity, thou profane professor of puppetry, little better than poetry. (*To the horse-courser, and cutpurse*) Then thou strong debaucher, and seducer of youth—witness this easy and honest young man. (*Then* CAPTAIN WHIT *and* MISTRESS LITTLEWIT) Now thou esquire of dames, madams, and twelvepenny ladies; now my green madam herself of the price. Let me unmask your ladyship.

LITTLEWIT

O my wife, my wife, my wife!

OVERDO

Is she your wife? *Redde te Harpocratem!*

Enter TROUBLE-ALL [followed by URSLA *and* NIGHTINGALE]

TROUBLE-ALL

By your leave, stand by, my masters, be uncovered.

URSLA

O stay him, stay him! Help to cry, Nightingale. My pan, my pan!

OVERDO

What's the matter?

NIGHTINGALE

He has stolen Gammer Ursla's pan.

TROUBLE-ALL

Yes, and I fear no man but Justice Overdo.

OVERDO

Ursla? Where is she? O the sow of enormity, this! (*To* URSLA

33 *formality* legal procedure
37 *enormity and spread* ed. (enormity, and spread F) wide-spread enormity (hendiadys)
42 *easy* compliant, credulous
49 *by,* Ed. (by F)
be uncovered take off your hats (as a sign of respect)

---

48 *Redde te Harpocratem.* Transform yourself into Harpocrates (the god of silence, born with his finger on his lips).

and NIGHTINGALE) Welcome. Stand you there; you, songster, there.

URSLA

An please your worship, I am in no fault. A gentleman stripped him in my booth, and borrowed his gown and his hat; and he ran away with my goods here for it.

OVERDO

(*To* QUARLOUS) Then this is the true madman, and you are the enormity!

QUARLOUS

You are i' the right, I am mad but from the gown outward.

OVERDO

Stand you there.

QUARLOUS

Where you please, sir.

MISTRESS OVERDO *is sick, and her husband is silenced*

MISTRESS OVERDO

O lend me a basin, I am sick, I am sick. Where's Master Overdo? Bridget, call hither my Adam.

OVERDO

How?

WHIT

Dy very own wife, i'fait, worshipful Adam.

MISTRESS OVERDO

Will not my Adam come at me? Shall I see him no more then?

QUARLOUS

Sir, why do you not go on with the enormity? Are you oppressed with it? I'll help you. Hark you, sir, i' your ear—your 'innocent young man', you have ta'en such care of all this day, is a cutpurse, that hath got all your brother Cokes his things, and helped you to your beating and the stocks. If you have a mind to hang him now, and shew him your magistrate's wit, you may; but I should think it were better

56 *you,* Ed. (you F)
58 *in no fault* not to blame
70 *at* to
72 *oppressed with* overwhelmed by

67 *Bridget.* The most probable explanation of the mention of this character, not heard of elsewhere in the play, is that Mistress Overdo, waking from her drunken stupor, imagines herself at home and calls a servant of this name.

recovering the goods, and to save your estimation in pardoning him. I thank you, sir, for the gift of your ward, Mistress Grace; look you, here is your hand and seal, by the way. Master Winwife, give you joy, you are Palemon, you are possessed o' the gentlewoman, but she must pay me value, here's warrant for it. And honest madman, there's thy gown and cap again; I thank thee for my wife. (*To the widow*) Nay, I can be mad, sweetheart, when I please, still; never fear me. And careful Numps, where's he? I thank him for my licence.

WASP

How!

QUARLOUS

'Tis true, Numps.

WASP

I'll be hanged then. WASP *misseth the licence*

QUARLOUS

Look i' your box, Numps. [*To* OVERDO] Nay, sir, stand not you fixed here, like a stake in Finsbury to be shot at, or the whipping post i' the Fair, but get your wife out o' the air, it will make her worse else. And remember you are but Adam, flesh and blood! You have your frailty. Forget your other name of Overdo, and invite us all to supper. There you and I will compare our 'discoveries', and drown the memory of all enormity in your biggest bowl at home.

COKES

How now, Numps, ha' you lost it? I warrant 'twas when thou wert i' the stocks. Why dost not speak?

WASP

I will never speak, while I live, again, for aught I know.

78 *estimation* reputation
81 *Winwife*, Ed. (*Win-wife* F)
85 *fear me* fear for me, doubt it
90 *Look* Ed. (Loke F)

78–9 *in pardoning him* ed. (inh im F). The Folio reading does not make sense. The purely conjectural insertion of 'pardoning', on the assumption that the compositor omitted it, as he omitted other words, balances 'recovering the goods' and fits in with the conclusion of the comedy. 'Pardon' is not an unusual word at the end of a Jonsonian comedy. Justice Clement tells Brainworm that he 'deserues to bee pardon'd for the wit o' the offence' (*Every Man in His Humour*, V.iii, 113–14), and Face asks for, and receives, Lovewit's pardon (*The Alchemist*, V.iii, 83).
82 *pay me value*. Because Quarlous is now Grace's guardian.
91 *a stake . . . shot at*. Finsbury Fields were a place of recreation for the citizens of London, and one of its attractions was archery contests.

OVERDO

Nay, Humphrey, if I be patient, you must be so too. [*To them all*] This pleasant conceited gentleman hath wrought upon my judgement, and prevailed. I pray you take care of your sick friend, Mistress Alice, and, my good friends all—

QUARLOUS

And no enormities.

OVERDO

I invite you home with me to my house, to supper. I will have none fear to go along, for my intents are *ad correctionem, non ad destructionem; ad aedificandum, non ad diruendum.* So lead on.

COKES

Yes, and bring the actors along, we'll ha' the rest o' the play at home.

[*Exeunt*]

THE END

THE EPILOGUE

Your Majesty hath seen the play, and you
  Can best allow it from your ear and view.
You know the scope of writers, and what store
  Of leave is given them, if they take not more,
And turn it into licence. You can tell
  If we have used that leave you gave us well;
Or whether we to rage or licence break,
  Or be profane, or make profane men speak.
This is your power to judge, great sir, and not
  The envy of a few. Which if we have got,
We value less what their dislike can bring,
  If it so happy be, t' have pleased the King.

101–2 s.d. *To them all* ed. (not in F)
102 *pleasant conceited* merrily disposed
2 *allow* sanction, license
3 *store* Ed. (*store*, F)
8 *speak*. Ed. (*speake*? F)

107–8 *ad . . . diruendum*. To correct, not destroy; to build up, not to tear down.